Disenchanted India
and Beyond

Disenchanted India and Beyond

Musings on the Lockdown Alternatives

Bhabani Shankar Nayak

LEXINGTON BOOKS
Lanham • Boulder • New York • London

Published by Lexington Books
An imprint of The Rowman & Littlefield Publishing Group, Inc.
4501 Forbes Boulevard, Suite 200, Lanham, Maryland 20706
www.rowman.com

6 Tinworth Street, London SE11 5AL, United Kingdom

British Library Cataloguing in Publication Information Available

Library of Congress Cataloging-in-Publication Data

Library of Congress Control Number: 2021931961

ISBN 9781793642790 (cloth)
ISBN 9781793642806 (electronic)

To
My youngest brother
Siddhartha Shankar Nayak
With love

Contents

Acknowledgements

The collection of articles and commentaries in this book have been published in different newspapers, journals and web portals like *Oxford Political Review*, *South Asia Journal*, *Eurasia Review*, *Law School Policy Review*, *Outlook*, *Student Struggle*, *Frontier Weekly*, *The Frontier Post*, *Economic and Political Weekly*, *Counter Currents*, *Counterview*, *Kashmir Times*, *South Asia Times*, *The Citizen*, *Media Scanner*, *Morning Star*, *India News Diary*, *Sabrang*, *The News Room*, *Times Now News*, *Eleventh Column* and many other online media platforms. The essays and commentaries in this book attempt to engage with everyday issues in a disenchanted world and attempts to unlock some existing alternatives. I am thankful to all the editors.

I am immensely grateful to Khushboo Mattoo for designing the book's cover page. Her sublime and subtle painting represents the vastness in ocean, challenges in mountains, potential alternatives and hopes in the sky.

I am thankful to Pritam, Ernesto, Geeta, Mahmood, Suresh, Safraz, Nazia, Suhas, Usha, Subir, Indrajit, Smeeta, many friends and family members for all their encouragement and support. I am grateful to Maa, Bou, Bapa, Tuku and Sansia for all their support. I am particularly obliged to my youngest brother Siddhartha for all his inspiration. He is the one who asked me to write this book. I dedicate and gift this book to Siddhartha for successfully completing his high school. I am particularly thankful to Joseph Parry and Alison Keefner of the Lexington Books for their timely editorial help and support in the making of this book. All inadvertent mistakes are mine only.

Bhabani Shankar Nayak
London, 29 November 2020

Introduction

The disenchanted world did not start in 2020. But the year 2020 has started with mass franticness as the contagion of COVID-19-led deaths and destitutions continue to keep people under lockdowns. It has accelerated the pandemic of prevailing inequalities, exploitation and authoritarian dominance, ethnic and racial violence, hunger, homelessness and unemployment issues. These are not apocalyptic signs but products of the capitalist system before the COVID-19-led growth of global health crisis. The social maladies and religious carnage, civil disorders, political unrests and economic crisis are creating havoc in every nook and corner of the world. The wistfulness of the will and disenchanted environment move together in an unending treacherous road. But capitalism and its systems are flourishing when masses suffer under multiple forms of miseries. The religious right-wing groups, conservative political parties, socially reactionary and authoritarian forces in the United States, United Kingdom, India, Pakistan, Brazil and many other parts of the world have exploited the mass discontent against neoliberal economic crisis and marginalisation. These forces have mobilised the masses with their populist slogans based on religious, nationalist, cultural and narrow political lines. These forces were successful to capture state power to reinforce authoritarian neoliberalism in service of the corporates.

The disenchanted world beyond India is a product of such a praxis. People are disenchanted with the neoliberal, authoritarian and reactionary political culture in which electoral democracies were used as a method to capture the state power that serves corporates. The states and governments are abandoning the idea of citizenship rights and civil liberties of people in Asia, Africa, Latin America, Americas and Europe. The market-led democracy destroys the welfare abilities of the states and governments and makes them conformist institutions to provide security to the corporates for capital accumulation.

The security state is a blessing to capitalism and a curse to the growth of democratic society. In this way, the neoliberal project and its praxis have created a perverted culture of utilitarian monopoly, where citizens are converted into customers. The amoral mass media and fictitious celebrity culture help in spreading consumerism worldwide. The culture of consumerism has not only destroyed our unique culture of consumptions based on local production, but it also writes the final epitaph of our own lives and fate of our own society.

Such a disenchanted trend in the society is not confined within India. This worldwide disenchantment is a product of crisis-ridden capitalism as an economic, political and cultural system, which is opposed to the idea of freedom, prosperity and peace for the masses. It survives by spreading its culture of crisis, conflicts and contradictions. It outsources its problems by forming alliance with religious and right-wing forces in politics. These forces insulate capitalism from collapse by stopping the growth of class struggles. This dysfunctional anarchy of capital destroys everything that is human, social, secular and sustainable. The capitalist governance based on pure greed for power and profit is against life and planet. Distrust and disenchantments are twin outcomes of capitalism and fascism.

The lure of capitalist economy, culture and its deceptive political system is the foundation of an unavoidable gap between reality and dreams of people in their everyday life. It creates rootless belongingness. But the decadent society of orderly objects creates new desires to conceal everyday issues, dreams, aspirations and realities of life. The human labour within bodies have become commodities to survive and explore the world. There is no time to discover one's own self. Human beings are just meaningless numbers in the Excel sheet of computer screens. In this landscape, price and profit become twin pillars in establishing the value of relationships among fellow human beings. The bond between human beings and nature became functional essentialism to hoard more and feel less. The pestilence of pandemic made us to realise human touch, importance of nature and relationships. The lockdown stories talk about human longing for freedom from self-imposed loneliness. The quarantine body and free mind failed to enjoy the lockdown holidays. The material needs and desires have imposed limitation on freedom of individuals.

The tranquillity of time and harmony of human emotions are attached with commodities. We are all becoming moving objects where 'utility', 'pleasure' and 'satisfaction' determine self-worth. The humane tales of ethno-sphere is imprisoned in a society of happiness industry. The assassins of market waiting with their new products; their weapons to enslave human imagination within organised objects; the money; the god of all gods and goddesses, living in such a society create the foundation of a deceptive mountain of sand where everything looks like beautiful dreams from a deceptive distance. Like belongingness is a distant memory of long past, it is like an old boat for an elderly boatman. Emotion is weakness in the wilderness of orderly objects, where commodities reciprocate and replace relationships in a new civilisation called 'market'. It is global and local. It is omnipresent and omnipotent. It is new god and religion where metaphysical spirituality is replaced by credit card. It enables us to access the impossible in our society. It runs on the deficit of human values, emotions, necessities and human feelings.

Human feelings based on necessities are transformed into desires based on false promises of the commodities. From god to ruling and non-ruling elites of the society transformed themselves as salesmen and saleswomen of this false narratives. Our lives revolve around insatiable new desires for commodities. This propaganda is central to the survival of the power of god, religion and market-led desire-based society. The desires are always unfulfilled. They make us feel inadequate. A desire-based society continues to instil inadequacy and incompleteness in our everyday life. We work like machine to fulfil desires. We even pray and fear god to achieve our goal and feel complete by acquiring more and more commodities. This narrative is a trap based on desire and fear. It sustains power and dismantles collective and individual ability and imagination to be emotionally creative. The radical departure from such a deceptive experience is central to search emancipatory ideals in politics and personal lives.

The book engages with the lineages of the present disenchantment and everyday issues of people in India and beyond. Similar issues are confronted by people all over the world. The book depicts local, regional, national and global transitions in politics, economy and society. It rejects the ideals that promote 'there is no alternative' narratives. It unravels the way reactionary and right-wing forces weaponise pessimism that helps capitalist forces and undermines working classes and their creative potential and emancipatory power. The book examines existing and available alternatives for a prosperous and peaceful society. The book argues for pluriversal political and philosophical praxis to consolidate and defend the progressive achievements of the working-class struggles.

Chapter 1

Illusions of Globalisation, State and Democracy

Democracy is a product of struggles and sacrifices of the working classes. The October Revolution, French Revolution in Europe and anti-colonial struggles in Africa, Asia and Americas shaped the democracy. The struggles for freedom, equality and justice, anti-capitalist struggles, people's movements against war and terrorism, and social and political movements for livelihoods have helped to deepen democratic practices all over the world. The coronavirus pandemic is taking its toll on the rotten and inefficient political, economic and social systems. The human cost of the crisis makes present look gloomy and the future is inconceivable. The discontinuity with everyday lives and emergency measures create an illusion that normality will return to its own place and pace. These illusionary desires help the crisis-ridden bourgeois democracy and capitalist state to survive and continue to create havoc in the lives and livelihoods of the masses.

The decade-long practice of neoliberal market-led democracy eroded both the abilities of the states, governments and democratic political traditions to deal with different forms of crisis. As a result, the relationship between state and citizens is deteriorating along with the democratic traditions. The crisis not only shows the cracks within different democracies but also questions the very foundation of bourgeois parliamentary democracy. Any attempt to return to business as usual in a post-pandemic world will reproduce a dead-end for the masses under capitalist democracy. It is not the spectre of communism that is haunting the world today. It is the capitalist democracy that failed people with false promises of freedom, prosperity, empowerment and development. The rising tides of reactionary nationalism, populism of the conservative forces and neoliberal economic policies are further weakening the democracy. These forces are also depoliticising the democratic processes of development and public policymaking. The top-down bureaucratic approach of the technocratic policymaking is worsening the crisis within democracy.

The propaganda machines of the establishment hide all the failures and inefficiencies of bourgeois democracy and capitalist state. It gives an impression as if democracies and states have failed. So, the establishment today offers us an authoritarian alternative by killing the idea of citizenship, freedom and democracy; the greatest ideals, and achievements of twentieth and twenty-first centuries. The propaganda machines help in socialising the masses and normalise authoritarian neoliberal forces as permanent rulers of the world to manage chaos in which elites are secured by the state and the masses are left to suffer alone as individuals. The father of propaganda and modern advertisement Edward Bernays summarised this process in his seminal book *Propaganda*, published in 1928.

In the first two paragraphs of chapter one of *Propaganda*, Edward Bernays wrote that

> the conscious and intelligent manipulation of the organised habits and opinions of the masses is an important element in democratic society. Those who manipulate this unseen mechanism of society constitute an invisible government which is the true ruling power of our country. We are governed, our minds are moulded, our tastes formed, our ideas suggested, largely by men we have never heard of. This is a logical result of the way in which our democratic society is organised. Vast number of human beings must cooperate in this manner if they are to live together as a smoothly functioning society. Our invisible governors are, in many cases, unaware of the identity of their fellow members in the inner cabinet. They govern us by their qualities of natural leadership, their ability to supply needed ideas and by their key position in the social structure. Whatever attitude one chooses to take towards this condition, it remains a fact that in almost every act of our daily lives, whether in the sphere of politics or business, in our social conduct or our ethical thinking, we are dominated by the relatively small number of persons – a trifling fraction of our hundred and twenty million – who understand the mental processes and social patterns of the masses. It is they who pull the wires which control the public mind, who harness old social forces and contrive new ways to bind and guide the world.

These prophetic words of Edward Bernays resonate with our everyday experiences with bourgeois democracies and responses of the capitalist states to the crisis in the world.

Such a crisis within democracy is a product of neoliberal politics and policies led and determined by the manipulative market forces. The rise of poverty, unemployment, hunger, homelessness, environmental disasters and ill-health are the products of the failures of bourgeois democracy and capitalist state. These disruptions to democracy can be a catalyst for exposing the limits and illusions of bourgeois democracy under capitalist system. It is important for the citizens to kill their false hopes on the failed democratic project of capitalism, which reduced democracy to voting and festivals of periodical elections. It is the time for reckoning within the opulence of miseries for the masses and island of prosperity for a small number of elites.

The brazen greed of the few billionaires has hijacked our democracy and state. It destroyed our hopes, fate and futures for the sake of their profit. These ultra-rich men are morally bankrupt and politically screwed to uphold the interests of the masses. It is time for majority of the people to reclaim the political space and transform the state that belong to the working-class masses. History tells us that the capitalist classes always relied on crisis to maintain their hegemony over the masses. Crisis produces power for the capitalist classes by reducing the power and autonomy of the working classes. Therefore, poverty and unemployment are not crisis but opportunity for the ruling and non-ruling capitalist classes. Peace, prosperity and employment create conditions of empowerment of the masses and threaten the power and positions of elites.

History is the witness to the power of working classes in shaping the democratic state and progressive society. All empires and dictatorships collapsed with the power of working-class unity and struggles. Marx and Engels summarised it in *The Communist Manifesto*: 'The history of all hitherto existing society is the history of class struggles'. These struggles can only create alternative conditions for real democracy and shape our futures in which 'the free development of each is the condition for the free development of all'. The market forces are not the friends of democracy, freedom, peace, prosperity, happiness, individual liberty and spirituality but represent the perverted form of these ideals that serves their purpose to domesticate the masses. Therefore, it is important to ensure that the principles of peace, prosperity, freedom and democracy are four pillars of all our future movements for justice and equality. There is no shortcut to progressive mass movements, which can change the course of history and fortify our democratic future. It can only be achieved through collective struggles based on our collective interests.

GLOBALISATION OF CAPITALIST CRISES

The post-pandemic economic recovery looks uncertain and the economic growth projections look gloomy in every stretch of policy paradigm within capitalist imaginations. The strong and existing multilateral cooperation within the Westphalian international system is falling apart and facing its existential threats due to its entrenched Eurocentric bias, democratic deficits and institutional dominance by the erstwhile colonial powers. The world is moving into a long-term crisis within capitalism. The capitalist system has failed to offer any viable alternatives to recover from the crises. It is rather deepening the globalisation of crises and miseries among the masses. The predicaments of hunger, homelessness and unemployment are growing. The idea of accessibility, availability and distribution of essential goods and services are becoming difficult. The markets are shrinking and sinking. Both the producers and consumers are facing the crises in their everyday lives.

The follies of globalisation and its flickers continue to be in denial mode. These illiberal charlatans of power live in the cocoons of their privileged ghettos and argue vehemently that the current crisis is not a capitalist crisis or crisis of globalisation. There is concocted propaganda that the crisis is a product of greedy and irrational individuals, inefficient governments and unproductive states. The free-market-led systems are only viable and competent alternatives. These reactionary and ahistorical narratives help capitalism by arguing that the current economic, social, political, environmental and coronavirus-led global health crises are products of state and government failures.

The right-wing economists, liberal commentators, salary-seeking intellectuals and consultants in different think tanks continue to glorify and provide ideological justification to capitalist globalisation by hiding its absolute failures in deepening egalitarian democracy, peace and prosperity. The globalisation of crises under capitalism serves four objectives of the ruling and non-ruling classes. First, these ridiculous propaganda makes people reject the state and the government they have formed with the help of their collective will. Second, it diminishes citizens faith in their own abilities and own intellect. It weakens and diverts them to analyse and reflect on their own realities. Third, it weakens the state and destroys the capabilities of the governments as instruments of social, economic, political and cultural change for common good based on scientific spirit and progressive future. Finally, it destroys democratic cultures by replacing it with authoritarianism that is concomitant with the requirements of capitalism for its growth. In this way, the fake narratives of reactionary politics and global capitalism help to achieve these four specific objectives, which are central pillars in establishing authoritarianism accelerated by crises. The globalisation of capitalist crises means globalisation of authoritarian politics and vice versa.

The world is facing six major immanent capitalist crises: (i) coronavirus pandemic-led global health crises, (ii) environmental crises, (iii) economic crises, (iv) political crises, (v) military crises and (vi) crises of governance. These six crises are integral to each other. One crisis triggers the other. It is impossible to address them separately. Therefore, it needs an integrated and pluriversal approach to understand and address these crises together and find reliable alternatives.

CORONAVIRUS-PANDEMIC-LED
GLOBAL HEALTH CRISES

The coronavirus pandemic reveals that spillover of virus from their natural habitat to human body is associated with the burgeoning wildlife trade, deforestation and loss of natural wildlife habitat due to over-exploitation of nature under capitalism. The monetisation of nature for profit is the foundation of health pandemics. According to a recent research, two viruses enter into human body from their natural hosts every year for a century now. The coronavirus-led health crisis and other forms of global health crises are products of capitalism, which considers human body and nature as resources to be used for the expansion of capitalist profit. It also uses sickness as business opportunities for health insurance and pharmaceutical corporations. The profit-driven healthcare and economic system breeds health crises across the globe. The coronavirus-led pandemic is aggravating existing health crises due to privatisation of public health infrastructures and corporatisation of health services. The alternative is to look at health as human rights and abandon the economic model that seeks profit from illness and business of sickness. The nationalisation and universalisation of healthcare is the only alternative.

Environmental Crises

The unprecedented environmental crisis is not natural. The environment is degraded and destabilised by the growth of a desire-based society under capitalism. The magnitude and severity of environmental crisis reveal that capitalist economic system creates grave imbalance within the ecosystem by over-exploiting natural resources. The issues of global warming, pollution and contaminations are the products of the productivist and utilitarian ideology of global capitalist system, which monetised the environment for profit maximisation without thinking about the planet and people. It has ruined the land, water and air. The outbreak of air and waterborne diseases are products of environmental crisis manufactured by capitalist system. The irreparable damage to environment is a threat to human lives. The environmental crisis aggravates global economic and health crisis. The reversal of profit-driven, desire-based capitalist economy is inevitable for a sustainable economic and social future.

Economic Crises

Economic crisis is integral to capitalism. The faux neoliberal narrative of austerity as an economic policy alternative to recover from economic crisis is the logic of market on steroids. Austerity is not an economic policy, but it is an economic project of the capitalist classes, which enforces economic miseries, political despondency and social alienation on majority of population. The voodoo of austerity and its alconomics culture reproduces crisis and empowers market forces by transferring public resources to the private pockets of the capitalist classes. The only way to recover from the crisis in short run is to abandon austerity-driven neoliberal economic policies. The permanent alternative from crisis is to destroy capitalism and all its cultures with the help of popular struggles for a sustainable economy and society based on community and democratic control over resources.

Political Crises

The neoliberal shift in economy led to the shift from welfarist social democracy to bourgeois democracy, where uninhibited market forces rule with their invisible free hand. The growth of island of prosperity and continents of miseries are the net outcomes of such a system, which led to the declining legitimacy of the democratic political forces. In this context, there is the rise of reactionary religious and conservative social forces are not only filling the vacuum but also providing legitimacy to the rule of capitalist politics in the name of culture, religion and nationalism. The recent political upheavals within liberal democracies in different parts of the globe reflect this right-wing shift and reactionary trend in politics. The political crisis is an opportunity for the capitalist classes to dismantle all democratic norms and values in support of authoritarianism. In this decisive period of structural crisis of capitalism, it is only authoritarian politics that can help capitalism to further accumulate at this stage of its growth. The collective politics with collective vision is the only alternative for the survival of the masses.

Military Crises

The authoritarian and reactionary political regimes breed conflicts, disputes and wars to stay in power and control resources. The global growth of nationalist war hysteria is producing military crises in land, ocean, air and space. It is also fuelling international arms trade. The colonial, imperialist and capitalist powers consider military crisis is an opportunity to expand their economic base by selling weapons of mass destruction. The guns and capitalist globalisation move together. The military-industrial complex is deepening the idea of security state led by the defence forces that ensures security to capital at the cost of human lives. The states and governments are spending all their resources on military equipment when citizens are suffering in hunger and homelessness. The military crisis puts citizens' welfare in the dustbin. The global growth of defence spending is a threat to environment, human lives, peace and prosperity in the world.

Crises of Governance

The world is witnessing the growing crisis of global, regional, national and local governance. The crisis of governance means crisis of rule of law, transparency and accountability. The criminogenic character of capitalism prefers a non-transparent and unaccountable system, which provides absolute freedom to the mobility of capital and control labour and its mobility with different legal mechanisms. The laws are for the masses and the capitalist classes live with legal impunity. This capitalist duality is central in creating crisis of governance. The growth of economic and social inequalities and the rise of political illegitimacies and illiberal thoughts also led to the crisis of governance. The struggle for liberal, progressive, egalitarian, cooperative and democratic governance is the only alternative which is destroyed by capitalism in regular intervals.

These six crises are intrinsic capitalism to overcome its own internal contradictions. The different incarnations of capitalism reveal that capitalism is an incubator of crises. There is no alternative to solve crises within capitalism. The globalisation is the diminuendos of capitalist world economy, which promised peace and prosperity but in reality, it is globalising crises and miseries. The astrologers of capitalism have lost all their gods and worshiping false god of propaganda has expired its usable date. The idolatry of capitalist falsehood is not an alternative to recover from the crisis of its own making. It is time to learn from our experiences with capitalist catastrophe and its history of crises. There is no individual freedom within capitalism in which majority suffers. Our individual freedoms are interlinked with collective emancipation. The glocal emancipatory struggle against capitalism is the only alternative for a collective future based on liberty, equality, justice and fraternity. The national socialism is only possible with practice of internationalism. The worldwide collective actions and resistance movements can revise and re-establish the hidden glory of socialism as the only alternative.

NEOLIBERALISM AND ITS CRIMINAL CONFESSIONS

The pandemic has shaken up the neoliberalism as an economic project of capitalism. The economic architecture of neoliberalism based on austerity, liberalisation, privatisation and globalisation has failed to provide basic dignity of life in terms of basic health, education, home and food security. The rise of unemployment, hunger and homeless are the direct products of neoliberal economic policies followed by the states and governments around the world. The neoliberal capitalist reincarnations have failed to provide dignity even to the growing number of dead bodies in the disposable bags as a result of COVID-19.

The master of neoliberal prophesies and their prophets like Mr Klaus Schwab, the founder and executive chairman of the World Economic Forum, argues to re-evaluate the global economic system based on neoliberal ideology of free market fundamentalism, which led to the emergence of global corporate monopolies at the cost of eroded workers' rights and economic securities of people. Such criminal confessions from the shibboleths of neoliberal architecture of capitalist classes are part of the strategy to revive the legitimacy of a criminal economic and political system that took away dignity from human life and destroyed the planet in search of profit. It has destabilised countries and pushed regions into war and conflicts in the name of spreading free market democracy, the other name of neo-colonialism, which manufactures inequalities in a global scale.

Mr Klaus Schwab argues for sustainable development and green business for economic recovery for launching the 'fourth industrial revolution' with the help of technology and digitalisation and ensures our collective commitment to capitalism. He further argues that social progress is the result of capitalist entrepreneurship, efficient allocation of resources by the market forces and risk-taking abilities of the capitalists. These arguments are not only factually incorrect but also based on myopia driven by an ideology of fraudulent economic system called capitalism. There is not an iota of truth in it.

The contradictory ideas of Mr Klaus Schwab are not based on his ignorance or lack of knowledge. It is based on a long tradition of capitalist propaganda and its diversionary strategies. Deception is a crime but innate to capitalism as an economic, political, social and cultural system. Capitalism produces social miseries, economic alienation and political marginalisation, which destroys all forms of social progress based on science and technology by forming alliance with reactionary religious and authoritarian forces. Democratic deficit is part of the neoliberal free market economy that destroys the abilities of states and governments to pursue social and economic welfare of its citizens. His concerns for climate change and green economy are dubious as capitalism grows by destroying environment and exploiting people. Therefore, human dignity, freedom, democracy and sustainable development are not concomitant with capitalism as an ideology of exploitation. The new kind of capitalism with human and green face is another propaganda to hide the inhuman character of capitalism in all its forms. The pragmatic steps of capitalism are in the dead-end. Capitalism can never be resilient, cohesive and sustainable.

The World Economic Forum has designed a set of 'Stakeholder Capitalism Metrics' during its 2020 annual meeting in Davos. The core of these values is based on environmental and social governance. Governance indicates transparency, accountability and rule of law. The rule of law is designed by the ruling classes and makes it compatible with the requirements of the capitalist classes. Accountability and transparency are twin dangers to capitalism. Therefore, capitalism does not engage with any system that is accountable and transparent. But unfortunately, the entire model of neoliberal governance is designed to protect the shareholders of capitalism. It is neither accountable to labour nor environment that produces profit for capitalism. Sustainable values are anathema to capitalism. It destroys everything that is sustainable. The profit under capitalism is not based on creative destruction. It is based on absolute annihilation of all creative abilities if labour and nature. It requires repetitive labour, which works in compliance-based regulatory regime. The dead capital is free but labour with life in bondages. It treats labour and nature as commodities.

The neoliberal economic policies and its austerity projects are dead but neoliberal political infrastructure is very much alive and thriving. The authoritarian and right-wing political regimes are growing and giving breathing space to capitalism at the cost of lives and environment. Therefore, any form of economic reimagination of economic alternative needs to reimagine the political system. The alternative political economy in the post-pandemic world needs to focus on the conditions of production, distribution and exchange relationships. The market can be based on the direct relationship between producers and consumers with the help of information technology. The fourth industrial revolution and its economic system need to follow the models of workers cooperatives based on human needs and desires concomitant with environmental sustainability. These principles are fundamental to the 'Great Rest' the post-pandemic economy, politics and society. The shared progress, peace, prosperity, human health and dignity and environmental sustainability depend on human abilities to overthrow capitalism and its rotten system. The survival of planet, people and prosperity depends on forward march humanity towards the ideals of equality, liberty, justice, fraternity in a world free from all forms of exploitation.

End of Economic Globalisation, Rise of Surveillance Capitalism and the Search for Alternatives

The colonial and imperialist militaries, political and economic systems are defeated by the mutilating powers of the pestilence. The COVID-19 virus is controlling our so-called modern lifestyles and quarantining ourselves within walls of our rooms to reflect and reimagine. The 'end of history', 'clash of civilisations' and 'there is no alternative' were three rotten ideological theses advanced to established market-led liberal democracy. The narratives were constructed and propagated to make people believe that capitalist world order is the only available alternative. However, the worlds of Prof Francis

Fukuyama, Samuel P. Huntington and linages of their ilk come to an end as coronavirus pandemic batters the world and its capitalist economic systems. It shows the limits of capitalist globalisation. It is also revealing a very frightening future with the rise of surveillance capitalism and its state apparatus.

The grandeurs of propaganda advocating the principles of *laissez-faire* economy promoted by capitalist globalisation undermined the abilities of the states. The welfare states within capitalist frameworks have failed to perform their welfare responsibilities for citizens. The weakening of welfare states under capitalist globalisation transformed basic necessities like lifesaving medicines as mere commodities in the market where ill-health is a great source of profit for the corporations. The world is reeling under lockdowns and death rate is increasing in the United States, United Kingdom, France, Spain, Italy, Belgium and the Netherlands, whereas China, Vietnam, Cuba, Odisha and Kerala in India have managed to contain and control the spread of the coronavirus pandemic. The myth of Western hubris and delusions of capitalist invincibility are falling apart.

It is not a surprise that the capitalist states have failed in emergency response preparedness to combat the coronavirus pandemic. It shows the limits of capitalist state and market-led healthcare systems dominated by big pharmaceutical corporations which laid the foundation for public health disasters. The big pharmaceutical corporations consider pandemics and all forms of health disasters as opportunities for making profit. It is clear that pharmaceutical corporations are the biggest obstacles for fighting coronavirus pandemic.

The neoliberal illusions of capitalist globalisation and its ideological roots have exhausted all its arguments. There is nothing new and liberal about neoliberal capitalism as a system in all its forms. There are attempts to expand its life span with the help of wars, dictatorships and by killing liberal democracy and democratic cultures around the world. All attempts have failed to save capitalism from itself. But capitalism continues to reinvent itself by forming new partnerships. This time, it forms alliance with regional, religious and reactionary political forces to sustain itself by spreading all kinds of hatred, risks and fear, which led to the growth of surveillance regimes and security states.

There is surge of surveillance capitalism after the outbreak of COVID-19 pandemic. It is a threat to individual liberty and freedom. The digitalisation citizenship reduced democratic polity as a mere number-crunching exercise in electoral marathons. It can be misused by the state, governments and corporations to control individual life as per the requirements of the capitalist structure. Prof Francis Fukuyama might have postponed his end of history thesis. Prof Samuel P. Huntington might have abandoned the clash of civilisation project. Prof Henry Kissinger's dream of American world order is halted for now. It is time to write the final epitaph Prof Francis Fukuyama, Samuel P. Huntington and their ideological followers who swindled the progressive promises of twentieth and twenty-first centuries by developing a system that helps few and marginalises many. Crisis and fear are the twin weapons of such a process of capitalist pandemic that thrives on war, dictatorships and economic exploitation.

The coronavirus pandemic associated with economic crisis reveals rotten economic and political system that treats human lives as disposables. It cannot be business as usual any longer. The world needs a new political and economic order. The working classes suffer the most in all public health crisis and economic crisis. It is imperative for the working-class population to fight for their alternatives based on their common experiences and common sufferings under capitalist globalisation and pandemics associated with it. The reversal of capitalist globalisation is possible and inevitable. The starting point is to nationalize health services by de-commodifying medicine and its business. The capitalist globalisation offers us to choose between *Laissez-Faire and Laissez Mourir*. It is not a choice between capitalism and socialism. It is a choice between capitalism and life.

The experiences of the coronavirus pandemic guide us to make a clear choice. Let's choose life and defeat capitalism. This is the only alternative, which can help us to survive the ordeal. Our economic freedom depends on the political choices we make today for the future survival of humanity. Nothing can stop emancipatory movements. In spite of all propaganda to socialise masses within capitalist social, economic and political order, revolutionary upsurge does not die. Human desire to emancipate from the bondages of capitalism finds news ways of expressing itself. It counters ugly realities of everyday lives under capitalism. The human cost of coronavirus pandemic immeasurable but it offers us an opportunity to completely destroy capitalism as a system. If we do not take this historic opportunity, our lives will continue to suffer from everyday pandemic of surveillance capitalist state and pharmaceutical corporations. Let this pandemic be a catalyst for universal healthcare and human emancipation from all forms of illness promoted by capitalism as a social, economic and political system.

The history of revolutionary struggles for political and economic alternatives is *sombresault* of continuous processes. It is hard to write and very difficult to predict. There is no doubt that human beings love for reason and science, dream of freedom and struggle for human emancipation win all the way to the end for a better future.

DANGERS FOR DEMOCRACY WITHOUT OPPOSITION

As people battle with the deadly coronavirus, the world is sleepwalking into an authoritarian future to keep capitalism alive with the help of brute force. The parliamentary and presidential forms of democracies are running the government without effective oppositions. The majoritarian governments in the United States, United Kingdom, Brazil, India, China, Pakistan, Bangladesh and many other countries are busy in bending inclusive, secular and progressive rules and regulations to please global capital at the cost of people and their lives. The parliamentary, presidential, liberal and constitutional democracies are falling apart by breaking democratic traditions as outlined in the constitutional traditions.

The authoritarian politics is becoming the oxygen for the survival of capitalist economy and its profit-driven system. The bourgeois cavalry of the ruling class is pushing democracy, democratic ethos and democratic institutions into its temporary graveyard on which neoliberal authoritarianisms can flourish. It is not only about one country anymore but from Europe to Americas, Asia, Africa and Oceania, there are visible signs of rise of authoritarianism and its assault on democracy. There are attempts by the governments to normalise illiberal and undemocratic practices with the help of majoritarianism. The right-wing shift in democratic praxis is not new in the history. The authoritarian and anti-democratic forces have always tried to subvert democracy to regain their unfettered control over people and resources. It is argued that strong leadership and stable politics is essential for peace and prosperity. Such a myth is promoted by the reactionary forces to continue their hegemony in different spheres of life.

The history is full of examples of both successful and failed democratic movements but never failed in promoting radical ideals, democratic values and cultures, whereas the tyrannical, reactionary and right-wing forces have always failed after their transient success. The undemocratic and authoritarian states and governments are spreading misinformation and fake news to keep people in dark about their diminishing freedom of choice in every step of their lives. The diversionary strategy helps to hide the failure of ruling classes and promote their failure as the failure of state, government and democracy. Both the weak states and compliant governments or strong states and powerful governments under dysfunctional democratic set-ups are useful for the expansion of capital. The reactionary political regimes are allies of capitalist classes. These forces are using every opportunity and platforms to defame, discredit and delegitimise opposition political parties, democratic and progressive movements to create political climate, where politics becomes the ideology of ruling classes. It even uses judiciary to criminalize political opposition to the ruling establishments. These deceptive tactics have been used in different parts of the world to use crippled democracy merely as a poster hide reactionary politics and capitalist exploitation.

Democracy is a tool of social, political and economic transformation. Democratic deficit or crisis of democracy delays transformation towards progressive future. The world needs to embrace the urgency of mobilising a radical mass movement to revive, restore and consolidate democratic developments in a progressive path, where the culture of political opposition is not strangulated. The politics of dissent enhances democratic traditions and sharpens decision-making processes. The opposition political parties are becoming inseparable from the ruling class ideology and policies. It looks as if they are the two sides of the same coin. The ineffective opposition or the absence of opposition diminishes democratic praxis.

The popular opinions based on beliefs are not always reasonable, objective and scientific. Therefore, it is important for the majority to respect the minority voices based on progressive and scientific ethos. It is an important tool of checks and balances within a democratic system. The alternative to democratic failure is more democracy to be successful. The authoritarian regimes can never be an alternative to democracy and its abilities towards a progressive transformation. Both the essentialist and emancipatory logic of democracy and its critiques are central to decentralisation of power and authority to ensure democratic praxis for common good. The opposition's questions and critique of the government is essential for social, political and economic transformation of governance mechanisms based on needs and desires of people. Such a democratic tradition and political culture allow multiple voices and exchange of different perspectives for larger goal of emancipation of people from different forms of structural inequalities and exploitation. The ideals of individual liberty, equality, justice and freedom are the gifts of democratic movements.

From the Solonian, Cleisthenesian and Ephialtesian traditions of Athenian democracy to Chartist character of parliamentary democracies with Westminster styles are products of working-class uprisings against ruling class authoritarianism and exploitation. The police brutality and unjust judiciaries have failed to protect the ruling classes and their undemocratic regimes. The Peterloo massacre in Manchester to anti-colonial struggles in Asia, Africa, Americas and Oceania are testimonies to the sacrifice and struggles of common people to establish democratic politics that represents the interests of the masses. The distributive justice, liberty and equality are foundational and governing principles of these working-class struggles for democracy.

Historically, the democratic struggles have used both 'reform' and 'revolution' as twin weapons of social, economic and political progress. The reforms are not working any longer. The survival of democratic ethos and principles are under threat now. The democratic state and governments are no longer representing the needs, desires, interests and aspirations of the masses. The states and governments are standing behind the global, regional and national capitalist classes and upholding their interests. The masses are suffering in hunger, homelessness, inequalities and multiple forms of alienation. This is a global trend and not confined within a particular territory and population. The forward march of this global trend needs to be halted for the sake of survival of human life, citizenship rights, dignity and peace in the world. It needs an internationalist approach with local actions and regional solidarity networks with global outreach acknowledging distinctive understanding of regional requirements based on people's needs. The hegemonic universalism promoted by Eurocentric understanding of bourgeois democracy needs to be transformed and replaced by pluriversal democratic practices moving beyond empiricist electoral framework of majority or minority.

CRISIS OF AMERICAN DREAM

The political turmoil in American presidential election reflects the limits of capitalist constitution and crisis of market democracy in the United States. Both Mr Donald Trump and Mr Joe Biden represent different versions of American capitalism. The imperialist foreign policy and domestic security states are twin pillars of American governance system. These twin pillars are going to stay whoever wins this presidential election. It will neither benefit the American society nor conducive for the world. The American Constitution limits emancipatory political and economic alternatives to flourish. The American constitutional democracy was shaped by Anglo-American legal frameworks, which promotes propertied classes and corporates for the growth of capitalism with constitutional protection. The American political and economic dreams are shattered by the capitalism ingrained within American constitutional law and its practice.

The unfettered culture of individualism and consumerism emanating from the capitalist praxis did not help in the growth of individual freedom within American dream. It fortified the processes of capitalist accumulation within American constitutional and legal framework, which led to the freedom of legal contracts of private property. The industrial revolution in the United States led to the further consolidation of capitalism by integrating American working classes within its culture of mass production: the foundation of American dream. The need-based American society was converted into a desire-based society in twentieth century to sustain, expand and globalise American capitalism. The economic dynamism of American capitalism gets its strength from the American political system sustained by its constitution. It has managed to emerge as the most successful and powerful system in the world.

American constitutional capitalism and its market democracy is showing all signs of its deteriorating democratic culture and marching towards authoritarianism led by political oligarchy of two-party system. The U.S. Supreme Court has enough judicial power granted by the American Constitution which forces federal constitutions to serve its purpose of centralisation of power. The centralisation of power is central to capitalism, and American presidential system is designed in consonance with the requirements of capitalism.

From the pre-industrial or agricultural period prior to mid-nineteenth century and from the corporate industrial period of late nineteenth century to corporate capitalist monopoly of twentieth century and finance capital of twenty-first century, American capitalism in all its forms gets its full support from dominant forces of American politics. Therefore, concentration of economic power in the United States is a product of political consolidation of powerful forces in American society. Senator Boies Penrose was a Republican Senator from Pennsylvania during late nineteenth century. He told big businesses directly that 'you send us to Congress; we pass the laws under which you make money and out of your profits you further contribute to our campaigns funds to send us back again to pass more laws to enable you to make more money'. This is the foundation and fate of many democracies in the world today. From Westphalian democracies to postcolonial democracies, the corporate-led market forces are dominating the political forces.

The spirit of capitalist accumulation moves along with American democracy and complement each other. It is the rule of capitalist classes within the constitutional frameworks. The constitutional frameworks are adjusted as per the changing circumstances, needs and desires of the capitalist classes in America. The political regimes, constitutional laws and economic structures are interwoven with each other and work together to uphold the class rule, which mass produces inequalities in all areas of American life. Therefore, the political freedom does not breed economic prosperity for majority of working-class Americans. There is a growing gap between political freedom and economic liberties within American society.

In this way, the constitutional capitalism in the United States has established a lopsided society based on marginalisation, exploitation and inequalities. The economic alienation reduces American citizenship to a mere symbol of political freedom without material foundation for empowerment of citizenship rights and liberties of majority of Americans. The issues of unemployment, debt trap, hunger and homelessness are exposing the dubious American dream, which converted human lives into orderly objects within a market-led society. Deaths and destitutions are posing a serious threat to American democracy and destroy many progressive, transformatory and positive aspects of American Constitution.

The American experiments with constitutional capitalism have reached its dead-end. Socialisation of risk, marginalisation of individuals and their democratic rights and privatisation of prosperity cannot be a model for governance in a liberal and constitutional democracy. The constitution cannot be selective upholding rights and ownership of corporates and landed elites in the United States. The American capitalist classes get all forms of immunities of law with the help of different contractual clauses like; contract clause, equality clause, due process clause and commerce clause. These clauses enjoy absolute freedom. The 'freedom of contract' derives its ideological origin within Adam Smith's doctrine of laissez faire. The so-called free democracy is imprisoned within a capitalist economic framework within the provisions of constitutional laws shaped by the capitalist classes in the United States.

The self-inflicted crisis of American dream is inherent within capitalism as a political, economic, social and cultural system. The commodification of nature, human creativities and lives are primary source of profit making within capitalism. The commodification produces metabolic rift between interests of the capitalism and human necessities. These fundamental contradictions reflect in every step of human life in the name of efficiency and economy that serves the capitalist classes. Any search for alternatives needs to understand these social, political and economic dynamism of capital within America and beyond. Therefore, the struggle for alternatives within and outside America needs to demand transformation of capitalist foundations of constitutional laws. The struggle for political, economic and cultural democracy and freedom based on shared peace and prosperity can be the only alternative for the present and future. Let's start our struggles to save our present and fortify our future beyond boundaries as global citizens of this planet.

TROIKA OF IMPERIALIST PROJECTS FROM NATO, QUAD TO D-10

The colonial and imperialist powers have imposed bipolar world order after the Second World War by establishing the North Atlantic Treaty Organization (NATO). The idea was to destroy every alternative like USSR experiments and establish capitalism as the only political and economic ideology. The hegemonic world politics emanating from it during 1945 to 1953 had created conditions for the growth of the Cold War from 1953 to 1962. The temporary peace during détente has ended with the renewed tension between Washington and Moscow. From the Cuban Missile Crisis of 1962 to the Euromissile crisis of late 1970s, the world has witnessed the imperialist manoeuvres to dominate political power and control economic resources of the newly independent countries in Asia, Africa and Latin America. The newly independent postcolonial countries were denied in their attempts to be free from these twin power blocks by following independent foreign policy under the Non-Aligned Movement (NAM). The neo-colonial economic policies and imperialist military adventures by the European and American powers have destroyed the abilities of the NAM countries to pursue independent foreign and economic policies. The defeat of American imperialism in Vietnam was a temporary jolt to its imperialist missions. The American imperialism restarted its military engine under the leadership of President Ronald Reagan by establishing international arms race under the programme called 'Strategic Defence Initiative' (SDI) led by the NATO on 23 March 1983. The cold war ended with the fall of the Berlin Wall in November 1989 but the imperialist war machine did not stop. It was further strengthened by forming new imperialist alliances after the fall of Soviet Russia in 1991.

The United States emerged as the dominant imperialist power after the fall of Soviet Russia. The U.S. and European imperialism led by the NATO has produced deaths and destitutions in Asia, Africa, Eastern Europe, Middle East and Latin America. The NATO continues to play a significant role in consolidating American imperialist hegemony till the rise of China as a formidable power, which can challenge the dominance of American imperialism today. The powers in Washington are recklessly on overdrive to reverse the conditions for a multipolar and democratic world order. The salvo of U.S. imperialism is threatening world peace by reviving its anti-Asian imperialist projects by setting up regional and global formations against China. In this new age of imperialism, there is no competition among imperial powers for dominance. The collaborations have replaced competition among erstwhile imperialist and colonial powers. The NATO was the first major form of imperialist collaboration, which continues to exist and expands its military adventures to change political regimes in the name of democracy. In reality, the NATO prefers right-wing and authoritarian client states and dictatorial governments. From Asia to Latin America, Middle East, the NATO has played a major role in the withering away of democracy. The groupings and regroupings of nation states by forming economic, political, religious and cultural blocks are shaping new forms of imperialist polyverse within the fragile world order.

The imperialist and colonial collective called the NATO as an organisation should have been abandoned after the fall of Soviet Union. But NATO has started consolidating and expanding its base in different forms in the name of expanding free market democracy. From the Conference on Security and Cooperation in Europe (CSCE) to the creation of the Organisation for Security and Cooperation in Europe (OSCE), the NATO has played a key role. The military campaign was not enough to defeat alternative forces fighting against the NATO. The anti-communist Visegrad Group was also established by the NATO to implement its imperialist military ideology. The Central European Free Trade Agreement (CEFTA) was a product of this ideological narrative of the NATO within the framework of free market democracy to consolidate European and American capitalism. The social, economic and political perils of Europe today are products of its own making. The imperialist military-industrial and corporate alliances are destroying liberal democracies in Europe and diminishing its economic strengths by marginalising Europeans. The proposed Transatlantic Trade and Investment Partnership (TTIP) between the European Union (EU) and the United States is a further consolidation of transatlantic capitalism, which will accelerate further marginalisation of working people in Europe.

The NATO and its ideological frameworks of capitalism, colonialism, imperialism and wars ideologies are de-territorial by nature. Its global ambitions cannot be confined within a territory. It intends to dominate the world both in political, economic and cultural terms by expanding capitalism alias free market democracy with the brute force of military. It forms alliances with reactionary religious, cultural and political forces to dismantle and replace democracies with dictatorships and authoritarian regimes. The NATO's wars for democracy are regime change by military means in reality. The wars and conflicts in Latin America, Africa, Middle East and Asia are part of the NATO's design to establish friendly regimes concomitant with interests of American and European imperialism upholding the interests of the capitalist classes.

The NATO has established an informal strategic forum called the Quadrilateral Security Dialogue (Quad) between the United States, Japan, Australia and India. The mission and vision of such a strategic forum were shaped by the NATO think tank called the Center for Strategic and International Studies (CSIS). The CSIS Alliances and American Leadership Program is pushing the Quad towards a formal military alliance like the NATO in Asia Pacific region. So, the Quad can be called 'Asian NATO'. The CSIS calls such an alliance as diamond. Shinzo Abe has called it as an 'Arc of Freedom and Prosperity'. It sounds exactly like the Charter of Paris for a New Europe based on the principles of the Helsinki Final Act, which proclaimed to 'build, consolidate and strengthen democracy as the only system of government'. In reality, it accelerated the establishment of unfettered capitalism in Europe. In reality, the Quad (Asian NATO) is against Asia and interests of the Asian people in letter and spirit. The central idea is to contain and destroy Chinese model of economic development by fuelling regional wars and conflicts between India and China. It is against the peace and prosperity in Asia. It is against regional and world peace. It was informally created during the natural calamity like Tsunami and attempts are being made to formalise it during global health crisis. How does military exercises help in disaster relief and rehabilitation of people? The human tragedies are inseparable part of imperialist designs. The outcomes are not going to be different. If the dreams of the Quad become a reality, it would be a disaster: threatening peace in Asia and destroy prosperity in the world.

The Group of Seven (G7) countries – Canada, France, Germany, Italy, Japan, the United Kingdom and the United States – are expanding their political, economic and regional base by formally adding South Korea, India and Australia into the group. It is rebranded as new D-10; a group of ten leading democracies in the world. It is promoted by Washington and Westminster to isolate China and its role in world politics and economy. There is no political, economic and ideological coherence between these countries. The anti-Chinese, anti-socialist alternative and unfettered capitalism are three defining binding forces for such an alliance. It does not care about issues of people and their living conditions in these ten countries. The D-10 is an extension of American and European capitalism and its dominance. The countries like Spain, the Netherlands, Sweden and Poland are going to be occasional participants. Boris Johnson calls it as golden opportunity for 'Global Britain'.

From NATO, Quad to D-10, the troika of imperialism in all its reincarnations follow its old maxim outlined by Hastings Ismay in 1949. The maxim was to 'keep the Soviet Union out, the Americans in, and the Germans down'. In 2020, the maxim is to check the rise of peace and prosperity in Asia by fuelling conflict between China and India. The conflicts and wars in Asia will accelerate economic growth in America and Europe with the help of defence trade. The military-industrial complex will be net beneficiaries at the cost of people, their lives and livelihoods. It will ruin both in their path towards economic and social progress. Historically, old and new imperialisms in all their reincarnations are against peace and human values of freedom and democracy. It is within this context; the world needs an anti-imperialist front to struggle against all forms of imperialism at home and abroad. India and China need to understand and realise these imperialist designs for the fall of Asia again. Therefore, Japan, India and China need to work together for peace by developing mutual trust among themselves and among their immediate neighbours to defeat these new imperialist designs. The regional peace and prosperity in Asia depend on Japan, India and China, whereas world peace depends on its international commitment to fight imperialism in all its forms.

MANIFESTO AGAINST DEMOCRATIC DEFICITS AND THE CAPITALIST WESTPHALIAN NATION STATE

What is happening to democracies across the globe? Democratic deficit, neoliberalism and rise of authoritarianism moving together by dismantling social harmonies and states. The rise of Donald Trump in the United States, Narendra Modi in India, Boris Johnson in the United Kingdom, Erdoğan in Turkey, Jair Messias Bolsonaro in Brazil and many others are not only examples of the symptoms but also the results of democratic deficits in the world today. The local, national and international politics is driven by ethnic, racial and religious conflicts in Asia, Africa, Americas, Europe and Middle East. These populist upheavals did not change the old-world order rather reinforcing it more vigorously. God, national glory, lawlessness, vulgar wealth and huge inequalities are five common features between old and modern world. It creates the foundation for reactionary nationalism and authoritarian capitalism across the globe. Democracy and states have become tools of such a dangerous worldwide process.

The pioneers of globalisation and lovers of free market argued that it will bring peace and prosperity by ending war and conflicts. They also argued that it will help in the growth and establishment of vibrant and multicultural democracies. But in reality, globalisation has expanded the conflicts and old-world inequalities. Rich became richer and poor became poorer. The class, gender, race, caste and regional fault lines continue to grow under capitalism. The neoliberal capitalist project outmanoeuvred the ideal alternatives of October Revolution, French Revolution and promises of anti-colonial struggles. And all idealisms are in downward spiral now. How do we analyse these upheavals? Is it a sign of end of Westphalian nation state?

It is impossible to offer alternatives for a better tomorrow without understanding present predicaments and its history.

THE LINEAGES AND TRANSFORMATIONS

The democratic deficit of the state is embedded with history of capitalist Westphalian nation state. The peace Treaty of Westphalia in 1648 consolidated capitalism by establishing nation states based on the idea of territorial sovereignty. It helped to end thirty years of savagely war in Europe. It also helped Europe to plunder the world with colonial rule in different parts of the world. The resources of the colonies were used to establish different institutions of economic development and democratic governance in Europe. Therefore, Westphalian states are innately colonial, capitalist and authoritarian by nature but dressed up as democracy. The referendum results and debates over Britain leaving EU is a classic example of democratic deficit and its relationship with European capitalism led by EU.

The postcolonial states emerged after the success of anti-colonial struggles. The postcolonial states promised democratic governance based on ideals of liberty, equality, justice and welfare of all its citizens. The anti-colonial struggles had positive influence on European states. It transformed the nature of state in Europe by making them more democratic, secular and multicultural in terms of citizenship rights with welfare orientations. But the neoliberal Washington consensus led to the universalisation of neoliberal welfare state by ending ideals of democratic and welfare state. The centralisation and securitisation of state became order of the day to uphold the interests of the private capital which grown enormously after the implementation of neoliberal policies of liberalisation, privatisation and globalisation.

We live in a world today where *Vox Populi, Vox Dei* (the voice of the people is the voice of God) is replaced by the order of the capitalism where market and money dominates every social, economic, political, cultural and religious sphere. It is within this context, democracy and state face challenges from capitalist world system accelerated by Westphalian ideals. Neoliberal authoritarianism emanates from such a political and economic project that creates a culture of democratic deficit and unreliable state. The legitimacy crisis of state creates the vacuums where ruling and non-ruling elites control the masses and all resources with the help of securitised, centralised and authoritarian state. The ideological narrative of neoliberalism was based on individual freedom but in reality, we live in a society today where people are in free prisons of market where prices are independent and free. It means the dead capital is free and lively labour in captives.

THE QUEST FOR ALTERNATIVES MANIFESTO

The crisis created by democratic deficit, neoliberal authoritarianism and rise of reactionary right-wing politics is a global phenomenon. Local and national contexts are important in search of alternatives, but the current political and economic crisis needs international solutions. It is imperative to develop pluriversal praxis that is applicable to the world today.

The first step is to dismantle the structures of Westphalian capitalist state system and all its affiliated supranational and international organisations. This is only possible by creating solidarity of all grassroots movements for alternative democracy for peace, environment, development and prosperity as inalienable citizenship rights. It is important to have continuous solidarity of struggles to develop conditions for non-discriminatory and pluriversal and inalienable rights based on progressive and scientific thoughts.

The second step is to develop conditions where local communities can control and manage their local resources based on their needs and desires with egalitarian distributive mechanisms.

The third step is to develop local, national and international struggles against all conflicts, wars and industries affiliated with it including nuclear weapons. Defence industry creates wars to expand its profits.

The fourth one is continuous struggle against all forms of authoritarianism and all forms of discrimination in every sphere of life.

The fifth one is about creating a decentralised, democratic, progressive and egalitarian state where individual rights and right to self-determination are inalienable.

TOWARDS THE FORWARD MARCH OF WORKER-LED ALTERNATIVE GLOBALIZATION

Is globalisation over after the COVID-19 pandemic? There are three visible signs during the unending coronavirus-led health crisis, which substantiates the end of globalisation thesis. The first sign indicates reversal of capitalist globalisation led by market integrations. The people and their nation states are fighting the pandemic alone. As a result, there is growth of ultra nationalist and right-wing forces during this pandemic. The second sign comes from the response to the global health crisis and search for anti-coronavirus vaccine demands more coordinated international response. Many countries are cooperating with each other in research and development of vaccine. The third sign comes from the failure of capitalist states and their healthcare facilities to deal with the pandemic. The liberalisation, privatisation and globalisation did not help people during this pandemic. The last two signs reveal that it is imperative for global engagement for better health, sustainable happiness, lasting peace and prosperity for all. It is impossible to have an island of peace and prosperity when the majority of world population suffer in different forms of crisis. Therefore, the search for an alternative system that puts people before profit during all forms of global crisis.

Both the progressive and right-wing forces oppose globalisation today. The progressive forces oppose globalisation as it marginalises the masses and destroys environment by exploiting both human beings and nature. The right-wing forces oppose globalisation for their narrow and nativist Malthusian predicaments. During this pandemic, the progressive forces blame the capitalist state and its failures to face the challenges of coronavirus crisis, whereas the right-wing forces oppose Asians, Chinese and migrants for the spread of the pandemic. In this context, there is a great deal of debates about the extent to which reshaping of globalisation is necessary to transform global economy and politics in post-pandemic world. The transformation depends on understanding our own experiences with the history of globalisation. It is time to move away from the preoccupation with the analysis of virtues or perils of globalisation. Such cost-benefit analysis of globalisation is unhelpful to develop an alternative and universal narrative, which keeps people and environment at the core of its analytical vision. The ferocity and proliferation of this pandemic obscures the fundamental global challenges and threats faced by the humanity due to the globalisation of capitalism.

Historically, globalisation of capital is the most dominant force for last three centuries of world history. In terms of the relationship between capital and labour, globalisation has passed through three different but interrelated stages. The first stage of globalisation was a period when labour was absolutely free during the processes of production, consumption and distribution. The second phase of globalisation was dominated by Western colonialism in Asia, Africa and Americas. During this phase of globalisation, colonial capital was free to exploit both labour and natural resources in the colonised continents, whereas the movement of labour was limited based on the requirements of the colonial powers. By the end of the Second World War, there was further limitation on the mobility of labour but there was relatively higher freedom for the capital. The third phase of globalisation started with the capital-labour accord with the Washington consensus, which led to greater economic integration of markets driven by free trade in the world. During this phase of globalisation, the developed countries have followed protectionist economic policies and imposed free trade on developing and underdeveloped countries. The free trade was designed by the erstwhile colonial powers in a way that led to the concentration of wealth in the hands of few in the Western world.

In order to succeed, the new era of globalisation needs to conceptualise globalisation in a different way by moving away from both protectionism and free trade under capitalism. The policies of both protectionism and free trade help in the concentration of wealth and serve the interests of the same capitalist classes. The processes of concentration of wealth trickled down to the capitalist classes based in the postcolonial countries. This created the conditions for the global capitalist alliances to control global resources in which states have become the facilitators. The welfare orientations of the states and their role in providing public healthcare facilities were transformed and privatised to pursue profit by the capitalist classes, who took over all state resources and facilities. As a result, the states have failed to face global health challenges like coronavirus pandemic. The competitive and hierarchical culture of capitalism has failed to face this global health crisis.

In this context, the intellectuals, public policy makers and leaders need to articulate a new wave of globalisation breaking away from its old colonial and capitalist lineages. The ideological and structural delinking of globalisation from its previous regimes and phases is significant for a new wave of globalisation. The ideals of pluriveralism need to be the organising principles of globalisation driven by the workers of the world. The ravages of coronavirus pandemic and other threats to the survival of human lives and environment depend on our commitment to the principles of cooperation. The framework of democratic dialogue between individuals, states and societies can create meaningful and sustainable alternatives in the world, where 'one lives for all and all live for one'. The shared vision for a collective global future and its success depends on our ability to embrace differences and celebrate our acentric uniqueness. The articulation and fundamental commitment to this principle can start a new era of globalisation, which is free and fair for all. Such global perspective can radically transform world economy, where workers become shareholders of capital they produce. In this distinct phase of globalisation, it is important to create cooperative governance systems, which can transform gun, god and globalisation into workers internationalism.

The workers' internationalism is not a utopia. The technology and digital revolution can help in realising the goals of workers' internationalism guaranteeing peace and prosperity. The workers-led democratisation of ownership of technologies and digital revolutions can shape global economy in four significant ways. First, the use of technology increases productive power of labour. The growth of productive power means labourers need to get their higher share of value that they add and produce by which they can enjoy more leisure time with their families and fellow human beings. Second, the workers-led digital revolution reduces competitiveness among workers, which can create conditions for greater cooperation among workers. Third, the use of technology reduces cost of production. It can help consumers to get their everyday products in low cost. The quality of life increases with the declining cost of living. Finally, technology can help in providing information on conditions and cost of production to the consumers. The flow of information can create an interactive process and environment for the greater understanding between consumers and producers. In this way, technology can create social market as a means of exchange by dismantling digital divide.

The forward march of workers-led globalisation based on internationalism is the only way to realise greater goal of the universalisation of global citizenship. This new wave of alternative globalisation and all its possibilities depend on our progressive struggles and commitment for a better world.

Chapter 2

State, Pandemic and Business

'To be or not to be productive' is an old constructed dilemma that surfaces during the coronavirus pandemic. This Shakespearean tragedy is pushing people in two contradictory directions. On the one hand, the states and governments are asking people to stay at home and stay safe during the lockdown period. The inevitable lockdown and physical distancing policies produce social alienation and economic distress for the masses. On the other hand, the centuries long capitalist socialisation with the ideal that unproductive indolence is immoral. It forces people to engage with time and creativity for self-improvement by busy in work. The social media accelerates such socialisation process during this pandemic. The battle of productivity during the pandemic undermines individual creativity, mental health and accelerates public health crisis.

The policymakers are ignoring the miseries of individuals and communities while looking for ways to recover after the pandemic. Many commentators on public policy are trying to draw lessons from the wartime economics to create a new narrative for productivism as the foundation of welfare state. Such narratives also glorify workers' sacrifices. The glorification of the spirit of work ethics is central to capitalism, which derives its strength from all major world religions. Religion and capitalism are twin pillars of such a contradictory narrative that promotes productivist society. In such a society, time is considered as money. People compete with each other and with nature to convert their time into money by working hard. It creates an illusion that working hard is a means to pursue one's own dream and uplift one's own self from economic miseries. The desire to recover from economic misery puts people in an illusion that diverts people's attention from their working conditions and the processes, which controls and exploits their work. The workers work hard in every field and they are the most productivist people in the world, but they suffer the miseries the most. The productivist societies normalise and naturalise inequalities and exploitation. So, the society based on productivist philosophy is inherently exploitative and unsustainable. The unsustainability of such a productivist system is revealed by this pandemic. The human alienation is the net outcome of both the pandemic and the productivism.

The history of productivism as an ideology emerged during early agricultural society based on the growing needs of people. The need-based society was transformed into a desire-based society with the growth of intensive expansion of agriculture for higher production. The production is not only for consumption requirements but also for sale in the market and for export to distant places. The ideals of productivism became the everyday ideology of the industrial revolution. Productivism continues to be the answer for problems created by the capitalist economy in different parts of the world. The ideology of productivism in twenty-first century demonstrates three specific dimensions: (i) concentration, (ii) intensification and (iii) specialisation. These three dimensions have played significant role in destroying environment and weakening the power of labour to serve the interests of the owners of the capital. Both the liberal and neoliberal policymakers use these features of productivism as policy prescriptions during economic crisis. The global health crisis due the coronavirus pandemic is bringing back these old ideals of productivism for the survival of capitalist system, which further weakens the working classes all over the world. Some countries have already removed the protective measures by reforming labour laws, which is used to provide safety nets to the workers. The historical experiences of all productivist societies in different parts of the world expose the limits of productivist ideology that upholds the interests of the capital and weakens labour power.

The productivist ideology of capitalism imposes economic and moral logic to allure the working classes to the world of work that diminishes the meaning of life. It individualises the working conditions and production processes which destroys the collectivist foundation of society. It is in this process, the workers face all forms of social, economic, cultural and political alienation that is concomitant with the alienation people face during the pandemic-led lockdown. The outbreak of coronavirus has also manufactured unprecedented uncertainties in global scale. The capitalist class is trying to capture their lost profit by increasing working hours. The trade union laws are being diluted to serve the interests of the capitalist class.

It is within this context, the workers need to start writing their own narratives by disengaging with capitalist productivist framework in which work is individualised, standardised, disciplined and commodified. There is a little room for the creative growth of workers and their skills. This crisis is an opportunity for the workers to create their own workers cooperatives and other labour organisations to coordinate different factors of production. The workers can create their own conditions of work, where the work is meaningful for the society and meaningful for the workers themselves. The workers can shape their own experiences by working independent of the productivist logic of a death cult called capitalism. The lockdown period is a period of reflection on life. The human happiness and health depend on the quality of life, which is denied in the productivist work culture.

The French philosopher Pascal said that 'all problems of the humanity come from the inability for the man to sit without doing anything in a room'. Pandemic-led lockdown period is the apt period in which people are made to feel impatient for being idle. It is time to understand the vices of productivist life and celebrate virtues of laziness. The iconic works like *On Laziness* by Christopher Morley, *An Apology for Idlers* by R. L. Stevenson, *In Praise of Idleness* by Bertrand Russell and *Why Are Beggars Despised?* by George Orwell have provided enough justification to celebrate the virtues of being lazy. It gives an opportunity to the workers to consolidate their time and energy for a more meaningful life that is disengaged from the system. The workers' non-cooperation with capitalism and its productivist philosophy can only help workers and make the world more sustainable for the future. The freedom of workers from capitalism depends on the quality of their laziness. It is time to dump the busy schedule in search of collective meaning of life, liberty, individual dignity, equality, humanity and happiness.

CORONAVIRUS, BUSINESS OF SICKNESS AND THE SOCIALIST ALTERNATIVES

The coronavirus pandemic is battering lives and wreaking havoc in world economy at the same time. This worldwide health and economic crisis reveals the inherent structural fault lines within neoliberal economic system dominated by global corporations. The fault lines are further exacerbated by the amoral market-led states that protect interests of big businesses and pharmaceutical corporations. The incoherent, incomprehensive and reluctant strategic response to this crisis by the developed counties like the United Kingdom and the United States reflect utter failure of the neoliberal ideology that promotes business of sickness by privatising public health.

The Thatcherite and Blairite neoliberal economic policies are destroying the National Health Service (NHS) in the UK: one of the best healthcare systems in the world. The NHS is suffering from funds crunch, shortages of doctors and nurses due to under investment in health infrastructure for decades. How do we expect the NHS to face complex challenges of coronavirus pandemic? The conservative government's response to the crisis is pumping up money to sustain business and less focus on fighting the pandemic. The focus is more on the survival of the businesses than lives of ordinary people. The Tory government's failure to face such a crisis is giving rise to racism and maskophobia against Chinese and other migrant population.

Donald Trump calls coronavirus as Chinese virus. Such statements fuel racism and anti-Chinese sentiments in the society. His government's policy response abandons poor American's ability to access healthcare during this pandemic. It puts nearly 58 per cent American lives in risk. His government is an utter failure to deal with coronavirus in the United States. The American imperialist trade embargo is directly responsible for the higher percentage of deaths in Iran due to coronavirus pandemic. It is important to demand for the removal of American trade embargo on Iran on humanitarian grounds. But capitalist geopolitics is all about business.

The business of sickness is an integral part of neoliberal ideology and its economic system. This pandemic is an opportunity for profit hungry pharmaceutical corporations, private healthcare providers, insurance agencies and other businesses. The stockpiling of essential goods by people is selfish, nasty and brutish. But such Hobbesian solitary behaviours are reinforced by the neoliberal economic policies practised over last four decades. The individualistic response to crisis is a product of neoliberal capitalism that reshaped us from social beings to mere customers under a market-led society and state. Therefore, it is important to break away from such a system that promotes death and destitution by using pandemic as an opportunity to make the empire of profit.

Courtney Davis and John Abraham in their book *Unhealthy Pharmaceutical Regulation: Innovation, Politics and Promissory Science* argue that drug regulatory agencies in the United States and EU are corrupted. These agencies and their policies promote commercial interests of the pharmaceutical industries and undermine the interests of the patients for last three decades. People in Italy, Spain, United Kingdom, France and the United States are in the receiving end of such policies.

This pandemic calls for structural reforms both within economic and health systems across the world. Kate Pickett and Richard Wilkson in their book *The Spirit Level: Why Greater Equality Makes Societies Stronger* argue that egalitarian societies are healthy societies. There is a strong link between inequality, poverty and poor health. Poor people are more vulnerable to coronavirus. Therefore, all government policies need to steer towards poor and working-class people both in short run and long run. Emancipatory politics and policies are only alternatives that the state and governments need to emulate. Nationalisation of pharmaceutical industries, private hospitals and medical facilities, universal access to medicine are few primary steps in fighting coronavirus pandemic.

China was the epicentre of coronavirus pandemic. State capitalism or socialism with Chinese character with all its limitations has managed to contain and reduce the spread of coronavirus. China and Cuba provided medical aid to Italy when EU looked the other way. In spite of all liberal criticisms, Cuba has managed to develop infrastructure to produce highest number of doctors, nurses and medical professionals in the world. Cuba has established the *BioCubaFarma group* which is rolling out *Interferon Alpha 2B* drug that can be used to treat coronavirus. Unlike developed capitalist countries, Cuba shares the technology with many countries like Finland, China and the United States. Cuban doctor Luis Herrera, the creator of the *Interferon Alfa 2-B* medication, argues that 'health is not a commercial asset but a basic right'. Cubans provide medical aid, many doctors and health professionals are working in many African and Latin American countries.

This crisis offers the limitless possibilities of socialist alternative which means borderless solidarity, sharing economy and technology for people and caring for healthy environment. It is our choice for a healthy and harmonious economy for the present and future. It is time to fight for socialism together or perish together under pandemic incubator called capitalism.

WHAT HAPPENED TO 'FAILED STATE' THESIS?

The policy practitioners in the World Bank, OECD and other development agencies used the term 'fragile state' during 1990s before using of the term 'failed state'. The failure to provide security to the citizens, failure to provide public services including health and monopoly of state violence are three central components that define 'failed state'. The incubation and spread of deadly diseases are one of the many features of failed state as outlined by the United States Institute of Peace (USIP) in its 2004 report. The *Dutch Advisory Council on International Affairs (AIV) on Issues of Public International Law* has defined failed state or state failures as 'the impotence of the central government'. The bourgeois intellectuals started using the term without questioning the validity of its core concepts. The *Failed State Index* was designed by the *Funds for Peace* in 2005. There is no empirical evidence or justification behind such an index. But the think tanks and academicians started using such a sham index to rank states in terms of their abilities, and efficiency in dealing with different forms of crisis and frame policies accordingly.

The coronavirus pandemic and failures of capitalist states provide an opportunity to interrogate the ideas and objectives around the 'failed state' and expose its conceptual ambiguity, theoretical absurdity and empirical fallacies. The 'failed state' thesis and its narratives were developed in the form of blistering critique of postcolonial states in Africa, Asia and Latin America. The motivation was to undermine postcolonial states, their development promises, processes and legitimacy in the eyes of their own citizens. The stages of economic growth, modernisation and development theories were offered as alternatives within Eurocentric paradigm that ignored the historical conditions and contemporary limitations to reflect on the realities of uneven developments in world economy. The idea behind such a narrative is to hide the imperialist and colonial plunders, which led to the economic underdevelopment in postcolonial states and their failures.

Further, the neo-colonial trade policies undermined the postcolonial states' ability to engage with international trade and business. The terms of trade during globalisation are not only unequal and unfair but also exploitative. The colonial aid for trade policies were designed in such a way that led to exploitation of natural resources of postcolonial states. These are some of the causes that led to the failure of postcolonial states in delivering public goods such as basic health, education, security, roads, transportation and communication infrastructures. The predatory ruling regimes and their cronies were promoted by the Western powers, which accelerated weakening and collapse of postcolonial states. The states in Afghanistan, Iraq, Syria, Lebanon, Egypt, Nigeria, Somalia and Serra Leone have collapsed due to different forms of imperialist and neo-colonial interventions. But these states were branded as failed states.

The failed state as a concept developed to organise these weak states and control their resources necessary for the survival and growth of capitalism. Failed state was a pretext of imperialist interventions to establish a political regime that works as per the orders of the capitalist states in Europe and America. It is capitalism and its international institutional apparatus developed the failed state thesis to hide the exploitative colonial past and imperialist present. The failed state as a concept needs to be discarded as it does not serve to analyse and explain the conditions of development and underdevelopment within the historical contexts of state formations. The Failed State Index is historically flawed and analytically poor. It does not help us to understand the subjective and objective conditions of state failures. It cannot guide policy framework in any positive direction.

The capitalist states like the United Kingdom and the United States have abandoned their constitutional responsibilities to protect citizens from the COVID-19 pandemic. The pestilence-led lockdown impels to rethink, reflect and reject the Eurocentric ideological narratives of 'Westphalian nation-states', capitalist in letter and spirit. It is also the time to rewrite the ideological narratives and dominance of the so-called success stories of Western states and their universalising tendencies of capitalism as only alternatives. In reality, capitalist states like the United States has not only failed to face the pandemic, but also the USDA under the Trump administration is making all efforts to strip away nutrition benefits from more than a million Americans who depend completely on food stamps. The UK under Boris Johnson-led conservative government has failed to provide basic safety nets to frontline workers. The government is planning to further weaken the working class by freezing the wages and removing triple lock system on pensions to fund the debt and to compensate the deficit occurred due to coronavirus crisis. This is morally indefensible but Malthusian capitalist state in the UK lacks moral compass. The capitalist states in France, Italy and Spain have also failed to protect their citizens during this pandemic. These Westphalian states were formed to consolidate capitalism during mid-seventeenth century, but they failed miserably to face the challenges of public health crisis during 2020 coronavirus pandemic. The failure shows the limits of the capitalist states and fallacies of failed state as a narrative. The countries like China, Cuba and Vietnam were successful because of their swift, scientific and collective response to the crisis. But this is unacceptable to the advocates of failed state thesis.

However, the rise of radical right-wing political parties and their reactionary nationalist politics is giving breathing space to the failed capitalist states. The popular discontent is externalised by conspiracy theorists and their propaganda machine to undermine the success of China, Cuba and Vietnam in dealing with the coronavirus crisis. The rising tide of xenophobia gives the capitalist states more power to hide their failures under security cover that undermines civil liberties of citizens during lockdowns. The emergency measures and suspension of normality help the capitalist states to divert the democratic discontents and resistance movements that empower the citizens. Deaths and destitutions are the twin net outcome of the coronavirus pandemic accelerated by capitalism.

The capitalist states have failed to respond to the global health crisis and other ancillaries of the pandemic. The people are facing alienation and discontent in life within lockdown for survival. The dreadful days of coronavirus pandemic will come to an end at one point of time and people will take off their mask of fear. But let us not forget to unmask the capitalist state and its healthcare systems that failed the masses. The atomised individualism promoted by capitalist system is also busted during the unavoidable lockdown-induced lethal loneliness. All forms of alienations are organic to capitalism that the failed states aggravate during this pandemic. There is an adage that one learns from everyday experiences of the present crisis that the capitalist state and all its machineries have failed in the face of pandemic. Therefore, social and political solidarity is the only alternative against capitalism and all its alienating experiences.

Societies, states, governments, economy, culture and politics exist for the people and because of the people. These entities and institutions are meaningless without people. So, it is imperative to reflect on the directions of our life, society and states. There are two directions. The first one is to continue with business as usual with the capitalist system and suffer under its profit-driven barbaric pandemic of inequality and exploitation. The second option is to break away from such a system and focus on people and their well-being. This is a historic opportunity to make a clear choice for our present and future. The coronavirus pandemic provides an opportunity to transform the state apparatus and overthrow capitalism that destabilises human existence and failed citizens, states and societies around the world. It important to move to an unwaveringly international, regional, national and local political and economic system that puts people and nature at the core of its agenda.

CORONAVIRUS CRISIS AND THE
FUTURE OF MASS MOVEMENTS

The spectre of pandemic-led crisis and its relationship with social transformation is not new. The *Plague of Justinian* and the *Black Death* had huge impact on weakening of feudalism in Europe. It did not pave the path for democratic movements in Europe but made people conscious about the difference in sufferings. The masses suffered in different plagues while the feudal ruling class protected themselves within their forts and castles. The political landscape in Europe changed after the pandemic. The agrarian capitalism in England, decentralised oligarchical commercial capitalism in Italy, partnership between aristocracy and monarchy in France and Spain led to the consolidation of capitalism and rise of authoritarian state in Europe. People's resistance movements and sacrifice paved the path for democracy in different parts of Europe. The history repeats itself during this coronavirus crisis in which rich live with their abundance, and masses suffer in deaths and destitutions. There is also growing tendencies of authoritarianism within and outside Europe.

Since the beginning of this pandemic, the world is experiencing higher growth of poverty, hunger and unemployment. The capitalist states have failed to respond to the crisis in any meaningful manner. Faced with the inability to find solutions, the right-wing ruling classes have unleashed reactionary nationalism as a weapon that provides breathing space to market forces to recover from the crisis. The market forces are doing everything in their power to capture the resources of the state. The states and governments are using lockdown as an opportunity to destroy the democratic space by spreading fear and xenophobia. Many governments are using this crisis to dismantle labour laws that protects the workers and handing over national resources to corporations. The pandemic works like a political lifeline for the authoritarian bigots and capitalist classes. The crisis is proliferating like the mutating power of the coronavirus. The policy of physical distance is branded as social distancing, which further erodes social ties in the name of defeating the coronavirus from spreading. The social distancing policy is a way of reconfiguration of social and political relations necessary to socialise the fear of the virus and naturalise the crisis in the society.

The American and Eurocentric intellectuals are trying to normalise the crisis as a cyclic process. Such a narrative is already outlined by Willian Strauss and Neil Howe in their book *The Fourth Turning: An American Prophecy-What the Cycles of History Tell Us About America's Next Rendezvous with Destiny*. The Strauss–Howe generational stage theory is essentialist and functional. It lacks empirical evidence. The old fault lines of class, race and gender continue to exist among different generations. The categories like baby boomers, generation-x and millennials are not helpful to understand social and political transformations. Willian Strauss and Neil Howe's ideological narrative reflects American determinism based on exceptionalism and perceptions. These perceptions can neither be universal nor can be applied even within American context. Such a myopic theory is reviving during this pandemic as a tool to normalise and naturalise the crisis by diverting attention from the limits of capitalism.

It is within this context, the liberal, progressive and democratic forces need to develop alternative imaginary based on collective experiences of people during this coronavirus pandemic. The days of top-down approach of managing movements are over. The other traditional forms of social and political mobilisation for a mass movement are not possible under the current situation of social disconnectedness. The social disconnection is the breeding field of apolitical culture that depoliticises the public consciousness. These are some of the serious ideological and structural constraints for a mass movement against the capitalist plunders during pandemic.

Historically, revolutionary movements emerged during crisis. It is time for the intellectuals, activists and progressive leaders to articulate hopes and dreams of a better alternative that resonates with people, and their everyday experiences. The principle of listening and learning from the people can create conditions of collective empowerment and solidarity. The collective imagination can help in creating political spaces of possibilities of a mass movement, with both short-term goals of achieving people's basic needs and long-term visions for future transformations based on human emancipation from poverty, hunger, homelessness and all forms of inequalities. Constructing alternative narratives for this struggle mean rethinking the capitalist conditions of production, distribution and exchange mechanisms within international economic system. It is not about opposing technological automation; technology after all is a product of labour. So, it is about giving labour its due for a comfortable, dignified and leisurely creative life. It is about stopping further environmental damages. The framework of shared experiences and common visions can be used to shape local, national and transnational struggles for liberty, fraternity, equality and justice. The struggle based on sharing and caring can only transform the solitary atomised life under capitalism accelerated by the coronavirus pandemic.

Crisis breeds mass movements both in its progressive and regressive forms. Mass movements lead to social, cultural, economic and political transformations. The progressive, secular, liberal and democratic transformation of society and state depends on the emancipatory agendas of the mass movements. It is only the progressive mass movements, that fortify our present, shape our future and it will provide ideological directions to all future movements. The digital renaissance depends on our resolve to uphold the spirit of science and reason in one hand, and to fight against individualist market dogmas of capitalism and religious fundamentalism on the other hand.

How can we fight capitalism and coronavirus pandemic? History offers successful tools for revolutionary mass movements. The Non-Cooperation Movement was one such movement which was launched by Mahatma Gandhi against British colonialism in India. The movement crippled the British colonialism in India as Indians stopped working for the British and boycotted British goods in Indian markets. The motto of the movement was based on the simple idea of independence and self-governance. The 'Non-Cooperation' as a tool can be used to mobilise and implement resistance movements even during this lockdown. Digital revolution and technological innovations can facilitate the resistance movement. Non-cooperate and boycott all forms of capitalist framework in everyday life can be the starting point in search of a better alternative to the pandemic of capitalism.

TALE OF TWO STATES IN INDIA DURING CORONAVIRUS PANDEMIC

The coronavirus pandemic has aggravated existing economic and social crisis in India. The country is witnessing incomprehensible distress among the migrant workers, farmers and poor masses both in urban and rural areas. In such a situation of utter crisis, Mr Narendra Modi, the Prime Minister of India, is busy in manipulating Indian public by false propaganda to hide all his failures. And the Government of India is busy in satisfying the needs of capitalist class while poor suffer. Modi-led government in the centre and BJP-led state governments are busy in destroying all rules and regulations that protect the workers. It surrendered itself before the capitalist classes in India. It did not provide any relief to the poor and migrant workers. Modi government has failed miserably to face and manage the crisis. Its inherent inabilities are products of false confidence, arrogance of power and ignorance of understanding the crisis. But the state governments in Kerala and Odisha tell two different successful stories of humanism and became the beacon of hope for the masses during this unprecedented public health crisis in India.

The communist parties under the leadership of Chief Minister Mr Pinarayi Vijayan and Health Minister K.K. Shailaja proved that Kerala is no more a communist utopia. The political consciousness, effective government policies and committed leadership helped to manage and contain the spread of coronavirus with lowest casualty (four deaths) in a population of 35 million. The state has not only quarantined 170,000 people but also provided accommodation and three times food to 150,000 migrant workers. The state is ready with further emergency plans to face the challenges in future by requisitioning of hotels, hostels and conference centres to provide 165,000 more beds. It shows proactive leadership, participatory planning and speedy implementation of policies with scientific spirit that helped the state in combating coronavirus crisis. The Kerala's success story is neither a miracle nor an accident. It is a product of systematic long-term decentralised planning of development and democratic investment in public health and educational infrastructure. The politics of the poor and their partnership with the state through decentralised local self-governments have led to the success of Kerala in its fight against coronavirus.

The state of Odisha under the progressive, secular and committed leadership of Chief Minister Naveen Patnaik managed successfully to contain the spread of coronavirus. The chief minister personally appealed to the people to cooperate with the government's initiatives to fight the coronavirus. He developed an effective partnership with the local self-governments by directly engaging with the heads of 6,798 villages in the state. He made them to take oath to keep their areas free from the COVID-19. The pledge reads as follows: 'I take pledge to sincerely work towards containing the spread of novel coronavirus in my panchayat for the public good. I will ensure keeping the people coming from other states in quarantine and look after their stay, food and treatment'. Such progressive steps by the head of the state gave a sense of ownership to the citizens in fighting the pandemic. As a result, there are only five deaths due to COVID-19 in a population of nearly 47 million. The swift planning, immediate implementation of policies, clear communication of risks, regular updates, devolution of power to the local bodies and proactive bureaucracy helped Odisha to deal with the pandemic. The state capital Bhubaneswar is declared as coronavirus-free zone.

Odisha as state is truly the best-kept secret of India. The national media continue to misrepresent and ignore the state of Odisha and its potentials. The state is making progressive policy interventions in shaping its development destinations and claims its rightful place in national discourse. Odisha is leading by example when it comes to combating coronavirus pandemic. Odisha has established thirty-four dedicated hospitals to deal with the COVID-19. The Government of Odisha provides around 1.52 crore meals to the people in the affected districts. The Government of Odisha has provided free bus services to all migrant labours to return to their homes in the neighbouring states. While the central government is cancelling the dearness allowances, the Government of Odisha has raised the dearness allowance by 10 per cent for state government employees. The state's experience of disaster management during natural calamities became very helpful in dealing with the coronavirus-inflicted public health crisis.

Kerala and Odisha are different from each other but similar in many ways. The Kerala is ruled by the communist parties whereas Odisha is ruled by a regional party called Biju Janata Dal. Political consciousness is higher in Kerala than Odisha. Therefore, the political systems and their ideological trends in the making of public policies are different in these two states. The unflinching commitment to secularism is the similarity between the two chief ministers. Both states are inclusive, secular and progressive coastal states in India. Odisha is relatively larger both in terms of geography and population. Odisha has thirty-four dedicated COVID-19 hospitals whereas Kerala has twenty-seven. Kerala has higher health budget to deal with the pandemic than Odisha. Both the states are leading examples for India and international communities to deal with the pandemic.

Kerala and Odisha proved that only state interventions can work efficiently during the crisis. The state can only ensure the welfare of the masses. These two states are debunking the neoliberal market myth that state is inefficient in dealing with crisis. The people-centric state can only bring development by providing right to public health. It is not profit but public welfare determines the nature and sustainability of the state and its relationship with the citizens. Kerala and Odisha are two Indian states setting international standard to test, track, trace, treat, isolate and contain the spread of coronavirus. The political will combined with reason, science and mass support, Pinarayi Vijayan-led Kerala and Naveen Patnaik-led Odisha are doing remarkable work and emerging as hopes for the people during this public health disaster. The political will and commitment for public health and welfare by both the state governments led to effective management of this unprecedented public health crisis. Let these two states and their experiences in dealing with COVID-19 guide the future of public policy for health and development in India.

MIGRANTS AS CITIZENS AND STATE PLANNING
FOR RURAL DEVELOPMENT IN INDIA

The pandemic of coronavirus has exposed all limitations of free market economies and anomalies in capitalist global economy. The world economy is in shambles. The unprecedented restrictive and unavoidable lockdown measures by governments across the world has led to the loss of livelihoods, growth of unemployment, economic stagnation and crisis. It is one of the biggest challenges in world history. In this context, Indian economy looks gloomy. The pandemic has crippled the manufacturing and service sectors in Indian economy. It shattered the urban economy in India, which led to reverse migration from urban areas to rural areas. So, it is time to revisit the role of state and planning to invest in rural economy, which can absorb migrant labourers for a sustainable future.

The authoritarian, neoliberal, market economy free from state planning is no longer an option to revive agrarian and rural economy in India. It is important for the state planners to shift their focus from economic growth–led capital formation to labour empowerment. The investment in rural workforce, environment and agricultural land are three areas on which the governments need to focus for the revival of Indian economy. The unbridle privatisation of natural resources must stop. The governments must use natural resources in the rural areas to generate revenue to invest in rural development. The availability of sustainable livelihoods, investment in rural infrastructure in health, education and healthcare facilities can help to reduce rural to urban migration. It can reduce urban-biased development programmes. It can reduce population and other pressures on urban areas. It can help in accelerating national economic development in long run. There is no alternative to public welfare–driven states and governments. The recovery from the pandemic-led economic crisis depends on revival of state planning for rural development.

The rural development in India was in disarray before the outbreak of coronavirus. The state planning was considered obsolete and completely abandoned in search of economic growth. The market forces were given free hand to decide. The practice of neoliberal capitalism and its technocratic approach with the help of analytical development tools destroyed rural economy and reinforced agrarian crisis in India. Poverty, hunger and unemployment are the net outcome of the withdrawal of state from planning for rural development. The decline of rural agriculture and economy led to mass migration of rural labour and agricultural workers to urban areas and cities in India. These migrants were treated as disposables during the outbreak of coronavirus pandemic. The majority of migrants were left to their own fate. Many migrants survived the ordeal by walking thousands of miles from Indian cities to their rural hamlets. Their citizenship rights and human dignities were taken away by the very system that profits from their labour. The progressive states like Kerala and Odisha are two beacons of hope for the migrant population. These two states have taken enormous steps in bringing back their own migrants and sending back migrants from other states. It is time for the return of the state for planning and development of rural India by developing an abiding partnership between migrant citizens and the state.

Odisha Model of Crisis Management

The state of Odisha is an agrarian economy, which continues to face challenges of natural calamities in regular intervals. The regular natural calamities like floods and cyclones destroy the economy and cause deaths and destitutions in the state. It is because of state planning for last two decades, the Government of Odisha has managed to reduce human casualties to single digit and sometimes to zero causality due to natural calamities. The Odisha way of disaster management can be emulated by other states in India and countries across the globe.

In spite of limited resources and apathy of the central government, the state and the Government in Odisha is making remarkable progress. The state government has worked relentlessly for the welfare and rehabilitation both Odia and non-Odia migrants in Odisha during this coronavirus-led pandemic. The Government of Odisha has announced a package of 17,000 crores for sustaining livelihoods in the rural areas. The idea is to engage the migrants in different rural livelihood programmes by developing sustainable infrastructure such as roads, school buildings, agriculture land, irrigation facilities and so on. The government provides incentives for the people to engage in the handlooms and handicrafts sectors. The handloom producers and workers are provided economic stimulus to carry forward their production activities so that the rural economic chain continues without any disruption.

The Government of Odisha has developed partnership between the citizens and the state to empower the women and rural poor with the help of the Self-Help Groups. It is an important policy platform of praxis, where 70 lakh women are directly involved. It gives an edge to Odisha over other states in India. The Self-Help Groups are the biggest institutional asset of the government for the implementation of rural development policies for the revival of rural economy in the state. These groups help in creating local livelihoods through production of daily needs and using locally available raw materials.

The agrarian economy in Odisha provides employment to majority of population in the state. The crisis is an opportunity to diversify agriculture in Odisha to absorb more people and increase the per capita income in agriculture. The revival of farmers-led agricultural marketing, storage and distribution cooperatives are important in long run. The small-scale agriculture-based industries with focus on food processing can provide livelihoods to a large number of people. People returning from other states with skills can be employed in these industries with little training and skill development. The contribution of farm sector to Odisha's economy is about 30 per cent, which can grow in these difficult times with the help of government interventions. The returned migrants are not going back to the cities outside the state of Odisha. It is important to create facilities to engage their skills and labour for the development of rural economy.

The coastal line in Odisha connects seven big districts in the state. It is important to accelerate coastal economy under the guidance and leadership of the Coastal Development Councils. The fisheries, tourism and agriculture are the three areas the Coastal Development Councils need to focus for the growth of rural employment and economy. The state is also gifted with large rivers like *Mahanadi*, *Brahmani*, *Budhabalanga*, *Subarnarekha*, *Baitarani* and *Rushikulya*. The river basin covers large parts of Odisha from north to south. The fertile river deltas need to be utilised properly for the further growth of agriculture.

The state of Odisha dominates the mineral map of India. Odisha is endowed with mineral resources. The mining sector contributes immensely to the state's economy but the poorest of the poor live in the resource-rich regions of the state. It is time to make the indigenous and rural communities as the shareholders of mineral resources of the state. However, the sector's potential for the growth and development of Odisha is restricted by the successive central governments. Therefore, the Government of Odisha is demanding greater financial federalism and greater control over its mineral resources for the development of Odisha, Jharkhand and other mineral resource–rich regions of India. The centralisation of power by the Government of India is destroying the framework of cooperative federalism for economic growth and development of rural population in India. The Government of Odisha is committed to the democratic decentralisation of development and empowerment of rural poor. The experience of Odisha reveals that participatory method is the only alternative to manage all crises in future.

The resource constraint theory in response to crisis is not an alternative. It is a product of neoliberal capitalist logic to control the state and its abilities for public welfare. Such an argument needs to be discarded. Austerity is not an economic policy but a religious philosophy. It has no place in economic planning for development. The pandemic has revealed that the prevailing free market economy with capitalist system has failed to manage the crisis it produces. It failed in developing an egalitarian system with distributive justice for the marginalised, urban and rural poor. It failed to provide permanent employment and safe working place to the majority of population. The history is the witness to the positive role of a people's state. It is only democratic state and governments can manage the crisis for the greater common good. The sustainable future depends on the abilities of the states and governments-led planning for economic growth and development in India.

THE PANDEMIC AND WITHERING AWAY OF THE WORKING CLASSES IN INDIA

The ordeals of the migrants and other working classes are not going to end if they survive from the COVID-19. The central and state governments are making sweeping changes to the labour laws to lure capital investments. There is no ideological difference between the BJP and the Congress Party when it comes to assault on rights of labourers. Both these national parties consider that capital and its interests are sacred whereas workers are disposables. The nationalism and patriotism are new drugs found in Indian politics, where ruling classes are addicted to uphold the interests of capitalist classes. The evil regimes of central government in New Delhi and state governments in Assam, Uttar Pradesh, Gujarat, Madhya Pradesh, Haryana, Himachal Pradesh, Rajasthan Karnataka, Punjab and Odisha are leading in labour laws reform processes in response to worsening economic situation during the pandemic. The economic situation was battered by the wrong economic policies and misplaced priorities of Modi government before the outbreak of the coronavirus. The unplanned lockdowns have further accelerated the grave economic downturn. Instead of finding sustainable alternative policies and programmes for economic revival, the governments are on overdrive to please capitalist classes at the cost of workers lives and livelihoods. The pandemic gives an undemocratic legitimacy to the governments to enforce legislative changes with ordinances, which are detrimental to working-class people.

The Uttar Pradesh and Gujarat governments have suspended thirty-eight labour laws in support of industries for next three years. The Madhya Pradesh and Odisha governments have reformed the Factories Act 1948, which provides various protective measures to the workers. The labour reforms are not only diluting the laws but also suspending it and exempting companies from following laws that safeguard workers' health, safety and well-being in industrial workplace. Several other state governments are also amending their labour laws to increase working hours and overtime work limit policies. Hire and fire is the sole motto of these labour reform policies. Such regressive and reactionary labour reforms are branded as untapped opportunities for employment generation and economic growth while it violates the ILO conventions and international commitments on protection of labour. The labour market reforms in India send a strong and wrong signal to the working classes that the states and governments are going to stand with capital and not with people. The lives and livelihoods of working classes are less significant than the mobility of capital in India.

The labour market deregulation is in deference to consolidation of capital by corporate power. It renunciates the idea of welfare state and redistributive government by accelerating the orthodoxies of neoliberal disposition in the name of reforms, which disempowers the masses. The consequences of comprehensive labour reforms are going to defeat its twin purposes: increase productivity and mobility of capital. It is empirically well-established that the productive power of labour diminishes with the weakening of workers protection, low wages, reduction of other entitlements and incentives of labour. The low labour morale creates low-productivity trap which weakens the mobility of labour. So the short-term luring of capital is neither in the best interests of capital nor in the interests of labour in the long run. So the pandemic-led labour reforms are thoughtless, nasty, illusionary and myopic. The economic framework of labour market reform is based on false economic promises to both labour and capital. These labour reforms are not only weakening labour but also slumping the economy. It weakens the republic too. Capital is attracted to productive and skilled labour market and not to the unemployed army of cheap and unskilled labourers. In a bid to avoid such a situation, the states and governments must reassert its protective and welfare responsibilities in the interests of the country and its people by reversing the unwanted labour reforms. It is the duty of every democratic and welfare states and governments to stand with its most vulnerable population during the global health crisis triggered by the coronavirus pandemic. But the pandemic-infused crisis is an opportunity for the ruling and non-ruling classes to further disenfranchised the working classes in India.

It is workers' sweat that transformed into capitalist profit in the excel sheets of their bank accounts and immovable assets. The labour is central to production process and economic growth. But the labour market reform framework is repositioning the working classes as secondary to capital. Such ideological praxis is the hallmark of right-wing political economy dating back to early nineteenth century. It is a great leap backward in terms of its objectives, analysis and outcomes. The economic and political logic behind these reforms lack social and economic rationales due to lack of historical understanding of labour and capital relationships even within capitalism and the declining relevance of illiberal laissez-faire political economy. The formidable resistance to right-wing political and economic onslaughts on working class is unavoidable for the sake of India and Indian workers. The organised struggle against the anarchy of capitalist loot is the only alternative for the survival of the working people in India.

The security to wages, work with dignity and secure workplace is a fundamental right of workers and precondition to egalitarian economic growth and

civilised development in India. History is the witness to the fall of civilisations due to adverse economic conditions, social and political breakdowns.
India is at a critical crossroads today due to directionless economic governance, arrogant politics, ignorant government and majoritarian dominance of
society by the Hindutva forces. It is time for the labour movement to fight and
ensure security of work in a secure workplace and move beyond the politics
of wage bargain. It needs to engage with broader realities of India, where
the divisive Hindutva politics is destroying working-class unity. Unless
this broader agenda is not undertaken urgently and seriously, the failure to
represent inclusive working-class interests creates the conditions for the rise
of reactionary politics of Hindutva with its capitalist spirit and actions. The
labour market is a serious warning sign for the future of working-class lives
and livelihoods. The future of the country depends on halting the forward
march of such a reform with united struggles in defence of working people
in India.

ALTERNATIVES FOR RURAL AND AGRICULTURAL DEVELOPMENT IN INDIA DURING AND AFTER COVID-19

The spread of COVID-19-infused crisis has huge impact on all aspects of life
and economy across India. It is particularly posing a serious challenge to the
social and economic development of rural poor, migrants and farmers. The
local businesses and communities are significantly affected by the coronavirus pandemic. The Government of India led by Prime Minister Narendra
Modi announced on 12 May that his government would provide a relief-cum-
stimulus package of Rs. 20 lakh crores. It is 10 per cent of Indian GDP. But
the reality came out in open when the Finance Minister Nirmala Sitharaman
revealed the details about the package. It is clear now that the stimulus and
relief package announced by the Government of India is just 1 per cent of
India's GDP. It too less to provide relief to the poor and rehabilitate the
Indian economy. It puts rural development in jeopardy thereby creating conditions for long-term rural distress and destitution.

The agricultural market reforms led by the BJP-led government in New
Delhi are not panacea for the serious agrarian crisis in India. The reduction of
tax on consumption and GST rate is a welcome policy initiative in right direction. But the reform of the Essential Commodities Act led to the removal of
cereals, edible oil, oilseeds, pulses, onions and potato from its purview. Such
reforms destroy both food security of the rural poor and destroy the farmers'
confidence to produce these items. The universal approach to food security
by public distribution system was diluted and destroyed by the previous

Congress governments in the centre. The BJP government is following the path initiated by the Congress government and ensuring permanent damage to food security and agricultural economy in the country. The policy of private investment in agriculture will create new landlords. What to produce? How to produce? When to produce? What will be the price of the product? The answers to these questions will be decided by the market forces. It will take away the farmers freedom to decide the production processes and price of their own products. The market forces will control the farmers creating conditions for the growth of a new era of neo-feudalism in India. The announcement of the allocation of Rs. 1 lakh crore by the Government of India is a bonanza for the private corporations for the development of agricultural and food processing infrastructure. The history of tax credit and fertiliser subsidies reveals that farmers are not beneficiaries of agricultural subsidies. Therefore, the Government of India and state governments need to redirect their policy focus to empower farmers and rural poor to expand rural economy.

There are several alternative policy options available within the existing development frameworks to revive the economy by reinvigorating rural development programmes. The existing cash transfer programmes in different states like *Rajiv Gandhi Kisan Nyay Yojana* (RGKNY) in Chhattisgarh, *Krushak Assistance for Livelihood and Income Augmentation* (KALIA) in Odisha, *Krishak Bandhu* (KB) in West Bengal, *Mukhya Mantri Krishi Aashirwad Yojana* (MMKAY) in Jharkhand and *Kishan* in Kerala are some of the good policy initiatives by the state governments which led to the creation of the *PM Kisan Yojana*. The cash transfer around Rs. 15,000 crore under the *PM KISAN scheme* by Modi government provides temporary relief. These cash transfer policies are beneficial in short term. But these policies are not enough to reinvigorate rural economy. These policies do not have potentials to revive agricultural distress. It can have long-term positive impacts if it is supported by long-term investment in agriculture and agricultural infrastructure.

The Government of Kerala has the most comprehensive and sustainable rural development policies in India. The Government of Kerala's policies follow an integrated approach by combining several policy initiatives together. For example, increasing rice, vegetables, spices and coconut production is combined with organic and technology-intensive planning. The biodiversity conservation and farm diversification combined with institutional mechanisms of the Agro Service Centers and Regional Farm Facilitation Centers create sustainable policy foundations that address rural economy and development issues in a permanent manner. The policies of crop insurance schemes, integrated pest management and group farming immensely help the rural poor and farmers in Kerala. The Government of Kerala also provides contingency programmes to meet natural calamities including pandemics like COVID-19. The public participation, decentralised development plans, market intervention support system, training programmes via virtual university and Rural Infrastructure Development Funds (RIDF) ensure confidence among rural poor and farmers. The involvement of Panchayat Raj Institutions in the processes of policy formulation to policy implementation ensures sustainable rural development and revitalises rural economy. The existing Kerala model can be adopted immediately and replicated in different states as per the conditions and local requirements of the people in the rural areas.

The consequences of coronavirus pandemic demand urgent attention on rural development. The rural development policies need to be revamped to address the serious issues of rural agrarian distress in different states in India. The specific objectives of the policy need to focus on farmers, agricultural workers and rural poor. The policymakers in India need to move away from technocratic short-term policy objectives by which the state can play a significant role in the revival of rural economy. The investment in rural health, educational, sports and recreational infrastructure can help in reducing rural to urban migration. It can reduce the pressure on urban infrastructure. The investment in irrigation, electricity, rural infrastructure, seed and fertilizer subsidies and higher minimum support price can encourage farmers to produce. It can generate rural employment in agricultural and regional rural crafts in different parts of the country. Such internal mobilisation of resources and labour power can revive rural economy and contribute immensely in reducing poverty, food insecurity and unemployment.

There is no surprise or radical about these policy suggestions. Most of the developed countries provide massive subsidies to farmers to increase agricultural production. The developed countries invest massively to reduce the gaps between urban and rural areas as a result of which rural areas are better in Europe than the European cities. India as a country has all resources, skills and labour power; only political resolve is missing. The political commitment to better public policy focusing on rural development can recover Indian economy from the brink of COVID-19-led catastrophe.

At the end, the states are as strong as their citizens. The states can never be powerful with weak citizenry. The success and failure of a state depends on the partnership between the government and citizens. The disconnect between the government and citizens led to the failure of the states and empires in history. The propaganda can only give temporary relief by diverting public attention but in long term people revolt against the state and ruling class that discriminates and disempowers them. The idea of peace depends on prosperity and the pursuit of prosperity depends on creating conditions for greater equality and liberty in political, social and economic sphere. India can do it if the governments of India show their political commitment for the all-round development of Indians. India lives in its rural heartlands. The future of India depends on the future of poor, farmers, migrants, women, students and youth in rural India.

IN QUEST OF ODIA RENAISSANCE

Historically, the idea of Bengali renaissance and anti-colonial struggles dominated the folklores of Indian intellectual awakening, political consciousness and social reforms led by upper caste and upper-class Hindus. 'What Bengal thinks today, India thinks tomorrow' reflects Eurocentric propaganda based on narrow nationalist glory. Such ideological narrative is based on singularity of Bengali renaissance, which dominated, destroyed and marginalised the representation of regional culture, language, local history and literature. It undermined multiple progressive modernities in different parts of colonial Bengal province. The Bengali colonial collaborators and reactionary nationalists were also responsible for creating internal and dual colonialism in Bihar, Bengal, Odisha and Jharkhand. At the same time, Bengali progressive culture and revolutionary politics has not only influenced the region but also shaped my own thinking.

As a child, growing up in a remote village during 1980s in Odisha, I looked up to Bengal and Calcutta in awe and envious admiration. My childhood stories were dominated by my neighbours, who used to be jute mill workers, ancillary factory workers and cooks in elite Bengali households in Calcutta. They used to bring Calcutta candies, chocolates and garments. Odisha markets were flooded with Calcutta products from pen and paper to bicycles, cars and other household items. The wonderful educational infrastructure in Calcutta used to be another attraction for Odias. The deindustrialisation of Calcutta ruined the Odias love affairs with the city. Kolkata is no longer a place of fascination for Odias.

I first visited Calcutta as a member of the Student Federation of India in 1994 immediately after my high school days. My first visit to Calcutta formed everlasting comradeships and lifelong friendships. Since then, I am in love with Bengali cuisine and developed lifelong bond with Bengali films, literature and music. Class politics, internationalist family outlook, personal sensibilities and accommodating Odia progressive culture resolved the narrow silo of nationalist dilemmas in spite of occasional experience of Bengali elite's supercilious behaviour towards Odias even within Odisha; particularly in the tourist town of Puri. I continue to visit Kolkata but miss passionate spark of radicalism in the city. The invincible red slogans are invisible in city walls today. It is replaced by populism of blue and white colour in the city of joy. Peace and prosperity are becoming distant dreams in Bengal. There is a growing sense of hopelessness in the city and in the state as well. The fall of Bengali renaissance and its politics of radical development promises need adequate interrogation. As deindustrialisation and disinvestment looms large and Bengal lags behind its erstwhile poor neighbour Odisha.

Odisha is one of the fastest growing investment destinations in India today in spite of regular occurrences of natural calamities in the state. Odisha's economy, its infrastructure and people are battered by super cyclones, storms and floods in regular intervals. It destroys lives and livelihoods of many, but Odisha continues to grow and show its resilience and capabilities in handling natural crisis and disasters. As the world is struggling to fight the outbreak of COVID-19 pandemic, Odisha shows its early success and commitment in containing the spread of the deadly coronavirus in the state. The experience of disaster management helped the Naveen Patnaik Government in Odisha, in its approach to fight COVID-19. Odisha can mobilise its own resources and invest in health, education and public infrastructure with a long-term vision. There is no alternative to state led development. Odisha's commitment to sports is unparalleled in the history of Indian sports. It brings international laurels to the state. The times are changing to showcase Odisha and its culture as an alternative in national and international horizons. It is important to continue the momentum in strengthening the state and its capabilities for the welfare of the people.

Many contemporary historians ignored the fact that the nation-state in Odisha is older than the Westphalian nation states in Europe. The secular culture in the state is as old as the state itself. The art and architecture in the Sun temple in Konark, Jagannath temple in Puri and Khandagiri and Udayagiri cave inscriptions are some of the classic examples that reflect iconic history, heritage and progressive culture in the state. The Jagannath cult, Buddhism, Jainism, Bhakti movements and non-conformist spiritual movements define the diversity and inclusivity of Odia culture. The history of mercantile trade shows the history of Odia capabilities and its internationalist sense and sensibilities as well.

These lineages of progressive ideological treasures of Odisha became the foundational principles of the state and inspiration for the Naveen Patnaik government to start a campaign called "Odisha for All". This pluriversalistic, inclusive and secular campaign was launched in Odisha in the backdrop of anti-Muslim propaganda and bigotry spread by ruling Hindutva forces in the country. It saved Odisha from the toxicity of hate and lynching of religious minorities in the state.

The hidden beauty of Odisha is in its classical languages, dance forms, music, cuisine, progressive history, heritage, culture and inclusive society. It is little known in and outside India. The state of Odisha was represented by national media as underdeveloped state with most inward-looking lazy people in India. The national political classes marginalised the state in terms of its share from national economic development processes. The natural resources of the state were exploited by mining-led industrial capitalist class. The central governments in New Delhi continue to act like rent-seeking landlords in Odisha. The politics in the state continues to be controlled by the erstwhile kings, landlords and few higher caste and class propertied families. These forces continue to work like political clients of national political parties and capitalist classes. The consolidation of caste and class combined power structure which denied its people, any agency to express their desire, and claim their rightful position in the national and international discourses.

What can Odisha and Odias offer? Odisha can offer peace and prosperity. Odias can offer the ways to achieve resilience to face crisis and successfully overcome it. The world needs Odisha as much as Odisha needs the world. It is time to break narrow silos and learn from each other. It is time for Odisha to rise like phoenix and spread the pluriversal, inclusive and internationalist hubris of Odia renaissance.

RISKS OF BANKING BROTHERHOOD BETWEEN INDIA AND CHINA

In the middle of a global pandemic, China has started an unprovoked border conflict with India. It is unravelling trust deficit and ties between two neighbours. As thousands of Chinese troops are occupying Indian territory, Mr Narendra Modi-led BJP government directs the RBI to allow the Bank of China to start regular banking services in India. The Bank of China will operate in India like any other commercial banks. This is going to put Indian banking industry in serious risk. The Bank of China has nothing new to offer to Indian banking sectors in terms of new technology and capital. It will only spread risks within Indian banking sectors. It looks as if the China has started this border conflict consciously to bargain its entry into Indian banking sector.

The post-2008 economic crisis followed by the 2015 stock market crash, debt crisis, capital flight and higher capital outflow, loss of foreign reserves, depreciation of Chinese Yuan against USD, fragile stock markets, high leverage, and soaring housing prices are some of the causes behind risks and instabilities within China's financial system. The dual track reform policies pursued by the Chinese government did not succeed. Before the outbreak of the coronavirus, the China Financial Stability Report (2019) was published on 25 November 2019 by the People's Bank of China. It revealed the seriousness of the banking crisis in China. The report found that 586 banks and 13 per cent of financial institutions were under high-risk category and some of the banks were declared bankrupt. The report did not reveal the name of risky and bankrupt banks, which are operating under the Bank of China. Many medium and large size Chinese banks have failed the capital reserve test and liquidity stress test conducted by the People's Bank of China (PBOC). It shows the level of risks and crisis within Chinese banking sector. The negative oil prices are exacerbating risks and crisis within the Chinese banking system.

The Chinese banks are preparing for worst case scenarios after the outbreak of the coronavirus pandemic. The net profit has fallen for the Industrial and Commercial Bank of China (the world's largest commercial bank), Bank of China, Agricultural Bank of China and China Construction Bank. These are the four biggest banks of China which are contracting in their operations and profit. The impact of the pandemic risks on Chinese banking system is going to be huge. It is argued that the rising bad loans as a result of loan defaults can rise fivefold within thirty largest Chinese banks. The China Banking and Insurance Regulatory Commission shows its helplessness under the current circumstances. There is no option before the Chinese banks but to sit on the mountain risks and crisis. In this context, the Bank of China intends to use internationalisation as a strategy to spread its risks. So, the Chinese banks are going global; such a trend was never witnessed earlier by the global banking communities.

The internationalisation of Chinese banks is prelude to the internationalisation of its currency. The Bank of China will perform four functions in India that will help Chinese currency in the process of its internationalisation. Firstly, the Bank of China will facilitate widening of receipts and payment functions by its own currency during cross border trade. Secondly, it will help in investment and financing by expanding China's interbank bond market. The first two functions will enhance the circulation of Chinese capital and increase Chinese currency valuation in international markets. Thirdly, it will serve to reduce Chinese debts and banking risks as a result of which, there will be financial stability within Chinese financial systems. Finally, as the central banks will have higher reserve of Chinese currency, China can use it as the modes of foreign exchange.

In this way, the entry of Bank of China into Indian banking sector is helpful to China by spreading risk and reducing its own banking crisis. It will leverage opportunities to expand its credit market within Indian banking sector. The Bank of China will not serve the interests of Indian people in anyway. The Government of India led by Mr Narendra Modi is providing security to the Chinese banks to pursue such an objective in India which is detrimental to the Indian banking sector. The banking sovereignty is paramount to the economic and political sovereignty of India.

IN DEFENCE OF CHINESE PEOPLE
AND THEIR REVOLUTION

The ugly head of racism is out in open air amid COVID-19 pandemic. The racism against Chinese people and propaganda against the achievements of the Chinese revolution spreads like coronavirus. The anti-Chinese media coverage also replicates the history of anti-communist propaganda and campaign against the Soviet Union from the days of its inception to fall. The anti-Soviet propaganda continues to appear in the front pages of mainstream media even after three decades of its demise. The ruling and non-ruling capitalist class, their well-paid right wing and liberal think tanks and intellectuals continue to argue that *there is no alternative* to capitalist world order after the collapse of Soviet Union. It means socialism is a utopia and it can never be an alternative to capitalism. The objectives of such ideological propaganda are to distort truth and hide incredible revolutionary achievements of the Soviet Union. Many anti-Soviet books, articles, newspapers, editorials, posters, advertisements, magazines, films, stories and documentaries were produced to sustain the narratives that uphold the interests of the bourgeoisies. The communists, socialists and workers parties were depicted like demons strangling the capitalist gods and goddesses of individual prosperity, liberty, democracy and freedom. The socialist alternative to capitalism is portrayed as apocalyptic culture of death.

History is the witness to the failed experiments and achievements of socialism in Soviet Union to Asia, Africa and Latin America. Our living experiences of capitalism in twenty-first century documents the inhuman stories of death, destitution, inequalities, hunger, homelessness, environmental catastrophises and war. Capitalism destroys our planet and all human values of our society based on peace, prosperity and solidarity. Throughout the world history, anti-communist and anti-socialist propaganda led by capitalist system has served the forces of tyranny. Dictatorships, authoritarian regimes, fascism, Nazism, xenophobia, growth of terrorism and reactionary right-wing forces are products of capitalism. The capitalist system is not a friend of democracy, freedom, human rights and human emancipation from illness, poverty and inequalities. In spite of all its powers and propaganda, capitalism failed as a system.

Deaths and destitutions due to pandemics are not new in human history. COVID-19 is not the first one and it is not going to be the last pandemic. But for the first time, there are attempts to delegitimise the state and government of China in the eyes of its people when human beings in general and working-class people in particular are facing annihilating economic crisis again amidst COVID-19 pandemic. The crisis is accelerated by racism and anti-Chinese propaganda. The specific objective is to defeat the achievements of Chinese people and their revolution that uplifted millions from hunger, homelessness, illness, illiteracy and unemployment. The general objective is to defeat all available experiences of alternatives to capitalism. The Western capitalist media plays a major role in achieving these twin objectives. Therefore, the capitalist media is spreading stereotypes on food habits of Chinese people and negative image of Chinese society, state and its government during this pandemic. The successful containment and reversal of COVID-19 is an achievement of the Chinese state and government. The capitalist states and governments in Europe and America have failed its citizens from this pandemic.

The incredible achievements of Cuba and China show that the alternative to capitalist healthcare system is possible and inevitable. The Cuban and Chinese medical aid to Italy, Spain and many other countries in the world shows that solidarity during a pandemic is only possible under non-capitalist healthcare systems. Therefore, it is imperatives for all working people all over the world to defend socialist experiences and achievements of Chinese people and stand against racial slurs against Chinese population outside China. It is not Chinese virus but COVID-19 which is a pandemic. It can only be defeated if we can reverse the business of illness spread by pharmaceutical corporations, private medicals and health insurance companies under capitalism. The failure to learn the lessons of history from the anti-Soviet propaganda then and anti-Chinese propaganda now will be an unimaginable defeat of working-class people all over the world. The pandemic of capitalism will continue to produce deaths and destitutions for its own profit. Human lives, animals and environments are disposables under capitalism. It is time to debunk the capitalist myths and celebrate socialist achievements even during this pandemic.

CHINA DIMINISHES ITSELF

The rise of China is not only a hope for the Asian people but also inspires working-class people all over the world. It instils hopes that there is an alternative to predatory capitalism of the West. The Chinese Communist Party (CCP) played a major role in transforming China as a major world power while uplifting many Chinese from poverty, hunger and homelessness. The Chinese state capitalism or socialism with Chinese character under the leadership of CCP has managed its economy, politics and culture in a progressive manner. The Chinese achievements are potential alternatives to Western capitalism. However, there are many issues that are confronting China today that limits the working-class politics. There is falling ideological appeal of the CCP among Chinese youth due to its top-down approach. There is growing disillusionment among the CCP members because of the growing gap between theory and ideological practice among the top leadership within the CCP hierarchy. There is huge growth of economic inequality among Chinese population. The growing gap between rich and poor shows the failures of the CCP in developing egalitarian economic policies. The gap between rural and urban China is another concern that CCP ignores in practice. Many of these problems are self-inflicted by the arrogance and dominance of the CCP. It is making the same blunders that USSR made and collapsed. These self-inflicted harms are avoidable for the sake of China, Chinese people in particular and working-class people across the globe.

The internal issues of discontent in Tibet, Hong Kong, Taiwan and fear among the Uighur Muslims reflect democratic distrusts between Chinese government, party and people living within China. It demands democratisation politics and decentralisation governance within the democratic traditions of communist ideology. The CCP-led Chinese government has failed to overcome the trust deficit within different regions and provinces in China. The trust deficit of China is accelerated by its aggressive postures in its neighbourhood foreign policy. China and India are two civilisational post-colonial states. These two countries share more than 3,440 km (2,100 miles) long border and have overlapping claims. These two nuclear armed countries can solve their border disputes with debates, discussions and diplomacy. The military confrontation between two diminishes their role both in regional and global forums. It sends wrong signals to regional and world peace. Both the countries need to focus on their own economic development and cooperate with each other for human welfare. China, Nepal and Pakistan are all weather friends. This is how neighbours should be in relationships but there is distrust of Beijing in Kathmandu and Islamabad. Vietnam, Philippines, Sri Lanka and East Asian countries are also good friends with China, but scepticisms are growing in these countries because of the highhandedness of Beijing. There is local resistance against Chinese investment and Chinese takeover of their natural and strategic resources. Similar trends are visible in African continent against neo-colonial modes of Chinese investments. The Chinese aggressive postures diminish the good will for China in different regions.

The ruling elites need to understand that these issues are serious liabilities in the long run. The sustainability of CCP and the rise of China depend on the good will it generates among people within its effective foreign policy praxis in dealing with neighbours and other friendly nations. The CCP can solve all these issues with a clear, coherent and democratic approach by developing uninterrupted trust between China and other neighbouring countries. It can solve its internal disputes and discontents with an open, honest, progressive and democratic manner. It needs political resolve that can further strengthen China within and outside its territory. But the Chinese aggressive behaviours diminish China and all its potentials. China is making the same mistakes as

Soviet Russia has made, which led to its disintegration. It was a major loss to the working-class people of the world. Similarly, the failures of China will further weaken the working-class politics in the world. In this context, the CCP-led China need to take responsibility and initiative for peace and development and transform itself within changing requirements of time.

The organisational, ideological and structural transformation of the CCP, Chinese state and government depends on various factors. These factors are local, regional, national and international. The understandings of these factors are central to the initiation of reform processes. The CCP's dominance and monopoly over Chinese politics and state needs serious reflection by which CCP can accommodate different political, cultural, social and intellectual voices within and outside China. The China is no more solely an agrarian economy. There are different sectors emerged in China during the post-1985 reform period. The Chinese party state needs to develop capabilities to engage with different professional classes and negotiate with their requirements. It would be political suicide to ignore the new class formations in China. The CCP, Chinese state and government can manage all these challenges and uncertainties if it engages with it in an open and democratic manner. The Chinese communists have nothing to hide but need to reform the way it functions.

China is a part of the global capitalist production and distribution networks. China is using these networks for its own national interests. But the national interests should not be the only criteria for a communist party state to determine its future course of actions in geopolitics. The national interests are not free from the interests of Chinese people and their Asian neighbours. If the CCP looks at its national interest only, it would be very difficult to sustain the Chinese model of economic growth and development. There are growing local resistance movements against special economic zones, industrial and technological parks due to the perilous working conditions and precarity of Chinese workers. In this way, China faces these uphill tasks and challenges during these uncertain times. The Chinese story can survive if Chinese ruling classes can transform themselves by reflecting on their aggressive, neoliberal governance within the country, poor public relations management and bullying behaviour with neighbouring and friendly countries.

Chapter 3

Lure of Hindutva Fascism in India

The feudal character of Indian society and Brahmanical Hindu religious order based on caste has become a fertile ground for the growth of Hindutva fascism in India. The seed of Hindutva fascism was germinated with the establishment of the Rashtriya Swayamsevak Sangh (RSS), the 'National Volunteers Organisation' established in 1925 by Keshav Baliram Hedgewar. Mr Hedgewar's mentor Dr B.S. Moonje was fascinated and inspired by European Nazism and fascist ideology, which shaped the organising principle of the RSS and its affiliated organisations. He has replicated it by establishing the Bhonsala Military School in India with an objective of militarising the minds of Hindu majority. The diversity within Hindu religion and diverse linguistic, cultural and social practices were the biggest challenges for Moonje and Hedgewar to replicate Hindutva fascism during its inception. These challenges were addressed by Madhav Sadashiv Golwalkar, who has shaped the ideological foundation of Hindutva fascism in India in his two books: *We, or Our Nationhood Defined* and *Bunch of Thoughts*.

According to Golwalkar, it is important to transform India into a racially pure Hindu nation with uniform Hindu culture and language. The religious domination and cultural assimilation were the two strategies adopted and prescribed by Golwalkar to achieve the objective of establishing India as a Hindu nation. Mr Golwalkar was also an ardent follower of European Nazism and fascism. His ultimate vision was to organise and produce ideally militarised Hindu manhood with a corporate personality. He found that caste is the only common organising principle among Hindus in India. Therefore, Golwalkar was a vehement supporter of hierarchical and discriminatory caste-based Hindu social order in the name of preserving unity in Indian society. Shyama Prasad Mukherjee and Deendayal Upadhyaya have played a major role in mainstreaming Hindutva politics in India. The ideals of

Moonje, Hedgewar, Golwalkar, Shyama Prasad Mukherjee and Deendayal Upadhyaya continue to inspire Hindutva politics led by RSS in India. The idea of one nation, one language, one religion (Hindi, Hindu and Hindustan) by the BJP today derives its philosophical and political outlook from these fascist ideologues.

In the name of establishing Hindu nation, the Hindutva fascists forces were allies of British colonialism and opposed Indian freedom struggle. The Hindutva fascists were the original anti-nationals of India. These forces were politically marginalised and did not appeal to Indian masses. The horrors of partition of India and its memories gave Hindutva fascists some breathing space in India. After killing Mahatma Gandhi, these forces were further marginalised in Indian politics and society. The rise of coalition politics and joint trade union movements based on concerns for working classes helped Hindutva politics to rise again within mainstream political culture in India. The Brahmanical caste mobilisation in northern India for the Ram Janmabhoomi movement and the demolition of Babri Masjid has helped BJP to get electoral dividends in both regional and national politics in India. The marginalisation of the masses by the neoliberal economic policies pursued by the Congress Party has created mass discontent in India, which gave the much-needed political space to the BJP and RSS to pursue their Hindutva fascist politics led by Mr Narendra Modi.

The bourgeois Indian media and reactionary regional politics have helped Modi to control the national narrative in the name of national, economic and cultural revival of India. Woe betide anything that stands in the way of Modi-led BJP, be it the youths, students, professors, lawyers, social and political activists and media, all are branded and demonised as anti-nationals. The Hindutva fascists (who were opposed to Indian freedom struggle) are distributing the certificates of patriotism but hiding their dubious educational degree certificates, much like their role in Indian freedom struggle.

India is ruled today by the so-called 'strong man' Mr Narendra Modi with a '56-inch chest', who believed to make India great again. The border disputes with neighbours, internal social strife, economic crisis and the global health crisis led by coronavirus pandemic are giving escape route to the Hindu fascists on the one hand and strengthening their political power on the other. The rise of Islamophobia, anti-Muslim riots and lynching, killing of rationalists, imprisoning human rights activists and political opposition, privatisation of national resources and diverting public money for temple construction are some of the achievements of the Modi-led BJP government. The vulnerable social groups, religious minorities and working people are living in poverty and bear the brunt of Hindutva fascism in India. The constitutional, liberal and secular democracy and independent judiciary are ruined to a point of no return. But the Hindutva fascists pretend as if everything is normal in India.

The disquiet transition in India today is moving into the absolute control of Hindutva fascism.

There is a growth of mass unemployment and mass alienation in India. The detached masses look for messiah in so-called strong men, who exploit them and marginalise them every day with the help of state power. Such a transition of Indian society is a breeding ground for Hindutva fascism. The growing inequality is no accident in India. It is a direct product of Hindutva political economy of deceptive development promise of Modi-led BJP. The Hindutva fascists take about the welfare of Hindus but in reality, they protect the interests of capitalist classes in India. Any secular political opposition to such a project is branded as traitors and parasites in the name of shared feelings of Hindutva culture of victimhood, bigoted patriotism, false pride and fake nationalism based on mindless but shrewd propaganda.

The assault on reason, liberal, secular and constitutional democracy in India is a part of the Hindutva agenda. The democratic institutions and constitutional practices are opposed to the fascist politics of Hindutva. So, the antidemocratic strategies are helpful for Hindutva politics to consolidate power and legitimise its authoritarianism via electoral means of majoritarianism with a hope that Modi can solve all the problems. The reality reveals the fairy tale of Hindutva politics in which the BJP rules and others are either silent or in prison. Hindutva fascist like their European brethren do not like dissent and democracy. They detest rule of law, transparency and accountability. These characters are visible in the political praxis of Mr Narendra Modi shaped by the RSS and BJP. The dismantling of constitutional democracy is a priority of Hindutva fascists in India.

The social media and communication technologies are helping the Hindutva fascists to spread their bigoted fake news and scandalous stories on political opponents to discredit them in public eye. The online media platforms are also helping the Modi government to hide all its failures from foreign policy, national security to economic development. The inclusive political and social struggles are imperative for Indian democracy to survive and work for the people by defeating Hindutva fascism. The defeat of Hindutva fascism and its ideological foundation is the only way to revive the present and future of India and Indians from this ruinous path. The peace and prosperity in India depend on the defeat of Hindutva fascism.

DECODING HINDUTVA POLITICS
AND ITS PERILS IN INDIA

Atal Bihari Vajpayee and L. K. Advani created the foundation for Hindutva forces to access power by forming BJP-led coalition governments in New

Delhi. This duo experimented with the troika of liberal, moderate and hard-line Hindutva slogans during the Babri Mosque–Ram Janmabhoomi movement to mobilise and expand their electoral base among the masses. They happily compromised their so-called RSS ideology of Hindutva as a short-term electoral strategy to gain state power. On such a foundation, Narendra Modi launched his electoral campaign by combining reactionary politics of Hindutva, neoliberal development and so-called nationalism of BJP and RSS.

When Narendra Modi-led BJP came to power in New Delhi with absolute electoral majority, RSS started implementing its long-cherished racist and fascist Hindutva ideology of hate towards Indian Muslims. The Modi government is a mute spectator of everyday lynching, violence and vicious attacks on Muslims in India. The Union Ministers in Modi government are openly garlanding Hindutva vigilante groups and perpetrators of violent crime. There is growing attack on artists, activists, academicians, journalists, intellectuals and rationalists. Modi government arrests leaders of various social, political and human rights movements on false and fabricated charges under draconian laws and puts them in prison. Any opposition to Hindutva forces and policies of Modi-led government is branded as anti-nationals.

The common Indians are reacting to these horrifying events, depressing and distressful developments with utter silence, shock and incredulity. Indian urban elites look at such intolerant and hateful climate as dispersed events and have no impact on their tinsel lives. While most of the Indian Muslims are reacting to this hateful climate with anxiety, anger, fear, deep dismay and disbelief having assumed their nationalist integrity and embeddedness with Indian way of life. Then Modi government launched the Citizenship Amendment Act, the National Register of Citizens (NRC) and the communalised National Population Register. These are steps in a direction to disenfranchise citizenship rights of Muslim population in India. The idea of India looks gloomy and the future of Indians looks uncertain if Hindutva forces continue to govern India for few more years. It is time to decode and defeat the ideology of Hindutva as a political and social practice.

The Hindutva forces and their ideological genealogy reveal the dangers of Hindutva politics in India. Hindutva political theology is no longer an imagined and isolated cluster of normative ideas about 'Hindu way of life' as defined by the Supreme Court of India. It is a pragmatic and exclusionary political practice carrying false claims to marginalisation of Hindus and their representation in history, culture and politics in mainstream India. Historically speaking, upper-caste Bengali spiritual leaders and intellectuals created the philosophical foundation on which Marathi political activists shaped the ideological and political narratives of Hindutva forces. The *Bhakti* movements in North India gave the mass base to Hindutva politics. The colonisers were patrons of Hindutva politics. So, Hindutva forces did not fight British colonialism. They did not participate in the anti-colonial nationalist struggle in India. These Hindutva forces formed partnership with the British to create Hindu Rashtra (Hindu state) in India. Such is the anti-national character of Hindutva forces in Indian history, but they create havocs in contemporary India in the name of nationalism.

From 1920s to 2020, Hindutva fascist forces managed to spread uncontaminated bigotry, violence and extremism in social, political and cultural life. In economy, Hindutva forces follow neoliberal economic policies to uphold and pursue interests of the capitalism class. There is absolute solidarity and harmony in the arranged-cum-love marriage between Hindutva and neoliberal capitalism. Such a combination marginalises rural and urban poor, religious minorities, women, farmers, Dalits and tribal population in India. It spreads prosperity for few rich and miseries for many. The growth of poverty, unemployment, hunger and homelessness is a product of economic policies pursued by the Modi government. India's external reputation is tattered by the Hindutva forces.

India is facing many challenges and dangers imposed by Hindutva forces led by Modi. The democratic rise of Hindutva forces by electoral means created a political culture of democratic deficit with the concentration of power in the hands of Modi. It is an organic outcome of fascist ideology of RSS which is opposed to the ideals of democratic decentralisation of power and empowerment of the masses based on citizenship rights. The representative and distributive function of Indian democracy has diminished further with the rise of Hindutva politics in India. It destroys the idea of India as a civilisational country within all its limitations. It destroys liberal, secular and constitutional democracy in India. The idea of India is meaningless without Muslims as they contributed immensely in shaping of the history and culture of India. The Hindutva forces want to destroy such a diverse and multicultural mosaic of India.

The Hindutva assault on secularism, liberal culture, democratic tradition, reason, science, history and everyday lives in India has started in an aggressive manner which was unseen and unheard in last seven decades of democratic experimentation in India with all its limitations. These dangers are no more early signs but at a maturing stage for the establishment of Hindutva fascism in India. The deadly combination of neoliberal economy, reactionary politics and authoritarian culture is growing. It is going to destabilise constitutional state in India and destroy Indian way of multicultural traditions and life. The political stability of Hindutva breeds social disharmony and economic marginalisation with a false sense of history and nationalist hallucination. The reversal of such a dangerous environment is only possible with collective struggles to expose the toxicity of Hindutva and its ideological practice.

The Hindutva politics has captured the space created by economic disillusionments after the 1991 neoliberal economic reforms which led to the concentration of wealth in the hands of few Indians. The neoliberal development dissatisfaction has accelerated the forward march of Hindutva politics in India. The five decades of Hindutva politics has become integral part of the neoliberal economic development model that it seeks to oppose in its earlier avatar. Hindutva is a democratic and development malaise that falters the secular, liberal and multicultural mosaic of India.

The ideology of Hindutva as a political practice is based on unadulterated hatred and violence against religious minorities. Hindutva is an opportunist pan-Indian alliance of perverted upper castes and propertied classes in India. Hindutva forces are working to establish social and religious hegemony of propertied and Brahmanical upper caste people and consolidate wealth of higher classes. Therefore, the successful opposition to halt of the forward march of Hindutva fascism depends on decoding and understanding the conceptual core in its ideological praxis. The opposition to Hindutva forces can never be successful with a series of contested dialogues during periodic electoral interventions. It only offers limited alternatives within the binary of electoral victory and loss. It is important to understand the social, cultural and economic base of Hindutva politics to fight and defeat it. The impending mass movement against Hindutva is a compelling need and crucial for the survival of the idea of India and Indians.

LYNCHING OF DEMOCRACY IN INDIA

Mr Narendra Damodardas Modi is a consummate practitioner of remorseless Hindutva politics of hate. He does not spare a moment to capture the headlines with his diversionary tactics, which makes him as one of the sharpest managers of media and prime master of propaganda. The Hindutva propaganda machine with the organisational network of RSS is erasing the idea of India in the name of building and converting India into a Hindu Rashtra. It is the end of secular, liberal and constitutional democracy in India. The tragedy of coronavirus pandemic does not shock Modi and his government. It a therapeutic opportunity for the Hindutva forces to clampdown on leaders and activists of democratic struggles, human rights defenders, students, youths, farmers, women and civil society leaders by using draconian laws. The mob lynching and rioters go unpunished. The criminals and frauds move around with all impunity. The rule of law for justice is no longer the governing principles of India under Modi. It is a message to the common Indians, who believe in the idea of inclusive democracy. Reason, science, morality in life and principles in politics are obsolete words in the ideological frameworks of Hindutva and its leadership.

The bigotry of Hindutva politics is destroying hopes, needs and aspirations of millions of Indians and their future. The BJP government led by Modi is using pandemic as an opportunity to subvert all democratic procedures, parliamentary traditions and constitutional conventions with the help of Hindutva majoritarianism. Modi promised cooperative federalism but practises despotic strategies for the centralisation of power in his hand. The Government of India is a one-man spectacle as a result of which the government has failed in all frontiers of governance. Modi-led BJP government has failed in social, economic, political and diplomatic fronts. The crisis is an opportunity for the Hindutva politics to accelerate its fascist rule. Deceptive, illiberal and undemocratic ideals are integral to Hindutva politics, which serves the cronies capitalist friends of BJP and Modi. The present and future are robbed from Indians by the politics and policies of Hindutva regime, which undermines and destroys democratic institutions and practices. It is worth asking, if India is still a democratic country under Modi.

The Modi government has passed the Farmers' and Produce Trade and Commerce (Promotion and Facilitation) Bill, 2020, and Farmers (Empowerment and Protection) Agreement on Price Assurance and Farm Services Bill, 2020, without a proper discussion in the parliament. It did not give any chance to the opposition political parties even to share their views on the bills. These bills are not only prelude to corporatisation of agriculture but also a death warrant for Indian farmers. The big farmers and corporates are going to be beneficiaries of these policy reforms. It will destroy the lives and livelihoods of millions of small farmers in India. This is not about two bills. It is about Indian farmers and their source of livelihoods. Modi continues to downplay the political opposition to the bill with his time-tested deceptive tactics.

This is not for the first time, Modi government is subverting rule of law in democratic India. Modi-led BJP governments have subverted democracy many times after it came to power both in states and in the centre. It is a final warning sign for Indian democracy. If Modi-led BJP government is allowed to subvert democracy in defence of corporate interests, it not only diminishes Indian democracy but also destroys the very foundation of trust poor and farmers have on Indian state and government.

The Modi government has always pretended and propagated to be the champions of India and Indian culture. Do Kashmiris, Adivasis, Dalits, students, youths, Muslims and other religious and linguistic minorities, farmers, rural and urban poor belong to India? Does the Modi government consider these people as Indians? It has demonised every political opposition and branded them as anti-national forces. In reality, the cultural, political and economic nationalism of BJP and RSS is a hoax. Modi government is an agent of transnational capitalist classes. It does not care for the people. Modi government hides behind police and prisons by scapegoating the vulnerable and vilifying the opposition parties. It is a historical trademark of fascist politics. The Hindutva fascists are no different. The Hindutva chauvinism survives by spreading falsehood on history, politics, economy, culture and society. It is fundamentally opposed to the idea of India and Indian way of life.

The lynching of democracy in India by Hindutva forces started with Adivasis, Dalits, Muslims and Kashmiris. The lynching of Dalits within apartheid Hindu caste order is not new. Similarly, the cultural and economic genocide of Adivasis is continuing for a long time. The open and full-fledged attack on Muslims, Kashmiris and people from North-East India started after Modi came to power in New Delhi. The political patronage to racist violence is an inalienable feature of Hindutva politics. It is not going to stop here as violence is a leverage of right-wing and reactionary forces. There is no recourse to justice. The next attack will be on all forces opposed to Hindutva politics.

The slow death of impartial judiciary and legal fraternity gives unbridle power to the Hindutva forces to expand their medieval ideology of governance, which weakens and ruins all institutions of democracy and its liberal traditions. The Hindutva politics has transformed Indian political landscape into a field of competitive consumerism of bigotry based on false propaganda. The stakes are much higher now. Without a serious mass mobilisation against the bigoted ideology of RSS and undemocratic politics of BJP, the lynching of Indian democracy is in its final stage. Its survival depends on people and their struggle for restoring liberal, constitutional and inclusive democracy in India. The building of a mass movement is not easy, but it is possible. The vitality, legitimacy and effectiveness of the struggles against Hindutva politics depends on solidarity among all progressive, liberal, socialist and democratic forces in the country. The democracy in India is a product of peoples struggle and its survival today depends on the progressive trajectories of peoples' struggle in defence of democracy in India.

LAWFARE, CRISIS AND HINDUTVA FASCISM IN INDIA

The Hindutva fascism is replacing seven decades of secular democratic traditions and liberal constitutional practices in India. The well-established decentralised institutions of governance are destroyed with processes of the centralisation of power by the BJP government led by Mr Narendra Modi.

The civilisational traditions of inter-faith dialogue and religious harmony in Indian society are ruined by the majoritarian politics of Hindutva forces. The Indian economy today is in its worst crisis in the history even before the outbreak of coronavirus pandemic. The growing Indian economy was stalled due to economic mismanagement, false economic priorities, irrelevant and arbitrary economic policies. The internal security, neighbourhood policies of India and its external relationships are tattered by the personality cult-driven Modiplacy. The economic, social and political crises in India are not isolated events. These are self-inflicted wounds by the ignorance and arrogance of Modi government, which is driven by anti-democratic and obscurantist ideology of the RSS. Where did India go wrong? What are the ideological factors that landed Indians in such a situation of desperation and despondency? How to characterise Modi government? The answers to these questions are central to understand the predicaments of India and Indians today.

The 'unbridle neoliberal capitalism' in economy, 'higher caste identity-based supremacist ideology in politics', 'authoritarianism in governance', 'evangelical cultural and religious outlooks' and 'false propaganda' are the five defining characters of Mr Narendra Modi-led BJP government in India. These features are central to the forward march of Hindutva fascism in India. These forces are transforming every democratic, judicial, educational, health and security establishments in India to kowtow before the RSS ideology, which derives its historical inspirations from the racist European Nazism and fascism. These forces have historical twin targets. Their first ideological target is to consolidate higher caste Hindus by spreading the politics of fear and hate. It helps in creating the culture of otherness, where religious minorities are branded as enemies of the Indian nation. The second target is to attack political left, human rights organisations and activists, progressive and democratic organisations and political parties. The objective is to destroy any form of opposition to the BJP-led governments in India.

The Supreme Court of India has given ideological breathing space to fascist forces by defining it as 'Hindutva is not a religion, but a way of life and a state of mind' in its 1995 judgement. It helped the BJP to get greater social and political acceptance among politically naïve liberals in India. The first part of the judgement is correct as Hindutva is not a religion. It has nothing to do with Hindu religion and spiritual Hindus. But second part is absolutely a biased conceptualisation. Hindutva is neither a way of life nor a state of mind. It is a political project of reactionary higher caste Hindu identity politics, which is against the democratic, secular and liberal ethos of Indian Constitution and multicultural ethos of Indian society. There is an interconnection between the Hindutva fascism, Indian judiciary and neoliberal capitalism, which is pushing India in a ruinous path of no return. This troika creates Indian form of lawfare, which is against egalitarian principles and promises of Indian Constitution and seven decades of judicial practices in independent India.

The Supreme Court of India destroys universalistic appeal of the Indian Constitution by not halting the implementation of exclusionary laws of the BJP government. The Citizenship Amendment Act (CAA), National Register of Citizens (NRC) and National Population Register (NPR) are unnecessary and unjustified attempts to institutionalise exclusionary form of citizenship and governance, which is antithetical to the Indian society and Indian constitutional practices. Some of the existing legal and parliamentary traditions help the Hindutva-led government to make new laws in Indian legislatures to destroy democracy and deepen social, economic, cultural and religious crises in India. The lawfare is a weapon to pursue the politics of the ruling classes. It is used to destroy any form of political opposition to the reactionary government in India. The lawfare in India provides legitimacy to reactionary political and economic forces by disciplining the masses. It enhances the power of regional, national and international capital and weakens the power of labour. The lawfare helps in socialising the policies and normalising the politics of Hindutva fascist forces in India.

The lawfare creates both conditions: institutions and regimes of capitalist accumulation with the help of Hindutva fascist forces. The social, economic and political crisis is an opportunity for the capitalist classes to capture the natural and other resources in the country. Mr Narendra Modi's successful bid to be the prime minister of India twice shows his media-made popularity; read it as manipulation helps him to pretend to be the messiah of the masses. He was successful in selling the false development narratives to the electorate by taking advantage of widespread anger against neoliberal economic mismanagement and corrupt practices of the United Progressive Alliance led by the Indian National Congress. However, after defeating the Congress Party, Modi-led BJP is following the same neoliberal economic policies with letter and spirit. The rules and regulations are made to facilitate the mobility of capitalism in India. It helps in the further consolidation of capitalism with the authoritarian governance and fascist politics of Modi-led BJP. This is the reason for which Modi is considered to be the darling of capitalist oligarchs in their local, regional, national and international incarnations.

The Ayodhya verdict of the Supreme Court of India has revealed that the lawfare in India is intertwined with so-called popular narratives and nationalist sentiments. The so-called popular narratives and nationalist sentiments are shaped by the propaganda of the *bourgeois* media and reactionary political forces led by BJP and RSS. It seems that historical facts and evidences are no longer sacred in Indian judicial practice. The insidious cult of RSS and BJP is looming large on Indian republic and its future depends on our collective conscious to comprehend the seriousness of the crisis. It would be hypocritic to be silent patriotic when Hindutva fascism is destroying lives and livelihoods of millions of Indians by implementing disastrous economic and development policies. It is time for political struggles to expose the fake nationalism of RSS and BJP and restore liberal, constitutional democracy in India. The progressive political struggle to defeat Hindutva fascism is the only alternative for the survival of India and its forward march towards a path of peace and prosperity.

DISASTERS OF NEOLIBERALISM AND HINDUTVA FASCISM IN INDIA

Neoliberalism as an ideology emerged in central Europe during early twentieth century in opposition to socialism as an alternative to imperial, colonial and capitalist plunder, war and economic crisis. The Department of Economics at the University of Chicago shaped neoliberalism as a strategy to shift the power from workers to the owners of capital by weakening the state and expanding the ideals of free market. These strategies were converted into economic policies and projects to undermine the power of labour by marginalising it both in economic and social terms. Neoliberalism today has become a political and economic project of capitalist classes to pursue their economic interests with the help of ruling classes. Such a project encompasses all spheres of social, economic political, cultural and religious lives of people.

The postcolonial economic and development planning helped neoliberalism to integrate itself slowly within the Indian context. From 1980s onwards, neoliberal economic policies were pursued as a strategy of economic growth which helped global, national and local capitalist classes. Such a strategy helped to consolidate capitalist classes and marginalised the masses in India. In the beginning, Hindutva politics used to support nationalistic economic policies and opposed to neoliberal economic policies as part of its populist and so-called nationalist narrative. But from 1990s onwards, neoliberalism consolidated its base in India. The national and regional mainstream political parties in India continue to articulate economic interests of the capitalist classes by pursuing neoliberalism as a project of economic growth and development.

The neoliberal economic policies pursued by the Indian National Congress have helped to create the conditions for the growth and consolidation of Hindutva fascists in Indian politics. Hindutva fascists helped the capitalist classes to consolidate their base in India. The undisputed neoliberal economic paradigm is redrawing the nature of relationship between politics, society, state and individuals as citizens in India. In such a context, the state has abandoned its own citizens and becoming a security state to protect the interests of the capitalist classes. The citizens are suffering under hunger, homelessness, unemployment, illiteracy, illness and hopelessness. The social and economic alienation produces political distrust and historic opportunities for the growth and consolidation of Hindutva politics in India. The abject condition of alienation produced by neoliberalism becomes life and blood of right-wing religious politics of Hindutva forces in India.

Hindutva politics plays two roles in India. It is in government led by Narendra Modi who pursues all economic policies to uphold interests of the global, national and regional capitalist classes. On the one hand, Hindutva politics is constitutive part of neoliberal project. On the other hand, it articulates the anger against neoliberalism and its political establishment. It looks like Hindutva politics has a contradictory relationship with neoliberalism. But in reality, the first role is an integral and organic relationship between Hindutva politics and neoliberalism. The second role is part of the half-hearted populist narrative to capture the state power by electoral means to pursue the first role. Therefore, Hindutva forces consolidate neoliberalism and neoliberalism consolidates Hindutva forces' position in society, politics and economy. There is no contradiction between Hindutva politics and neoliberal economic policies in India.

The forward march of neoliberal Hindutva politics is in its way to establish Hindutva fascism in India by converting India from a secular state to a Hindu state. In the process of establishing this dream project of the RSS, the Modi government is destroying institutions established by liberal, democratic and constitutional traditions in India. It is not an anarchy of Hindutva politics but a systematic shock doctrine to achieve their goal to establish a theocratic Hindu state. Neoliberalism and theocratic politics move together as twins. It serves each other's purpose. The theocratic political culture of Hindutva is established by the RSS which produces prejudice and hate. Such a culture diverts people's attention from real issues of their lives and livelihoods. The diversionary tactics of Modi government helps both the capitalist classes and fascist RSS to implement their agenda.

There are fundamental similarities between fascism in Europe and Hindutva fascism in India. The growing street violence, lynching and killing of Muslims, Dalits, Communists, prejudice against religious minorities, capturing state power by electoral means and infiltration of RSS into judiciary, universities, army, media, police and bureaucracy are some of the similarities between European fascism in early twentieth century and Hindutva fascism in India today. There is much resonant here. European fascism took a decade to evolve during 1930s, but Hindutva fascism is institutionalised and internalised nearly for a century in India since 1920s. Hindutva fascism is not only populist but also popular beyond the cow belt of Hindi heartland. It has expanded its support base from landed elites and business communities to rural areas of India. The neoliberal economic policies marked the difference between European fascism and Hindutva fascism in India. The all-out onslaught on labour laws and labour movements are common features between neoliberalism and Modi-led Hindutva fascist government in India.

Neoliberalism and Hindutva fascism is grounded on the twin idea of spreading fear and insecurities, which helps in the re-emergence of different reactionary religious and regional fault lines in the society. This helps Hindutva fascists to consolidate their power by using security infrastructure in the name of unity and integrity of India and Indian nationalism. Hindutva fascists are also committed to neoliberalism ideology as an economic policy strategy. Neoliberal and Hindutva fascist forces are suspicious of democracy. Both consider the ideals of debate, disagreements and dissents as existential threats. Therefore, there is diminishing support for democratic culture, individual dignity, human rights and individual liberty. Such developments are integral part of neoliberal political and economic culture concomitant with the interests of the Hindutva fascist forces in India.

The disaster that is unfolding in India today is a product of arranged-cum-love marriage between Hindutva politics and neoliberal economic policies. Such an alliance produces deaths and destitutions. Any search for alternatives in India depends on united struggle against Hindutva and neoliberalism. It is a common battle that can pave the path towards sustainable alternatives. The only option is to struggle continuously for alternatives by fighting against neoliberalism and Hindutva.

POLITICS OF HINDUTVA AND DEVELOPMENT THEOLOGY

The well-crafted shallow slogans of 'Shining India', 'Achhe Din (good days)' and 'Sabka saath, sabka vikas, sabka vishwas' (solidarity with everyone, development for all) are designed to hide failures of BJP governments and camouflage the hate-filled fascist ideology of RSS. These slogans also summarise the deceptive narratives of development theology. Mr Narendra Modi duped everyone with his propaganda of development theology. He behaves like an event manager whose entire motto is to increase the sale of RSS's falsehood in every aspect of life. The relationship between Hindutva politics, its dubious propaganda of development and false narratives on Indian nationalism are attempts to reconcile its history of betrayal during anti-colonial struggles and postcolonial nation-making in India. The art of dishonesty and spreading falsehood are twin projects inseparable from the history of Hindutva politics and its growth.

Hindutva politics evolved during mid-nineteenth century to consolidate upper caste Hindus to transform India into a Hindu Rashtra with the help of British colonisers. The Hindu Mahasabha, the ideological forefathers of Hindutva politics in India, collaborated with British and did not participate in Indian freedom struggle. These forces were promoters of two nations' theory well in advance of the Muslim League. The Hindu Mahasabha and Muslim League were ideological twins; both believed in the concept of parochial ethnic and religious nationhood borrowed from Western Europe. The divisive Hindutva politics is responsible for the partition of India. These original anti-nationals are trying to distribute certificates of nationalism and patriotism by destroying the idea of citizenship and secularism in India today.

The Hindutva politics and its populist cultural playbook is not well-equipped to handle the economic, social and development crisis faced by India and Indians today. The policy response demands the spirit of scientific inquiry, peace, solidarity and cooperation. Hindutva forces and their love affair with neoliberal capitalist development theology are antithetical to everything that people need during a crisis. Hindutva forces manufacture and exuberate the crisis to sustain in power by spreading false economic, cultural and nationalistic narratives like a snake oil vendor. The development theology of Hindutva politics helps in the consolidation of capital and helps capitalism to integrate within its reactionary and right-wing social, cultural, religious and political practices in India.

The Hindutva forces opposed to everything that is foreign. They talked about nationalist economic politics during their early days but in reality, their ideology itself is Western European in letter and spirit. It is opposed to Indian ethos of universal brotherhood and inclusive humanism. The arranged-cum-love marriage and reconciliation between Hindutva and capitalist forces in India reflects the inherent reactionary nature of capitalism as a system. 'Hate, abandonment of science and reason, unity of Brahmanical forces, unquestionable authority, false propaganda' are five principles which animate all varieties and various incarnations of Hindutva politics of faith and its relationship with capitalism.

The development theology of Hindutva politics is fascist and resilient during crisis. The genocide of Muslims in Gujarat 2002 and Delhi 2020, demonetisation and GST-infused economic crisis reveal that Hindutva forces are resilient. The Hindutva political resilience is a product of ritualisation of the idea of individual sacrifice for the Indian nation. The Indian media follows this norm and promotes false narrative of positivity as outlined by Hindutva playbook. Such propaganda creates unwavering faith in the ruling regime and a citizenry with herd mindset. These twin outputs were soothed by false assurances and great acting by Hindutva playboy in politics Mr Narendra Modi and his capitalist cronies.

The continuity of such a reactionary alliance between Hindutva politics and development theology of capitalism depends on political practice of resistance movements in every layer of Indian society. The resistance and opposition to Hindutva theology of development need to move beyond ritualistic habituations of fragile electoral democracy. These are the days of street fights with fascist Hindutva forces in India. These street fights need to shape its sustainable and alternative ideological narratives that are acceptable to the masses. The ideological narrative need to move away from narrow silo of Hindutva politics and advocate for a society based on peace, humanism, science, secularism, reason, prosperity, respect and solidarity. These principles are non-negotiable in the political and social practice of alternative politics. The defeat of Hindutva politics and development theology is the necessity of our times and it is inevitable.

LABOUR DIVISION BETWEEN HINDUTVA FASCISM AND CAPITALISM

History is about forgetting and remembering within different waves of time. If a society fails to view its present situation in the mirror of history, then that society condemned itself to the dustbin of future. The Indian society is in such a dangerous crossroad. The despicable ideology of Hindutva led by RSS, evil politics of BJP and horrific policies of Modi government threaten the lives, livelihood of Indians and weaken India and Indian democracy. The failure of Modi-led BJP government is written in all fronts of governance from home fronts to foreign policies.

The agricultural policies of Modi government ruined the life and livelihoods of Indian farmers and destroyed agricultural economy in India. The myopic foreign policies of Modi government have isolated India within the neighbourhood and outside South Asia. The vile of Hindutva politics and its inhuman actions have defamed India in the world among the community of nations. The dismantling of state-led welfare policies, planning and institutions by the Modi government led to the collapse of health, education and industries. Modi's economic policies have ruined small and medium businesses in India. The growth of unemployment, crime, hunger, homelessness and insecurities are direct outcomes of BJP-led Modi government and its directionless policies. These policies manufacture crisis that ensures suffering of millions of Indians. It is a Hindutva shock therapy that breeds enormous political power for the growth and stability of Hindutva fascism in India.

As India and Indians are suffering under multiple forms of crisis in different steps of their lives, Indian corporations and their multinational brethren continue to multiply the mountain of their profits. Hindutva fascism derives its economic, political, social and cultural strategy from European fascism and Nazism. There is a clear labour division between fascists and their capitalist crony corporations. The historical brotherhood between Nazis and corporate capitalism continue to thrive in India today as it has happened in Europe during and after world wars. The European and American corporations were not only sympathetic but also collaborated with fascists and Nazis for ideological reasons. Capitalism is concomitant with all illiberal and undemocratic forces in society today in search of profit. Their organic and historical relationship reveals itself with same motivation accelerated by Hindutva rule in India.

The Dehomag, a subsidiary of the IBM, has supplied technology to identify Jews during nationwide census operation in Germany. The company has also provided punch card machines and sorting systems devices to identify and exterminate Jews in concentration camps. It was a lucrative business for the IBM. The German auto designer Ferdinand Porsche and his company helped to develop the Volkswagen cars as per the order of Hitler. The Volkswagen had used slaves from the concentration camps to expand its car production and profit. Similarly, Hugo Boss has used slaves from the concentration camps to produce uniforms for the Nazi regime. He was also a sponsoring member of the Schutzstaffel (SS), the Nazis' paramilitary wing. The media corporations like the Associated Press have worked as Nazi collaborators. The Coca-Cola Company's Fanta business was booming with the help of Hitler's Youth wing. The corporations like the Kodak, Bayer, Ford, BMW, L'Oréal, Bosch and many banks were beneficiaries of Nazi rule in Germany. Human miseries were the foundation of corporate profit under Nazism. The death of democracy and freedom were twin foundations on which fascism and corporate capitalism grew together in nineteenth- and twentieth-century Europe.

The Hindutva rule led by Modi is not only following the ideological footprints of European Nazism and fascism but also following the strategy of labour division between politics and economics for the success of Indian and global corporations at the cost of Indian lives and livelihoods. The shameful alliance between Indian corporations and Hindutva fascism is pushing India and Indians into a miserable chapter of history by ruining the present. The Hindutva forces decided to control the state power with the help of electoral politics dominated by one party, whereas Indian corporations and their global brethren can control Indian economy and resources while Indians suffer under multiple forms of miseries. The democratic deficit, economic crisis, cultural and economic turmoil witnessed in India today is not a Hindutva method of madness but a clear and historical strategy of labour division between Hindutva and corporations.

Indian capitalist class and higher caste's complicity with Hindutva fascism breed all forms if crisis and conflicts in India. Social, economic, political and cultural crisis consolidates the power of fascists and their crony capitalists.

Both benefit from the crisis. The ever-willing industrialists and business partners of fascism and Nazism have failed to save Hitler and his rule. The Fuhrer's thousand-year plan has collapsed within a decade. Hitler died by suicide and his regime collapsed like a pack of cards with the horror of death and destitutions. But Hindutva forces will not find their hiding place. Like any other anti-fascist struggles, people will follow the path of unity, peace, liberty and justice. The Indian industrialists, celebrities, fashion designers, media houses and capitalist classes cannot save Hindutva-led fascist Modi government in India for long. All illiberal and undemocratic forces sink under the waves of historic liberation struggles of the masses. History has witnessed the collapse of all empires and dictators. Hindutva fascism can bite the dust sooner if we can resolve to fight both capitalism and fascism together. This is the only long-term alternative for the survival of India and Indians.

PERILS OF HINDUTVA-LED INDIAN ECONOMY AND ALTERNATIVES

The world is heading towards worst economic recession in its history. The governments are worried about their citizenry and future of their country. But Mr Narendra Modi cares very little as long as his popularity and electoral victory remains intact. Mr Modi fiddles with the future of India and Indians by manipulating the public mind with the help of mass media. His government spent over Rs. 3,800 crores on publicity in print and audio-visual media according to Mr Prakash Javadekar, the Union Minister for Information and Broadcasting in Modi government. According to the *Centre for Media Studies*, Modi-led BJP spent nearly Rs. 27,000 crores in 2019 Lok Sabha polls, which is about 45 per cent of the total electoral expenditure in India. This is the cost of maintaining Modi's image in public with the help of propaganda when Indian economy is going down in drains. The economists in the World Bank and International Monetary Fund are projecting a gloomy economic scenario for India. It is worst economic growth since the 1991 economic crisis and liberalisation.

In December 2019, Arvind Subramanian and Josh Felman in the Center for International Development at Harvard University published a working paper called *India's Great Slowdown: What Happened? What's the Way Out?*. The paper outlined the causes behind the slowdown of Indian economy. It argued that adverse impact of demonetisation and GST shocks, unsustainable credit boom in real estate market, fall in consumption expenditure and demand shortages are some of the causes behind the collapse of economic growth in India. The alternatives offered in this chapter follow the same old neoliberal paradigm that led to economic chaos in the first place.

All major economic indicators in India look extremely miserable now. Indian industrial and agricultural growth was in a downward spiral well before the outbreak of the coronavirus pandemic. The manufacturing and service sector is contracting. Unemployment is at forty-five year high last 2020. According to the Centre for Monitoring Indian Economy (CMIE), the employment rate fell to an all-time low of 38.2 per cent and unemployment rate rises to nearly 9 per cent in March 2020 which is highest in last forty-three months. There is also a sharp fall of the labour participation rate which is a very worrisome sign for Indian economy. The formal and informal sectors are both sputtering in Indian economy.

It is political arrogance and economic ignorance that defines the everyday economic policies pursued by Narendra Modi-led Hindutva government in India. The Indian economy and its development processes are at a crossroads. The centralisation of power and directionless of governance undermines well-established constitutionally mandated institutions of policy, planning and economy development that firefights crisis in India. The net outcome of such a process is loss of credibility and public trust on the abilities of state and its institutions. This is the dangerous outcome of populist promises and politics of Hindutva in India.

It is myopic to expect that Modi government will follow revolutionary economic policies and political economy of development which can permanently emancipate people from hunger, homelessness, poverty and unemployment. The modest liberal and Keynesian approach to Indian economic growth depends on stimulation of growth of internal markets and business competitiveness in the world markets. This twin project of economics depends on the political abilities of state and government in creating favourable internal economic environment by empowering labour forces both as producers and consumers. But Narendra Modi-led Hindutva government pursues every economic policy that disempowers producers and consumers in both formal and informal economy.

The asymmetry of economic growth is pursued to empower both Indian and foreign capitalist classes. The reactionary Hindutva forces and their myopic economist clans have little understanding that capitalist economic growth does not depend on concentration of capital accumulation in the hands of few. Such a process establishes a rent-based economy that destroys economic growth and development. So, Keynesians argue that economic growth depends on expanding demand, investment spending and enabling employment for higher consumption. This is not possible in a stagnant economic environment of jobless growth that defines Indian economy led by Modi government.

Modi government has failed to mobilise India's internal resources to face and overcome the economic crisis. It is possible to overcome the economic crisis by mobilising human, technological and natural resources in India. State intervention in the interests of many and not few is the way forward to revive Indian economy. But Modi government has already abandoned its responsibilities for the recovery of Indian economy after the COVID-19 pandemic. Modi government is not taking any initiative towards the economic recovery. It is madness when a government abandons its citizenry.

It looks like there is a method in Modi's directionless economic governance in India. Modi regime is accelerating economic, political and social disasters in India. It is a method of shock doctrine that inflicts extreme violence and pain on majority of population in pursuit of power. The economic policies pursued by Modi government is a shock therapy that helps Modi's crony capitalist classes whereas majority of Indian population suffers under hunger, homelessness, illiteracy, unemployment, ill health, deaths and destitution. Modi government is drunk with power. The cocktail of ignorance and arrogance keeps Hindutva ideologues in RSS and BJP in a state of bliss when the entire country cries for help. Hindutva can never offer any alternative to the people of the country because Hindutva is neither politics nor economics. It is a constructed cultural logic of perverted upper-caste capitalists in India. Their political and economic demise is the only way forward.

Resistance is the final and only alternative for the survival of India's democratic and secular traditions of economic growth and development. The defeat of ruling class represented by Modi is written in history. Indians must fight this government to write history and reclaim their republic for social harmony, peace and economic prosperity. There is always time for songs and poetry in dark times. It is important to remember and recite the last paragraph of the prophetic poem called *The Masque of Anarchy* by Percy Bysshe Shelley.

Rise, like lions after slumber
In unvanquishable number!
Ye are many—they are few!

FASCIST MODI, HIS SPEECHES AND
THE ART OF DECEPTION

India needs investment in health infrastructure by establishing more medical colleges, research centres and hospitals. Indians need more doctors, nurses, pathologists, pharmacists, medical technicians, laboratories and hospital managers. These facilities are central to public health infrastructure in India. Instead of providing these facilities, Mr Narendra Modi asks Indians to clap and light candles. Clapping and lighting candles will not help patients and doctors. It cannot stop the spreading of diseases and pandemics like COVID-19. India needs schools, colleges, universities, industries, employment and all other modern infrastructures. In every crisis, there is no policy response, but Modi addresses the nation as if his speeches can heal the broken republic of India. His speeches symbolise the art of deception, abandoning his constitutional responsibilities for the citizens of India during different crisis. In spite of all his failures, his popularity among Indians continues to surprise many.

There are three questions central to understand the rise of Modi, RSS and BJP. The first question is what explains the appeal of Narendra Modi to unforgiving Indian voters. The BJP won last two general elections under his leadership. The second question is how the fringe elements of fascist Hindutva cultural movement led by RSS become mainstream in Indian politics and society. The third question is how strong constitutional institutions became so fragile after the electoral victory of Modi-led BJP.

The answers to the three questions can be found in the works of German philosopher Erich Fromm. His book *Escape from Freedom* (1941) outlines that fascism and its leadership grow when citizens surrender their freedom and 'the readiness to accept any ideology and any leader, if only he promises excitement and offers a political structure and symbols which allegedly give meaning and order to an individual's life' (Fromm, 65:282). Manufacture crisis and fear are twin projects of Hindutva fascist forces in India. RSS and BJP provide a deceptive nationalist ideological narrative based on Hindutva symbols which are neither history nor Hindu religion. The strong leadership of Modi and RSS is based on false propaganda. Modi is a master of such a project that destroys very cosmopolitan fabric of Indian civilisation.

BJP and RSS pursued the politics of otherness by propagating the Hindutva politics of hate against Muslims and captured the political environment created with the failures of Indian Congress. It created a false sense of insecurity created by global war against Islamic terrorism. It helped BJP and RSS to pursue its politics of hate against Muslims. It also spread a false sense of threat to Indian national glory due to Indian Muslims allegiance to Pakistan, which is not true in reality. Indian Muslims are patriotic and nationalist like anyone else in India. Historically, RSS and BJP are the real and original anti-nationals of India. However, human beings desire for order and security under a strong leader provided grounds for the propaganda that led to the victory of Modi-led BJP.

The reality of Indian economy and society reveals failed politics of Modi-led fascist Hindutva in India. The menace of demonetisation, Goods and Services Tax, unconstitutional abrogation of Article-370 of Indian Constitution, CAA, lynching of Muslims, imprisoning human rights activists and political opponents and gunning down leaders of rationalist movements are some of the ideological achievements of Modi-led fascist BJP and RSS government in India. The rising tide of unprecedented social disharmony, unemployment and acute economic crisis is battering India today. These are self-inflicted pain induced to Indian society and economy by the architects of Hindutva fascism to manufacture crisis, fear and otherness. This is a Hindutva shock doctrine to transform secular India into a Hindu Rashtra envisioned by Hindutva fanatics inspired by Adolf Hitler. This shock therapy is essential to sustain and manufacture further crisis that will allow RSS and BJP to enjoy absolute power in India. It will cost Indians their freedom and constitutional, secular and liberal democracy.

The opposition to Hindutva fascism under the leadership of Modi and his deceptive political practice is inevitable for the survival of the unity and integrity of India. The opposition parties need to develop their own agenda and stop responding to the diversionary and deceptive tactics of Modi-led Hindutva fascism. It is important for the opposition parties to recover from their inner tiredness and political resignation. Political despair and depoliticisation are twin weapons that create fertile environment for the establishment and growth of Hindutva fascism in India.

The mass movement against Modi needs to create an alternative narrative to counter the misconceptions created by Modi's propaganda machine. It is important to highlight the ideological threats of Hindutva fascism in our society by looking at lynching of Muslims, Dalits and human rights activists. The movement based on reason, science, sense and sensibilities defeated fascism in history. This is our historical responsibility now to defeat Hindutva fascists to write the history of new India free from all forms of bigotry.

MR NARENDRA MODI: THE FAILED
PROPHET OF PROPAGANDA

Modi represents contradictory character of Hindutva politics to hide its fascist character. The political history of so-called Hindu nationalism is neither consistent nor chaotic. But it is a methodological contradiction in shaping the power of national and international capital in India with the help of state power. The people of India have been beguiled by the claim of Modi's consistent false propaganda that country under his leadership is moving towards the resolution of all problems. The groundless optimism did not take much time to reveal hopelessness in the republic. All his promises and claims have been discredited by tragic realities of everyday life. All reasons and sensibilities have been assaulted by aggressive nationalism of false patriots. The agendas of people were put into dustbin of politics by regular headline grabbing cow vigilantes, terrorism, love jihad, cultural and moral policing of our young generation. The despairs have been reduced to the result of past failures of previous governments and it is impossible for the current Modi government to reverse the situation. This symbolises naive hope of people and meaninglessness of despair lies within the structure of Modi government, where corporates flourish and people face the death cult of hunger, joblessness, cultural police and their test of patriotism before their journey to burial grounds.

India is in the brink of becoming the hotspot for the spread of COVID-19. The Modi government is planning to lift the lockdown when the coronavirus spread is in its peak. The unavoidable lockdown was imposed when the coronavirus spread was minimal. This reflects lack of reasonable planning and long-term vision in managing crisis. As a result of which the unplanned and authoritarian lockdown policy by Modi government failed miserably to control the spread of coronavirus. It is contributing to the deaths and destitutions of majority of poor and marginalised migrant workers in India. It stripes away the citizenship and dignity of human lives in India. It is a Modi made and Modi-led public health disaster in making. But the showman Mr Narendra Modi's unfettered popularity, his false promises and deceptive propaganda continue to rise while Indian states are combating COVID-19 pandemic. The directionless policy decisions of Modi government, explosion of misinformation combined with Hindutva hangover with pseudo-science creates challenges for India in its resolve against the pandemic. It undermines India's credibility and international image.

The secular, multicultural democratic dividend can only help to shape India and the future of Indians during crisis. The future of India depends on its people irrespective of their religious, regional, cultural and social background. Empowering people and enlarging democratic space is central to transform India into a successful welfare state. Food security, public health, education and sustainable development are some of the central issues that Indians face today. It is within this context, India needs planned interventions by mobilising its own internal resources. India lacks infrastructure to mobilise its own natural and human resources. So, it is imperative for the policymakers to create sustainable infrastructure with a long-term vision that can generate mass employment and other sources of income for the people even during the pandemics. The success depends on sustainable leadership that empowers people with clear flow of progressive and scientific information. Therefore, digital revolution can be used as a tool to realise this goal. All these ideals are missing in Modi government as it follows a very narrow reactionary vision of RSS. It did not miss any opportunity to blame the religious minorities for the spread of the coronavirus. Modi government is an onslaught on the future of India and Indians. Death toll grows due to COVID-19 and Modi's popularity grows due to propaganda.

The Modi-led Government of India is creating massive tax regimes for the masses but gives huge tax relief to the corporations. The neoliberal economists in Modi government have failed to understand the objectives of taxation as a concept and as an economic tool. Taxes are used to increase public investment to increase productive infrastructure for economic growth and development. Taxes are used to augment social welfare of the masses by controlling market mechanisms. It helps in creating economic stability by reducing, inequalities and inflationary pressures within an economic system. Modi government has failed to achieve the basic objectives of taxation. The corporates are beneficiaries of taxation policies of Modi government. It is economic illiteracy that defines this government, which puts masses in miseries.

Modi government did not provide any form of relief to the masses. It surrendered to the Indian industrial capitalist class by withdrawing the policy of mandatory wage pay during the lockdown period. While Modi-led central government surrenders before the Chamber of Indian Industries (CII), the BJP-led state governments in Uttar Pradesh and Madhya Pradesh have abolished important legal protection for the workers. In this way, Modi government enables conditions of bonded labour. The postcolonial Indian state as a political entity is a product of anti-colonial struggles of the working class. But the state in India today is taken over by the upper caste and class population in Indian society. It serves the purposes of industrial capitalist class and feudal-landed elites. It does not represent the Indian working classes any longer. It is clear that Modi represents the political rule of the capitalist class, where the masses cannot decide the future of democracy with the perpetuation of misery. It is the farmers, youths, migrants, labourers, women, Dalits and tribals who produce everything but suffer from misery in the midst of plenty. They produce food but die in hunger. The migrants build the cities, malls, hotels but live without a roof over their head. They build hospitals but die in illness without basic medical facilities. The lockdown period is a time for self-reflection and realisation for the working class that they need to work for their own emancipation from the bondages of work within a system that does not give opportunities for a dignified life.

The Hindutva regime led by Modi is losing control over very objectives, it had promised to the people of India. It promised strong leadership, economic prosperity and national security. Modi government has failed to achieve these three important promises, it has made in the election manifesto. Modi government is using the coronavirus-led lockdown to control the masses by putting student leaders, human rights activists and opposition leaders in prison. It is destroying Indian democracy by controlling the masses in the pretext of stopping the spread of coronavirus. In reality, the directionless lockdown has failed to achieve the objectives. The Modi regime began to turn against the people of India, accusing the non-existent opposition parties for the failure of the government. It ruined constitutionally approved well-established norms and institutions of policy and governance in India, as a result of which people are facing a very uncertain future. The country is facing troubled neighbourhood.

The mass appeal of Modi and corporate character of his government reflects contradictory character of Hindutva forces in India. It expresses itself in the way in which it seeks to achieve its reactionary objectives at the cost of Indian republic. The contradictions are ways to hide the real objectives of Hindutva politics that is incompatible with modern India and its people. The propaganda has failed to hide the contradictions and ideological elusiveness of BJP and RSS. The people of India are frustrated, and the government has betrayed their hopes and aspirations. The impoverish migrants, students, youths, farmers, women, rural and urban poor witness the paradox of plenty and so-called strongman Modi, the prophet failed them.

In such a context, Indian democracy is heading towards a street-level chaos. The chaos needs political direction and leadership to covert itself into a revolution that can shook Modi regime and its medieval ideological apparatus led by RSS. The failure of Modi government reflects the ideological bankruptcy and irrelevance of the RSS and BJP. The alternative political forces cannot be repressed for ever. It is time to struggle together to save the idea of India from the ruinous path led by BJP and RSS. India can only revive its progressive and democratic path by mobilising its own resources with the help of its own people. It needs change of political leadership, direction and ideological revamp to ensure its multicultural ethos. The establishment of social harmony, devolution of power to people and economic decentralisation can only help India in a path of economic growth and development. It is important to realise that peace and prosperity moves together.

HOW NOT TO BE A LEADER LIKE
MR NARENDRA MODI

The prime master of propaganda Mr Narendra Modi survives all ordeals of Indian politics with the help of media myth making and diversionary strategies. It gives Modi an immediate edge over other political opponents. The organisational network of RSS and BJP provides the ideological framework on which Modi pursues his politics of otherness. In short run, Modi and his ideological mentors in RSS will destroy the founding principles of India as a republic. The social and religious harmony, secular political culture and economic progress are three immediate casualties of Modi-led BJP government in India. Such a disastrous trajectory bound to fail in long run due to ignorance and arrogance of leadership.

The leadership in politics is not only about winning elections by hook or crook. It is about creative application of available ideas and resources for the greater good of the society. Creative politics is the heart of social, economic and cultural transformation which upholds democratic values, individual freedom and liberty and collective well-being at the top priority in everyday governance of the state and government. Such creative ideals transform a political leader into statesman or stateswoman who engages with issues of the present and fortifies a sustainable future for generations. Mr Narendra Modi does not care. His mission and vision are clearly shaped by myopic RSS, which derives its ideological inspiration from European fascism and Nazism. Such ideological framework is pushing Indian society into indefinite darkness of hate, hunger and homelessness.

Mr Narendra Modi lacks creative qualities as a leader. The propaganda can hide the failures and entice the population to vote for a while. But propaganda cannot change the ground realities of lives and livelihoods of people. Creativity in political leadership demands to step back and reflect on everyday realities of the masses and their future. The monumental blunders of demonetisation, failure of Goods and Service Tax (GST), mismanagement of economy, catastrophic pandemic of coronavirus and centralisation of decision-making, and foreign policy failures show that Mr Narendra Modi lacks qualities to reflect as a leader. A leader learns from his or her own mistakes or learns from people, but Modi has failed to learn from his own experiences or from other's experiences. The top-down and dictatorial approach to politics takes a leader to the dustbin of history. Modi is going to be another name in the list of many other fascists, who destroyed peace and prosperity for a long time.

A nationalist leader inspires confidence and taps ideas from diverse sources and encourages collaboration between different people to deliver public welfare. India's recent border conflict with China shows that Hindutva nationalism is a sham. It does not inspire confidence on national security. The BJP led by Modi does not believe in diverse perspectives. He is neither a team player nor a team builder. Mr Narendra Modi prefers one-man show in front of the camera. There is no attempt by Modi to develop collaborative culture to overcome the crisis in India. Diversity is an asset in the making of nation states, but it is an anathema to Modi as a leader. He promotes the RSS-led unhealthy culture of competitive bigotry in India. The authoritarian outlooks and fascist tendencies in Modi are the products of RSS ideological training. Good leaders are transparent about their strengths and weaknesses. By being open and liberal, leaders enhance innovation and diversity of decision-making. Modi is neither transparent about his life nor about his wife, degree and decision-making. Modi moves secretly under the cloud theory of stealth and invisible courage. His vindictive actions against political opponents show his cowardice as a leader.

A successful leadership follows the historical legacies of a society and celebrates its past to share the present and future. Mr Narendra Modi and his brethren in RSS and BJP are making every effort to destroy Indian history by rewriting it and replacing its mythology. The destruction of history is important to promote rootless neoliberal capitalism and its consumer culture in India. Capitalism only grows by destroying the society and its historical experiences. Modi helps in accelerating the wealth of his capitalist cronies by spreading miseries for many in India. Modi destroys all institutions of governance that stops his reckless policies and politics. It also helps in the centralisation of power that is concomitant with the requirements of capitalist accumulation of profit at the cost of people and environment in India.

An efficient and creative leader flames motivation and allows people to follow their passion in life but Modi follows people in social media, who give rape threats. Modi patronises social media trolls, who are violent and hate mongering invisible profiles. The people behind these invisible profiles are trained by RSS and BJP. The Modi government has reduced expenditure on health and education. The students and young people do not have any opportunities to follow their passion. The Hindutva forces impose their medieval mindset on students and youths of India by asking them what to wear, whom to love and marry, what to eat and whom to pray. These private and personal individual choices of everyday lives are restricted in the name of Indian culture and Hindu way of life in India. These reflect Talibanisation of Indian society by the Hindutva forces led by Narendra Modi.

A committed leader stands with people during crisis and shows the path to recover from the crisis. The empathy and sympathy are twin characters of a committed leadership, but Modi gives shock therapy to people and put them in indefinite crisis. It is easier to control people in crisis than people in prosperity. The myopic Modi has little exposer to history of radical resistance movements in world history. Like all religious and right-wing forces, the Hindutva forces have very little exposer to historical knowledge, science, social and political history. These forces are the life and blood of capitalist classes in India. Everything that is wrong with Mr Narendra Modi as a leader reflects the narrow and ruinous worldview of RSS and BJP as bigoted political entities.

The safety and survival of India as a modern, liberal and constitutional democracy and the future of Indians depend on defeating the fascist ideology of RSS and BJP, which produces fake and failed leaders like Mr Narendra Modi. The propaganda has limited time span. Nothing can stop the fall of commercial capitalism-led Hindutva forces in India. It is a matter of time before people will rise up against such medieval forces. These forces have no place in a modern and democratic society. The good leadership is a product of political struggles. It is time to pull together all liberal, progressive, nationalist, patriotic and democratic forces to fight and defeat Hindutva fascism in India.

MODI'S LOVE FOR ANIMALS AND POLITICS OF HATE

As Indians are sinking amid the coronavirus pandemic, the makeup dependent, camera addicted and selfie-savvy Prime Minister Mr Narendra Modi is busy sharing his multitasking photos, his photography skills and his love for animals, birds and wildlife. The utter economic and social crisis does not disturb his focus on camera. The positive vibe photos of Modi feeding peacocks at his residence are flooding social media timelines. The idea is to make people believe in the compassionate character of Mr Narendra Damodardas Modi and represent his simplicity and love for animals. The petting of animals and birds for company and entertainment is not same as unconditional love for animals. Some animal lovers are people haters. The feudal and authoritarian leaders have always used animals to project their leadership in terms of power, strength and courage. Jan Mohnhaupt (2020) in his book *Animals in National Socialism* depicts the way animals were used in Hitler's footage showing his love for animals and demanding obedience to his leadership. Adolf Hitler to Karl-Otto Koch of the *Schutzstaffel* (SS) of Nazi Germany were known for their love for animals and used pets for entertainment and diversionary strategy. The Nazi propaganda used animals to undermine political opponents. There was no contradiction between love for animals and Nazi death cult. Similarly, the love for animals cannot hide the evil Hindutva politics and policies of Modi-led BJP government in India.

Under Modi's watch thousands of Muslims were killed during the Gujarat pogrom of 2002; as the chief minister of the state, he watched it silently. The rise of hate crime, lynching of Muslims, attack on rationalists and activists continue to grow in India under Modi's watch as the prime minister of India. The recent Delhi riot has taken place directly under his watch. The ministers in Modi's cabinet are known for their Islamophobic views and anti-Muslim statements in public. There is no doubt that Mr Modi loves camera more than animals and considers Muslim not as citizens but as puppies. The hugging corporate heads and humiliating Muslims are twin pillars of Hindutva politics. The vilification campaigns against Muslims, secularists and political opponents are everyday affairs. The brazen abuses of civil liberties and celebration of riots are daily reminder of worsening of law and order situation after the formation of central government by BJP under the leadership of Modi. It is important to identify how the love for animals and Hindutva politics of hate moves together in India. The subjugation of minorities and undermining the secular and democratic character of India are defining features of Hindutva ideology in praxis.

Mr Narendra Modi is trying to seduce Indian masses by showing his love for animals and hide all his failures as the prime minister of India. The ambiance of Modi's photoshoot makes one feel as if Modi stays far away from the ugly realities of majority of Indians. No amount of propaganda can provide relief to the pain of hunger. No amount of media management can hide the agrarian and unemployment crisis in India. The social crisis and foreign policy crisis make India look as if there is no government in the country. The Hindutva anarchy is a systematic design to manufacture crisis, which can be used as a shock therapy to control masses with authoritarian culture of law, police and court. The making of democratic deficit is an opportunity for Hindutva fascist forces in India. The Modi's jubilant photoshoot is a project to hide the darkness and dangers of Hindutva ideology. The policies of Modi government display that it neither cares for animals nor for human beings.

The animal love narrative by Modi is myopic without loving fellow human beings irrespective of their religious background, food habits and dress patterns. The citizenship rights are no less than animal rights but authoritarian politicians like Modi use animal love to hide their sinister design to diminish citizenship, democratic rights and liberties. Hindutva politics of hate will not stop with Muslims; it will percolate to every level of Indian society. It is time to stand with Indian Muslims and other religious minorities to save citizenship rights and constitutional democracy in India. Make no mistake, the stripping of Indian Muslim's citizenship right is a threat to the citizenship of Hindus in India. The diversity is India's strength and Indian's pride. The Modi-led BJP is opposed to the idea of diverse India. The idea of Hindu nation by BJP is a cover for corporate rule in India. Modi's love for animals will not save Indian economy from plummeting to new low every day.

It is time to defeat Modi-led Hindutva's fake propaganda with facts. The failure to stop the forward march of Hindutva would push Indian society to perpetual conflict within the country. There will be no peace and prosperity in India as long as there will be Hindutva ideology. It is time to greet Modi's false euphoria with mass demonstrations and civil disobedient movements across the country to save the idea of secular, liberal and democratic India. The future of Indians depends on the defeat of Hindutva politics and its bigoted ideology. Political silence is no longer an option for Indians.

TRUST DEFICIT IN MODINOMICS

The revival of vibrant Indian economy depends on rebuilding public trust in economic systems and institutions based on inclusive politics and peaceful social coexistence in India. The prolonged geopolitical disputes with neighbours and self-inflicted communal conflicts are pushing Indian economy and society to uncertainties, which breed distrust and undermines economic growth and development. The pervasive inequalities help to accelerate the environment of trust deficit in the country. The growing discontents and Modi-led authoritarian governance models are twin setbacks to Indian economy. It does not help to revive trust and optimism; it rather deepens economic, social and political crisis. Therefore, it is critical to rebuild trust in society for economic recovery. There are important ways to restore trust for revival of economic growth story of India.

The Hindutva forces led by Modi are spreading rampant Islamophobia and anti-Muslim programmes in the name of cultural revival and cow protection. The patronage of the state and government is accelerating social and inter-religious conflicts in India. Modinomics and Hindutva politics has destroyed the social harmony, peace and stability which inspires producers and investor's confidence, and ensures economic progress. The social instabilities and conflicts are stumbling blocks in the processes of economic growth and development. The citizens' concerns about uncertainty, safety and security of life and livelihoods are seriously affecting economic productivity. It produces the culture of mutual distrust in India. The elusive speeches and media management by the ruling Hindutva regime does not stimulate economic recovery. The investment in non-merit goods like temples further alienates economic actors from the economic system. Such a trajectory is not sustainable both in short run and long run. The economic recovery will require a renewal of trust in secular, liberal and democratic society and politics. The egalitarian approach to accessibility and availability of goods and services are prerequisite for a vibrant economy based on mutual trust. The defeat of Hindutva politics is central to the progressive project of social, political and economic revival in India.

The narrow inward-looking attitude of Hindutva politics and Modinomics has destroyed regional peace and the future of regional integration is hanging in jeopardy. In the world of interdependence, regional peace, stability and mutual trust are three important ingredients to attract large capital investments. The capital investment and its mobility depend on social and regional peace and stability. The removal of regional barriers to capital and labour is central to regional peace, stability and economic integration. The bigoted politics of Hindutva and its chauvinism is an obstacle to the growth of regional trust. The Hindutva politics and Modinomics are twin disruptive forces that shatter public confidence in state and government. It will have serious long-term impacts on India and Indians.

Modinomics led by the reactionary Hindutva ideology is destroying Indian educational system and its scientific ethos by reducing funding and increasing the Hindutva mythology in curriculum. Such a trend in India will create an environment of unskilled and uncompetitive labour force in the age of artificial intelligence, automation and data-driven global economy. It destroys trust in the quality of Indian education and training which would compromise the creative, innovative, technical and scientific skills in India. The treacherous Hindutva road to economic development is a disaster.

The implementation of tangible and inclusive economic policies to support farmers, small-scale industries, entrepreneurs and consumers can revive trust in Indian economy. But Modinomics lacks vision and commitment to address citizen's concerns as a result of which citizens do not trust the government and question its ability to deliver. The Hindutva-led Modinomics is incompatible with the needs and desires of Indians. The shallow public relations exercise does not work. It is clear that Hindutva politics is subservient to capitalist classes in India and Modinomics is their project. These disruptive bigoted forces cannot create an environment of mutual trust for the growth and development of Indian economy. India and Indians need a new compelling political, social, cultural and economic narrative based on trust. Therefore, it is the responsibility of all Indians to develop a collective vision based on mutual trust to revive a sharing and caring economy that works for all.

Modinomics is a cocktail of deceptive promises and fabricated propaganda for electoral sloganeering. The economic salvation promised by Modinomics is a mirage branded and packaged well for electoral dividends. The fairy tale of Modinomics lacks any understanding and imagination of macro and microeconomic policy perspectives and directions. Indian economy lost its positive vibes due to trust deficit of Modinomics inflicted by the Hindutva politics. It is not personalities, but policies shape the economic directions with the help of constitutionally mandated decentralised institutions. The individual dominance destroys efficiency and legitimacy of the institutions. The weakening and dismantling of well-established economic institutions with centralisation power and decision-making has further accelerated trust deficits in Indian economic system led by Mr Narendra Modi under the guidance of the RSS. Modinomics is legalised plunder of national resources by the corporates. Modinomics is a neoliberal class war on poor in India. It has destroyed the opportunities for long-term economic development in India by ruining the confidence of producers, consumers and investors. Trust is an invisible currency, which has both use and exchange value in economics. The long-term economic growth and inclusive development depends on level of trust prevalent in politics, society and economic system. The resource transfer to the big corporates, giving tax concessions and tax cuts are myopic and a short-term stimuli that do not work in an unfaithful social and political environment. It is easy to destroy public trust in public institutions and difficult to rebuild it. The pandemic of trust deficit is integral to Modinomics. The only alternative is to abandon the political and economic project of Modinomics to revive Indian economy.

NIRMALA SITHARAMAN'S ECONOMICS AS AN ACT OF GOD IN INDIA

The Finance Minister of India Ms Nirmala Sitharaman in Mr Narendra Modi-led BJP government has attributed the pandemic-led economic downturn as an act of god. She is not alone in this 'act of god' bandwagon. The theological reasoning gives temporary relief to the ruling classes but failed to provide long-term hiding ground in history. The extraordinary economic fall out of the COVID-19 pandemic gives an opportunity to the ruling classes and neoliberal economists to hide all their failures. The neoliberal authoritarian governments always find a way to manipulate and outsource their ignorance and responsibilities to god. The COVID-19 pandemic and economic crises are neither 'an act of god' nor 'people force on themselves'. The market of wildlife consumption, destruction of nature, neoliberal capitalism and failure of states and governments are responsible for global pandemic and economic crises.

The 'act of god' theory of Ms Nirmala Sitharaman is putting herself in theological trouble. The Hindu religion has 33 million gods and goddesses, and religious Hindus pray more than 33 million registered and unregistered gods and goddesses. Some are mythological deities, and some are living deities too. It is difficult to fix the blame on one god or goddess. You may not have real choice in a capitalist supermarket as a consumer. There is no freedom of choice for consumers under neoliberal capitalism unless you have purchasing power and disposable incomes. But there is real freedom of choice in gods and goddesses in Hindu religion. Even the hierarchical caste and temple barriers have failed to be an obstacle in the choice of your gods and goddesses. There is no mystery here. India is a society of cultural diversity, which breeds religious diversity and vice versa. The religious and cultural diversity in India is a bane for Hindutva politics represented by Ms Nirmala Sitharaman. It would be easier for her to evoke *Karma theory* as outlined in the *Bhagavad Gita* to justify the government and blame all Indians or all the people in the world for the ordeals of global economic and health crises.

The *Karma theory* is the best way to escape from the constitutional responsibilities and economic ignorance of the leadership. The *Karma theory* not only individualises responsibilities and results of one's own work but also externalises individual problems to the results of the *Karma* in previous life. The *Karma theory* helps to naturalise and normalise the crises, structural inequalities, exploitation and risk-free accumulation of national and global capitalist classes in India. There is no business like the business of religion. It is risk free. The profit belongs to the priest and crisis is individual responsibility.

The Indian economy was knocked down by the mistaken economic policies, social insecurities and directionless politics. Do not blame Modi government for the demonetisation, GST, unplanned and authoritarian lockdown and lack of investment in public health and health infrastructure. All are pre-planned by god and destined to happen beyond the control of state and governments. These arguments are not only obnoxious but also reflect arrogant economic illiteracy of Hindutva leadership.

The hierarchical and Brahmanical Hindu social order-based 'caste' and 'capitalism' are the twin pillars of Hindutva politics in India. The *Karma theory* in Hindu religion provides theological and ideological justifications for such an exploitative and unequal society like other religions in other parts of the world. The act of god theory of Ms Nirmala Sitharaman hides her failures as finance minister, hides her government failures and provides breathing space to capitalist classes in India with all government support. The *Karma theory* would help Ms Nirmala Sitharaman immensely and provide cover up to her government failures. It would also discourage Indian citizens to resist the government as asking for one's own rightful share is a bad *Karma*.

The legal usage of 'an act of god' might help the corporates and insurance companies but it will not help the government to abandon its roles and responsibilities in long run. In this way, the *Karma theory* is a superior excuse than the 'the act of god' arguments. The *Karma theory* is not just about personal *Karma* in previous and current life, it is about seeing a life as a whole and justifying every actions of the power in the society. The *Karma theory* also domesticates production, consumption and distribution. It organises it with caste hierarchy. Therefore, it would be good for Hindutva forces to fall back on *Karma theory* to justify loot, corruption, dominance and deaths in Indian republic.

The markets, ruling classes and gods have failed the people in history. And governments are overthrown to the dustbins of history by the reasoning power of people. The collective experience breeds collective movements to steer society out of the crises. It is a matter of time when neither the acts of god nor Modi government can stop the emanating upheavals in India. The 33 million plus gods and goddesses in India cannot take the blames and witness to the deceptive politics of the BJP government led by Modi. Ms Nirmala Sitharaman's 'act of god' explanation has lost its relevance in history. It is illusionary like Hindutva promise of salvation of life under Mod's rule. The powerful mass movement can only save India and Indians from the disasters called Hindutva; a cocktail of arrogance and ignorance.

HINDUTVA HINDRANCE TO ECONOMIC GROWTH AND DEVELOPMENT IN INDIA

The perils of Indian economy are products of directionless economic policies of Modi government. It is led by ignorant leadership and arrogance of Hindutva politics based on exclusionary ideology, which is inspired by European Nazism and fascism. There is a method madness in the reactionary politics of BJP and RSS. It intends to convert multicultural India into a monolithic India based on Hindutva. It is a reactionary political outlook shaped by national and global capitalist classes. These forces have unrestricted access to national treasury and natural resources in India under Modi-led government. From deregulation, demonetisation, GST to pandemic lockdowns, Modi government did everything to dismantle both supply and demand side of the Indian economy. The collapse of two primary pillars of economy led to the growth of unemployment and declining purchasing power of the masses. The consumption and consumer demands declined immediately, which shocked Indian economy and pushed it to undeclared recession for the first time in Indian economic history. Modi government is doing everything to protect corporate interests, when people are trying to find ways to survive with hunger, homelessness, unemployment and coronavirus pandemic. Indian economic predicaments are inherent within exclusionary Hindutva politics. The economic recovery, growth and development in India depend on social, religious and political inclusive culture, where citizens are equal shareholders of economic opportunities.

Hindutva exclusionary politics is trying to hide all its failures and constantly diverting public attention. The advocates of Hindutva glorify mythological Hindu past and blame all previous governments for all ills of Indian society today. The current problems are products of past deeds. It is a perfect Hindutva recipe that derives its philosophical legitimacy from the *Karma theory* of the Bhagavad Gita. The current problems are products of Hindutva economic policies, which are geared towards upholding the interests of corporates in India. It is evident in the rise of corporate wealth and decline of per capita income of the working Indians. Hindutva uses neoliberal dispossession to mobilise the masses and consolidates its Brahmanical social and cultural order. At the same time, Hindutva politics accelerates neoliberal economic policies that dispossess the masses. These political and economic contradictions are integral to Hindutva politics. The mainstream mass medias are playing a central role in hiding these contradictions by promoting Hindutva agenda of dispossession and disenfranchisement of majority of Indian citizens; Muslims, religious minorities, lower caste, tribals, women and working classes. Hindutva exclusionary ideology is not only depriving Muslims from their citizenship rights but also accelerating deprivation of lower caste, women and working-class population from participating in economic opportunities by privatising national resources.

Hindutva politics is opposed to the idea of India as an inclusive, constitutional, liberal and secular democracy. It follows mythological theocracy, which is opposed to very foundation of scientific and modern India of twenty-first century. The Indian economic perils are products of such a reactionary and medieval ideology of Hindutva. It is shaping India with its Hindutva shock therapy based on prohibitions, controls and commands over everyday lives of people. Hindutva discourse is trying to dominate every aspects of Indian life from food habits, dress patterns, education, health to reproductive rights. These regressive outlooks are fundamentally opposed to economic growth and development in India, because social, political, economic, religious and cultural marginalisation weakens citizens, families, societies, states and institutions to mobilise internal resources of India. The centralisation of power by Hindutva forces further diminishes the abilities of local and provincial governments to mobilise local resources. The availability, accessibility and distribution of goods and services depend on production, demand and supply. Hindutva politics destroys every economic foundations of the country by creating social and religious conflicts and violently supressing political opposition and democratic decentralisation processes.

Hindutva model of economic and political governance of Modi government is based on multiple forms of exclusionary practices that hinder economic growth and development in India. Hindutva's innate hatred for Muslims is the first form exclusion, which diminishes more than 14 per cent of Indian population and their abilities to contribute to their individual lives and to the national economy. Hindutva politics considers women only as mothers, sisters and wives who can be prayed inside the house. Such a patriarchal approach discourages civic and economic participation for nearly 48 per cent of Indian women population. The apartheid Hindutva ideology believes in caste hierarchy, which disables social and economic abilities of nearly 25 per cent of lower caste and tribal population. It means 87 per cent of Indian population are living under the conditions of structural barriers that do not allow them to grow and be the shareholders of national life. The processes of marginalisation, denials of citizenship rights and lack of participation create social, political and economic conditions of institutionalised deprivation, which gives power to Hindutva forces. Therefore crisis, crime, dominance and deprivation are four weapons of Hindutva politics in India.

Hindutva exclusionary politics creates conditions of deprivation trap, which breeds unemployment, poverty, debt, destitution, marginalisation, illiteracy and illness. These outcomes are dangerous and weakening of India and Indians both in short run and long run. Social coexistence, peace and inclusive cultures are foundations of economic growth and development.

But the idea of inclusive culture and peace are alien ideals and antithetical to Hindutva politics. Therefore, Hindutva ideology is a hinderance to economic growth and development in India.

The Hindutva politics led by Modi can neither be reformed nor can be revised. The only alternative is to defeat it ideologically and politically till it becomes qualitatively and quantitatively irrelevant and illegal in India. Hindutva is Indian version of Nazism and fascism. It is detrimental to India, Indians and humanity. India and Indians will suffer social and economic underdevelopment as long as Hindutva rules the country. The institutionalisation of Hindutva discrimination destroys all potentials and conditions for economic growth and development. The struggle against Hindutva is struggle against caste, gender and religious-based discrimination in India. The united struggle against Hindutva politics must develop radical narratives based on social, political and cultural integration, inclusive of economic and development policies for peace and prosperity for the masses. These are essential conditions of sustainable economic growth and secular development of society in India.

HINDUTVA LEVIATHAN

The Hindutva governments led by BJP in India are brazenly attacking Muslims, students, journalists, writers, human right activists, youths, farmers and marginalising communities. These assaults are integral to RSS and its ideology of Hindutva politics. The suppression of civil liberty is growing. The independent judiciary and free democratic institutions are abjectly surrendering to the Hindutva project shaped by the crony capitalist classes in India. The BJP governments in centre and states are implementing economic policies that destroy the future of working classes in India. The BJP governments are also implementing social policies that ruin social peace and harmony. The ruthless Modi government is empowering lynch mob to control democratic dissents of the civil society. The assassination of democratic politics and liberal society in India by electoral means is near complete. It is a matter of time before Brahminical Hindu caste order as outlined in the *Manusmṛiti* becomes formal law.

The Hindutva politics is shaped by the bigoted ideology of RSS. It has revealed itself after forming BJP-led government with absolute majority under the leadership of Mr Narendra Modi. The Modi-led BJP government shows the essence of its politics of control, command and communalisation of individuals, families, societies, states and governments. It has revealed the vileness of RSS and its fascist ideology. The decisive victory of these forces undermines liberal, constitutional and secular traditions of Indian state and government. The intention is to replace Indian Constitution with Hindutva leviathan as outlined by the medieval outlooks of RSS.

The Hindutva leviathan is based on the Hobbesian idea of 'sovereign' without democratic accountability and citizenship rights. It does not believe in India as a modern state based on social, political and cultural contracts and cooperation based on democratic citizenship. The everyday curtailment of individual liberties is a regular affair. The rise of conflicts between different religious and regional groups is on rise after Hindutva forces came to power. Hindutva is an organised ideology of a political project of national and global capitalist classes to control society, domesticate consumption and dominate the economic system. It talks about cultural nationalism to hide its reactionary outlooks.

Hindutva forces spread hatred and fear to manufacture crisis based on false propaganda. The environment of crisis helps to suspend democratic politics in the name of unity, integrity and sovereignty of the nation state, where the government enjoys absolute power to control citizens without any questions in the absence of politics. There is no opposition to the government. Any opposition to the government is branded as anti-national. The original anti-nationals are in power today. The RSS is antithetical to the ideals of modern democracy. It did not participate in the Indian nationalist struggle against British colonialism. It formed ideological partnership with reactionary forces and weakened anti-colonial struggles in India. The same organisation distributes certificates of nationalism today; the irony dies its natural death in Indian politics.

There is systematic regular campaign against religious minorities and opponents of BJP and RSS. There is regular demonisation campaign against Muslims, Christians and rationalists in India. The idea is to domesticate and destroy the very foundation of democratic citizenship in India. RSS does not believe in the ideology of democracy. The nasty, brutish, selfish and authoritarian ideology of RSS and BJP derives its philosophical and political outlooks from solitary ruling-class ideology of Western Europe. The European fascists and Nazis provide ideological inspirations to Hindutva forces in India today. These reactionaries celebrate the ideology of ethnic cleansing.

The stripping away of citizenship rights from Indian Muslims, Christians and other religious minorities reveal the sinister design of RSS to destroy Indian democracy. It is time to stand up for the rights and liberties of Indian Muslims as citizens of India. The failure to defend Muslims in India will not only weaken Indian democracy, but it will also weaken citizenship rights of all Indians. Hindutva is not a defender of Hindus. It is an organised principle of fascism to look common Indians to empower and enrich Indian and global capitalist classes.

As capitalism completely consolidates its absolute power over Indian state and government, the marginalisation of people and conflicts between different communities will become a norm. In this way, Hindutva is pushing Indians into a situation of civil war. In such a situation, the Hindutva forces can exercise their power with impunity. Indians are waiting to face enormous risk of facing coercive state power under the guidance of Hindutva authoritarian ideology and government. There will be no political choice for people to elect their own government. It is going to be a society free from any form of individual liberty and rights. The basic survival will be under question mark.

From demonetisation, GST, lockdowns to farm laws, the Hindutva forces continue to manufacture crisis to obscure their arrogance of ignorance and hide all failures of governance. The populist politics of common sense and street smartness of the school dropout criminals have taken over all institutions of state and government in India. There is no organised opposition to Hindutva politics and policies of Modi and brethren. Such a dangerous situation puts India and Indians in a vulnerable position in a fragile world. There is no difference between autocratic regimes and Hindutva-led government in India. It is imperative for the masses to stand up against the arbitrariness of ideological politics, absoluteness of ruling-class power and order. After four centuries, Hindutva forces are implementing the Hobbesian ideology in India that Hobbes wanted to escape during early seventeenth-century Europe.

The struggle against Hindutva leviathan is the only alternative for the survival of India and Indians. There is no other way for the survival of India as a liberal, secular and constitutional democracy. The ongoing farmer's struggle against Modi government gives us hope that a democratic struggle is possible to uphold and expand the idea of democratic India by defeating the ideological and political apparatus of Hindutva leviathan.

Chapter 4

Indian Resistance against Hindutva Fascism in India

Hindutva fascism is no more an imaginary political depiction of reactionary and right-wing Narendra Modi-led BJP/RSS government in India. These reactionary forces are the original anti-nationals of India. Any serious analysis of forward march of Hindutva fascism in India needs to understand Indian social and economic conditions where caste, tribe, gender and class interact within a Brahmanical order both in rural and urban areas. It is the life and blood of Hindutva fascism. The social fascism emanating from Brahminism within exploitative Hindu caste order continues to be the foundation of propertied class that controls the state and political apparatus of the government. In spite of exceptionally favourable political environments, the liberals and progressive forces have failed to shake the authoritarian social and religious structures that enable Hindutva fascism in India today. The electoral defeat of liberal and progressive forces is inextricably linked with electoral opportunism, revisionist ideological policies and their earlier political association with regional reactionaries. Soft Hindutva cannot replace Hindutva fascism. In such a context, defeatism is a product of ideological ambiguity and political compromises of forming opportunistic electoral alliances. The result is gloomy.

From Gujarat 2002 to Delhi 2020, India witnesses continuous deterioration of the constitutional, secular, liberal values of a democratic state. The social, political and cultural normalisation of violence against Muslims and silence of the Supreme Court is unprecedented in independent India. The processes of law, order and justice were subverted to defend the organisers of pogrom as a patriotic act and depict the victims as anti-nationals. The mainstream media, judiciary, executive, police and other pillars of modern democracy are crumbling and working as the typewriters of Hindutva fascist power.

The magnitude of capitalist crisis and electoral victory of Hindutva fascists in last two parliamentary elections in India is neither unique nor surprising. It is the repetition of history in the rise of fascism. The Hindutva fascist murders provide cultural logic to apartheid caste order and capitalist crisis. There is absolutely no surprise in the policies and actions of BJP-led fascist RSS government in India. They are following their playbook of anti-Muslim pogrom in letter and spirit. In the long run, it is not only a threat to Muslims but also a threat to lives and civil liberties of all Indians. The unity and integrity of India depends on how we build up a mass movement in defence of Muslims and against the hate factory of RSS/BJP. The sporadic movements and opposition to Hindutva fascism in India are not enough. The task is to overcome this defeatism by reclaiming radical promises of Indian Constitution based on universal citizenship and democratic rights of Muslims in India.

Indian resistance against Hindutva fascism led by students and women that threatens the very foundation of old and new political cretins who consider themselves as aficionados of electoral democracy and parliament. But people are spontaneously forming their own resistance movements in different parts of India against Hindutva fascism. It is important to bring them together as a mass movement with alternative politics of hope, peace and justice. It is only possible by forming united front of Dalits, students, youths, women, Muslims, minorities, workers and all other progressive forces in the society. The priority of such a united front is to stand unconditionally in defence of Muslims.

The Hindutva fascists' deceptive narrative of nationalism needs to be exposed. History is the witness to Hindutva betrayal of Indian independence struggles. It is important to highlight the sacrifice and significant role of Muslims in anti-colonial struggle and in shaping the secular character of postcolonial India. These ideological praxis needs to be the foundational principles of India's resistance to Hindutva fascism. The broken republic of India needs such a resistance project which can help to nourish the social harmony and economic stability.

HINDUTVA: A POLITICAL AND ECONOMIC PROJECT OF SHARED LIES OF BRAHMANICAL CASTE AND CLASS ORDER

India is facing its worst crisis in its history. The Hindutva forces shaped by RSS and politically led by BJP are accelerating the crisis to undo liberal constitutional democracy in India. The political opposition is withering everyday with the help of media, puppet police, investigative agencies and judiciary. The Hindutva blueprint is to declare India as a Hindu Rashtra by viciously diminishing citizenship rights of Muslims, minorities and lower caste people. The success of RSS and BJP over last three decades is based on poisoning the minds of the higher caste Hindus with the help of deceptive propaganda. Hindutva politics is reactionary identity politics of higher caste Hindus, which destroyed the unity of working classes and used lower caste in their political project, which weakened the emancipatory politics of Dalits and lower caste politics. The Hindutva forces have converted mythology as history and deception as an art, which diverts people's focus on objective reality of their everyday life and material conditions of mass suffering. The Hindutva project is an assault on reason, science and society in India.

Hindutva is a distinctive political project of higher caste Hindus to ensure social, political, cultural and economic control of the masses in India. Every fraudulent control mechanism of Hindutva is essential to normalise all forms of exploitations and naturalise inequalities in India. The apartheid ideals of Brahmanical Hindu caste order are not compatible with constitutional democracy in India. The caste inequality is the foundation of Hindu social order. The deepening of democracy is a threat to Hindu caste order. Therefore, the Brahmanical forces are united behind Hindutva in the name of Hindu unity to uphold their control over Indian society. The colonial apologist Vinayak Damodar Savarkar has territorialised the bigoted idea of Hindu unity in his book *Essentials of Hindutva* and gave it a cultural outlook, whereas Keshav Hedgewar has shaped the political project of Hindutva by establishing the RSS. The fraudulent call for *Akhand Bharat*, construction of Ram temple in Ayodhya, and ministry for cow protection are not only political consolidation of Hindutva forces but also an establishment of cultural narrative for economic consolidation of capitalist classes and Brahmanical forces in India.

The fascist character of Hindutva is in consonance with the requirements of the Indian and global capitalist classes. As Indians are sinking in sorrow and suffering from loss of lives and livelihoods in large scale due to the mismanagement of global pandemic in India, the Indian capitalist classes are accelerating their profit in a massive scale. It is an opportunity for the capitalist classes in India to capture all national resources during the Modi-led BJP government. The capitalists have always celebrated dictatorships and authoritarian governments, which help in the expansion of their profit and consolidation of capitalist classes. The corporate capital in India gets massive tax concessions but people face welfare budget cuts. The corporates make money while people suffer in miseries. This is no accident but systematic economic strategy of the Modi government. The result is a visible disaster for India and Indians.

India and Indians are collapsing within the bottom of the development pyramid in all development parameters. India is ranked 94 out of 107 in the Global Hunger Index. The rampant growth of inequalities puts India in the rank of 147 out of 157 countries in the Oxfam Inequality Index. The Water Quality Index puts India in the rank of 120 out of 122 countries. The Air Quality Index puts India in 179 out of 180 countries in the world. The freedom of press is plummeting in India and the country stands in the rank of 140 out of 180 countries. The Environmental Performance Index puts India in the rank of 167 out of 180 countries. India is becoming the unhappy capital of the world ranking 144 out of 156 in the UN World Happiness Index. The health and educational infrastructures are collapsing every day in India, but the corporate propaganda machine hides all failures of Hindutva in the name of nationalism. But Hindutva nationalism is not anti-colonial nationalism in India. Hindutva nationalism is based on the idea of higher caste and class unity, which is the other name for fascist bigotry. The Hindutva nationalism a form of is narrow chauvinism based on hatred for religious minorities, lower caste and class people in India.

The love-cum-arranged marriage between Hindutva and neoliberal capitalism is no accident. The neoliberal capitalism has accelerated Hindutva politics as a dominant class and caste project in India. The RSS in all its political reincarnations from the Jan Sangh to BJP has always been a party of Brahmins and business communities and appealed to the dominant class and caste interests. The right-wing political movement led by Hindutva and reactionary economic policies of neoliberal capitalism have emerged together in India during the 1980s. They have strengthened each other over last three decades and helped to consolidate and expand each other's social, economic, cultural and political base. Both these forces have used lies and deceptive tactics for their growth. The neoliberal capitalism and Hindutva politics are twins. These forces are accumulating profit by both dispossessing and assimilating people based on false narratives of Hindu nationalism. These forces have a common goal: the goal of disciplining labour, diminishing citizenship rights and making people follow orders without questioning the power and authority.

The neoliberal Hindutva is a political and economic project of the capitalist classes in India. The institutional alliance between Hindutva politics and capitalist economy is a natural outcome in which capital accumulates with the support of the state and government and minimises capitalist conflicts and risks. Such an alliance and its outcomes are putting millions of Indians and their future in jeopardy. If this alliance between Hindutva and capitalism continues to grow deeper and deeper, the greater dangers are awaiting India and Indians.

In this context, it is important to develop political alternatives by forging all forces opposed to the troika of caste, capitalism and Hindutva in India. It is impossible to fight Hindutva and capitalism without fighting caste-based discriminatory social order in India. All liberal, progressive, democratic and left forces must realise the dangers of Hindutva fascism and its alliance with capitalism in India. Any compromise or surrender with these forces will breed miseries in large scale for all Indians irrespective of their caste, class, gender, religious and regional background. United struggle against caste, capitalism and Hindu right-wing forces can only save constitutional democracy in India both in short and long run. No progressive struggles have failed in the history and no struggle for alternatives will fail in India. Let's fortify our future by defeating these reactionary-force-led Hindutva politics, neoliberal economics and Brahmanical society in India. It is possible and immanent.

HALT THE FORWARD MARCH OF NEOLIBERAL ECONOMY AND HINDU RIGHT-WING POLITICS

On 15 August 2020, India celebrated seventy-four years of her independence from the British colonialism. The ravages of colonialism are still visible in her economic and political landscape, from class, caste division, regional disparity to partition of the country continue to owe its lineages to the divide and rule policies of the British Raj. However, the postcolonial India has achieved many things to her credit. There is no intention here to draw a balance sheet of her success and failures in the process of nation building but to locate its growth in the lanes of citizenship rights, regional and religious equality, social justice and economic equality.

The promises of Indian freedom struggle and achievements of the working class, lower caste, tribals and women under a constitutional and welfare state are under threat today. The twin dangers are hunting Indian working classes and the marginalised population: the neoliberal economic policies and forward march of Hindu right-wing forces in politics.

The neoliberal economic policies followed after the new economic reforms of 1991 has produced the shanty town of Dharavi (one of the largest slums in the world) besides twenty-seven-storey-high Antilla (the home of India's richest man, Mukesh Ambani). In a nation of 1.2 billion population, the neoliberal economic development has produced hundred richest people who own assets equivalent to one-fourth of the Indian GDP. India has now more than 123,000 millionaires who control more than $440 billion between them – almost half the country's GDP – whereas more than 300 million Indians live less than a dollar a day. It is better not to talk about access to food, water, electricity, housing, health and education. The visible and invisible paradox is part of the reckless liberalisation, privatisation and globalisation policies. It has not only increased the gap between rich and poor but also marginalised large section of rural population and their livelihoods. The agrarian crisis coupled with industrial stagnation today has not only created a jobless growth but also poverty, food insecurity and impoverishment. As per different reports, half of all Indian children under the age of five suffer from malnutrition. Safe drinking water is a dream for millions of Indians, but industries get perennial source of water with the help of neoliberal ruling class in different forms after the new economic reforms of 1991.

The new economic reforms have had immense negative impacts on the macroeconomic structure of India. They have not only led to the declining role of state in economy but also given rise to the growth of non-state actors (NGOs) in development planning and economy. The formalisation of development planning and declining role of state has helped to create a gap between the state and its citizens. This gap between the state and its citizens is often occupied by the Hindu religious right-wing forces by their NGO networks which is a threat to the secular social fabric, democratic polity and basis of welfare state in India.

The changing economic landscape with the growth of market-led economic development and withdrawal of welfare state led the foundation for the growth of many religious right-wing, reactionary and regional groups in India. Religious fundamentalism is the cultural logic of capitalist expansion because market that functions though the deterministic cultural hegemony under the support of the political process. The nationalistic ethos of post-independence India was well-manipulated by the Indian capitalist class to create a single national identity rather than divergent local identities. The unitary federal polity and constitutional state were created to serve the purpose of the market mobility which can aid capital accumulation by the national capitalist class. The Hindutva forces are suitable for this capitalist project in India and, as a result, the idea of Hindu ethnic nationalism has been growing with the process of liberalisation which is a threat to the pluralistic ethos of Indian society and secular polity of India. The evils of Hindu fundamentalism and market forces are accelerated by the industrial bourgeoisie, rural-landed elites both in terms of class and caste. In spite of many achievements, independent India has failed to alter the very basis of exploitative class relations and feudal social formations based on caste. The *growth, crisis and contradictions* in the contemporary political economy of India reflect changes with continuities as part of the historical process of postcolonial capitalist development which reproduces new and old forms of social and economic inequality. Hindutva-led neoliberalism in India is helping to sustain and expand this exploitative system.

Therefore, it is vital for the Indian working class and marginalised communities to develop class organisation based on their class experience and prepare themselves to launch an inclusive class struggle by looking at social, cultural and economic necessities of masses while defending its historical achievements of citizenship rights. This is only possible by halting the forward march of neoliberal economy and Hindu right-wing politics.

HEY RAM INDIA: JAI SRI RAM BJP AND CONGRESS – THE TWINS

'Hey Ram' were the last words of Mahatma Gandhi, the father of the nation. He uttered these words on 30 January 1948 while taking bullets from his assassin by a Hindutva terrorist Nathuram Godse. The Hindutva politics of hate-filled bullets from the Beretta automatic pistol killed Mahatma Gandhi. This was the first onslaught on the secular and multicultural fabric of independent India by the Hindutva forces. Like the three bullets that killed Mahatma Gandhi, the 6 December 1992, 9 November 2019 and 5 of August 2020 are three defining dates that killed secular India. These three dates are significant in dismantling of the secular character of Indian state and politics. These three dates are central towards the establishment of Hindu Rashtra in India. The process was started with the killing of Mahatma Gandhi. It continues to create havoc and enduring pain within the Indian republic.

The activists who belong to the VHP, BJP, RSS and other affiliated organisations were responsible for the demolition of the Babri Masjid in Ayodhya on 6 December 1992. The demolition of Babri Masjid has accelerated the deepening of Masjid-Mandir (temple) politics in India led by Hindutva; a bigoted political and economic project of Brahmanical propertied caste, class and capital. The landslide electoral victory of BJP in general elections led by Mr Narendra Modi has given pan-Indian political legitimacy to the Hindutva forces. But the Hindutva political project has received its judicial legitimacy, when the Supreme Court of India ordered the Government of India to create a trust to build the Ram temple in the disputed land and give five acres of land in another place to the Sunni Waqf Board for building a mosque. The Supreme Court's Ayodhya verdict has ended legal dispute between Hindus and Muslims. The contradictory judicial verdict is a victory of religious faith based on Hindutva mythology; the life and blood of Hindutva politics. The verdict did not punish the Hindutva forces and their organisations for dismantling a historic monument: 470-year-old mosque. The verdict has given new life to the political vandalism of Hindutva forces in the name of establishing a Hindu Rashtra by destroying secular India.

Amid the coronavirus pandemic, Mr Narendra Modi, the prime minister of India and the poster boy of Hindutva politics, laid the foundation stone for the construction of Ram temple in Ayodhya on 5 August 2020. He will also release a commemorative postage stamp called 'Shree Ram Janmabhoomi Mandir'. The many leaders of the Indian National Congress and opposition parties consider Ram temple in Ayodhya is a product of national consensus. It means Hindutva consensus. The Congress general secretary Priyanka Gandhi Vadra has not only endorsed the construction of Ram temple but also considers the ground-breaking ceremony of the temple as an occasion for 'national unity, fraternity and cultural congregation'. The Hindutva politics is immersed with hate, violence and vandalism. It cannot inspire national confidence, cultural unity and fraternity. The statement by Priyanka Gandhi shows the influence of Hindutva politics on mainstream opposition parties and its leaders in India.

The 'Hey Ram India' signifies the assassination of secular politics and state in India on 5 August 2020 by the BJP and Congress Party. The era of closet Hindutva is over. The launch of the culture of 'Jai Sri Ram' within Congress represents the rise of Congress model of Hindutva and the death of secular, Nehruvian and Gandhian Congress Party. There is no difference between Hindutva politics of BJP and Congress Party that helps to establish the higher-caste-based Hindu social order destroying multicultural fabric of Indian society. Both parties follow the same neoliberal economic policies that consolidate the powers of big businesses and capitalist classes in India. The difference in political flag colour and office locations does not matter. These two national parties are detrimental to the idea of India. Both political parties are a threat to life and livelihoods of poor masses in India. The circulation of elites defines both political formations, which failed to provide any alternative for the relief and rehabilitation of people from the pandemic of hunger, ill-health, homelessness and joblessness. The deceptive politics of BJP and Congress Party can never offer any form of alternatives to India and Indians during the current social, economic and military crisis. Both the political parties represent the interests of the local, regional, national and global capitalist classes in India. The Hindutva-led caste-based social, political and economic order is concomitant with the requirements of capitalism. The political consensus and judicial legitimacy have given a final touch to the process of writing the last secular and democratic epitaph for Indian pluriveralism.

It is truly the start of new India led by Hindutva, where there is money for temples and statues but there is no money for health and education. There is money to subsidise and write off debts of big businesses but there is no money for farmers, students and youths of India. Such a pathetic transformation did not happen overnight or over last six years. The casteist and conservative undercurrent of Hindu Brahmanical social order has received its political patronage from the Narendra Modi-led BJP government. This has helped the upper caste and class bigotry to become mainstream social, political and economic order in India. The idea of secular and democratic India was demolished with the destruction of Babri Masjid on 6 December 1992. The success of Hindutva political project in India was verified and reconfirmed with the start of the Ram temple construction on 5 August 2020.

The Hindutva triumphalism is undisputedly the new order in India today, where political despondency, social alienation and economic crisis rule. But hope comes up from unusual sources to inspire the resilient masses. Hindutva politics is a national shame, and it cannot write the final words on the future of India and Indians. The civilisation survived all onslaughts of time. The graveyards of time have swallowed all prides, empires and emperors within all its powerful waves and allow history to document the death of all the winners to give hope to a hopeless world in India. Hope redeems itself as alternatives. It is only the human heritage of peace that outlives time to tell stories of successful struggles for justice, equality, liberty and fraternity. It is time to conserve energy and fight for the future. The fake gully boys and their deceptive politics of Hindutva will fall like all other regimes drunk in power. This time shall pass and *Apna Time Aayega* (our time shall come) for the gullible masses to enjoy their freedom and dreams of life in peace and prosperity.

IS IT THE LEGAL TERROR OF *SONDERGERICHTE* AND *VOLKSGERICHTSHOF* OR THE SUPREME COURT OF DEMOCRATIC INDIA?

The Nazi regime in Germany has established the *Sondergericht* (summary courts or special courts) and *Volksgerichtshof* (special people's court) outside the constitutional framework. The objectives of these totalitarian courts were to destroy internal opposition to Adolf Hitler's mission in dominating and establishing absolute control over German state, government, culture and society. The legal systems were destroyed and reconstructed to support in the making of the Third Reich. The more special courts were established and given arbitrary powers to intimidate general public, execute and imprison the political opposition to Nazis. From 1933 to 1945, within twelve years, twelve thousand Germans were executed and more than sixty-six hundred thousand Germans were put in prison. These are manipulated and reduced official figures, but the realities were far worst.

During the Nazi period, the number of crimes declined, number of special courts increased and prison population have increased in Germany. These contradictions within the Nazi legal system revealed its political objectives and judicial compliance with the Nazi regime. These courts were working as legal and institutional deterrence against opposition to the Nazis. The trials were held in the forms of publicity stunts in public halls and in city squares to inflict psychological fear among the masses. The sole goal of the *Sondergerichte* and the *Volksgerichtshof* was to perpetrate legal terror in defence of the Third Reich. The legal institutions were used for the Nazi propaganda and censorships. It controlled art, architecture, literature, music, cinema, research, teaching, journalism and mass media. These special courts have eliminated civil liberties in Germany in the name of patriotism and nationalism. And justice disappeared in Germany.

The Supreme Court of India was established on 26 January 1950 to deliver independent and impartial justice by following both *niti* and *nyaya* as envisioned in the Indian Constitution. The first few decades of its establishment, most of the Indians have witnessed and trusted the impeccable and impartial nature of judgements from the highest court of the country. However, in recent times, there is a pattern emerging in the recent judgements of the Supreme Court, which questions its own foundational principles, missions and visions. The public display of political allegiance by some of the retired and current judges of the courts in India reduces its judicial legitimacy in legal praxis. Its verdicts resonate with the legal and political culture of the *Sondergerichte* and the *Volksgerichtshof* in Germany.

Like Nazis, the reactionary Hindutva forces swept away many of the freedoms in the name of nationalism, it is the duty of the Supreme Court to ensure and protect citizenship rights and individual freedom of speech and expression as enshrined in the Constitution of India. It is not malicious to criticise the governments and courts in a democratic country. It is not the tweets of lawyer Prashant Bhushan that threaten the 'very foundation of constitutional democracy' in India. It is the dubious silence and complicit of the judges that destroy judicial impartiality and independence of the Supreme Court of India. The Supreme Court's silence on human rights violation, marginalisation of civil liberties in Kashmir and diminishing citizenship rights of the Dalits, tribals, workers and religious minorities weakens the moral foundations of judiciary in India. There is a pattern growing today in India, where professors, doctors, students, youth activists and human rights activists are suffering in prison, but violent cow vigilantes, rioters and other criminals are roaming free with political patronage. Such a culture of justice empowers crime and criminals in India. If the majoritarian conscience determined by the ruling class becomes the foundation of justice, then justice is doomed in India.

The legitimacy and authority of the Supreme Court of India should not be based on spreading the fear of justice but the love to deliver and ensure justice by following the letter and spirit of both *niti* and *nyaya* as enshrined in the Constitution of India. The ideas of dissent and freedom are inalienable rights in a liberal democracy, sustained by the culture of criticisms. The monopoly of justice by judiciary and dominance of power by the government of the day destroys the very foundation of justice, freedom and democracy. It erodes public faith in different institutions in the country. The culture of criticism sharpens democratic and judicial values. It is imperative for a democratic and constitutional court to promote the culture of criticisms for its own survival and growth. The attempt to throttle the culture of criticism is pushing India with a medieval mindset, which is a leap backward. It is dangerous for the future of India and Indians.

It is time for the courts and leaders of the governing party to look at the history as their sole witness. The absolute power erodes quickly without any doubt. It is better to be conscious than be sorry. Justice survives in the moral canvas of struggles in history and all illiberal forces die their natural death in the dustbins of history. It may nor may not be televised, but the fall of power is inevitable. In spite of all legal support, political, economic and military power, all young people did not participate in the 'Hitler Youth' movement in Germany. The working-class youth organised under the *Edelweiss Pirate's* (*Edelweißpiraten*), the students organised under the *White Rose* group (*die Weiße Rose*) and the middle-class youths organised under the *Swing Youth* and *Jazz Youth* groups rejected Nazi values and fought against Nazi regime and its legal infrastructures. The students, youths, socialists and communists have played a major role in defeating Nazi rule and re-establishing liberal, social, secular and multicultural democracy in Germany today. It is within this context, it is the historic responsibility of Indian students and youths to fight and defeat Hindutva Nazis and save India and Indians from the ruinous path.

HUMAN COST OF SILENCE

In a haunting memoir, Piera Sonnino has narrated her devastating experience as a twenty-two-year-old Italian Jewish woman. She lost her parents and three brothers in the Auschwitz concentration camp in 1944. She is the only holocaust survivor in her family. Her memoir *This Has Happened: An Italian Family in Auschwitz* provides a moving account of unspeakable evils of Nazism. The horror started in 1938, when the Italian government promulgated the racial laws against Italian Jews and other minority native inhabitants of the Italian colonies. The discriminatory laws prohibited Jews from schools, universities and having any professional positions. The Italian Jews were banned from working in the armed forces and civil services too. It also banned marriages and sexual relations between Italian, Jews and Africans. Jews were rounded up and deported. The Jews community had lived in Italy for more than two thousand years and well-integrated within Italian culture and life. But the Nazis and fascists were responsible for brainwashing common Italians against Jews. The peaceful character of neighbourhoods started changing. The Jewish shops and homes were attacked and burnt down. The killers were not unknown faces but the neighbours and armed police. The people who lived together for centuries with peace and harmony have become Nazi vultures and fascist death squads.

The courageous Piera Sonnino has outlined her personal experiences in two sentences while reflecting on the last night of her family together. She writes, 'whatever I could say that time, it would not make sense translated into words; it would be a thin shadow of that reality. I would be stealing it from myself, from what is mine, desperately mine alone'. This personal memory reflects the collective pain of Jewish communities across Europe. Such a vile transformation was not a surprise. It did not happen overnight, accidentally or naturally. The majoritarian silence and disbelief of the minority communities have allowed the twin evils of fascism and Nazism, which engulfed Italian society and other parts of Europe within a couple of years. It does not reflect the success of Nazis and fascists. It reflects the silence of the majority. Silence was not the best choice, but the majority of people had silently accepted the government's official bigoted propaganda against the Jews.

The official optimisms of the evil regime did everything to hide the prevailing economic catastrophe, it diverted people's attention to constructed narratives against Jewish communities. The displacement, disintegration and deaths of the Jewish communities were the net outcomes of evil regime. The migration of Jewish communities to different parts of Europe did not save their lives. Only few people like Piera Sonnino survived to share the horrors of Nazism and fascism in which mere Jewish existence is a crime punishable by death. And prison becomes home to humanism, reason, rationality, ethics and the people who fought for the rights of the Jewish people. The partisans were perished in prison and bullets along with their Jewish compatriots. The communists and socialists were in the forefront in defence of Jewish people, and in the battle against Nazism and fascism.

Piera Sonnino's autobiography is not only a chilling history of a Jewish family in Italy but also a warning sign for the present generation to be vigilant about the rise of fascism of our times. Mass genocide, absolute devastation, disappearances and mass imprisonments are the human costs of silence in the face of fascism. As the poet Professor Michael Rosen warns us in his poem "Fascism: I Sometimes Fear" that contemporary fascism will not come in fancy dress, but they will come as if they are your friends to make you feel proud.

Piera Sonnino's devastating autobiography and Michael Rosen's poem is a daily reminder for all of us to be alert and fightback fascism in all its forms. Silence is not an option. As authoritarian regimes continue to grow with the help of religious right-wing forces and free market fundamentalists, it is time to raise our voice against these forces before they consolidate their power and positions. Majoritarian silence is not a fear but betrayal of their own existence. Active resistance is the only form of solidarity that the time demands from every patriotic Indians. It is the duty to provide unwavering support to all persecuted religious minorities and stand in solidarity with all struggles of working-class people across the globe. This is the only way towards peace, prosperity and survival of a secular, multicultural and democratic world. The united struggle against fascism is the only alternative for the human survival.

INDIA NEEDS UNITED FRONT
AGAINST HINDUTVA FASCISM

Electoral alliance and opportunism of national and regional political parties, neoliberal economic marginalisation and soft secular Hindutva line pandering to Hindu majoritarianism laid the foundation of Hindutva fascism in postcolonial India. It is in this context, Indians need to develop a broad front based on mass movements inside and outside the parliament which would ensure the defeat of Hindutva fascists and create effective political alternatives for the survival of the idea of India.

Hindutva fascism is not a movement for changing India towards peace and prosperity. It is a reactionary movement of the ruling and non-ruling elites in India. In the name of Ram temple, Hindu religion and cultural nationalism, it represents the interests of the national and international corporations. The capture and dominance of state power by BJP, RSS and Sangh Parivar accelerates the process of establishing full-fledged fascism in India. It is a matter of time before the bourgeois democratic methods: the electoral processes, rule of law and constitutional sancties become irrelevant. Like secularism, democracy is going to be a dirty word in India soon.

The narrative of Hindutva fascism is based on the politics of hate and disdain for reason, science, secularism, democracy and rule of law. Modi-led BJP and RSS are working on making this narrative as a pan-Indian narrative. Once this project is complete, Hindutva fascist will move from lynching Muslims and killing rationalists to everyday mass violence against any opposition to their politics and power. The democratic illusion, we see today, will evaporate very soon. The Hindutva fascists can brazenly represent monopoly capital and their control over Indian state and all-natural resources. Violence is going to be a tool and new normal in everyday lives of Indians.

Can we fight this evil called Hindutva fascist effectively with old electoral methods? The answer is written on the wall and we have crossed that stage. We need an anti-fascist movement in India based on a clear and revolutionary manifesto. We can shape the manifesto based on anti-fascists movements in history and our current experiences with Hindutva fascists in India. United

Against Hate (UAH) campaign is a good beginning but it is not enough. We have to create a united struggle against Hindutva fascism based on a manifesto which can include the following eleven programmes:

1. Fight against caste, communalism and capitalism is a common battle. We cannot fight Hindutva fascists without fighting the evils of caste system within and outside Hindu religion. Caste remains the foundation of Hindutva communal politics in India. Hindutva fascism is the life and blood of local, national and international capitalist class. Therefore, any attempt to fight Hindutva fascism depends on our commitment to fight caste, communalism and capitalism.
2. Ensure social, economic, political and cultural citizenships based on reason, science and constitutionally guaranteed inalienable rights of one and all without any form of discrimination.
3. Ensure freedom and rights of the minority communities based on progressive values.
4. Militantly fight against regional and religious reactionaries from all communities and within religions.
5. A democratic system which is more than periodic elections. Let the local people decide the nature of their development policies and manage their resources.
6. Ensure gender and sexual equality and broad unity among people.
7. Ensure scientific education and isolate blind believes and superstitions of all kind.
8. Isolate and defeat Hindutva fascists in social, cultural and political sphere.
9. Form alliance between all democratic, secular and progressive forces in India.
10. Ensure social and economic justice for all.
11. Promote peace, harmony and prosperity among all.

The strategies for united struggles against Hindutva fascism are about guiding the struggle to advance the cause of masses towards peace and prosperity. It is not about ideological puritanism of any political formation or party. The organisational strategies against Hindutva fascism is an adultery between individual and mass consciousness and struggle to advance the interests of the working-class masses (Dalits, women, Muslims, tribals, farmers, minorities, workers, rural communities, students, unemployed youths, students, rural and urban poor). Fighting Hindutva fascism is central to the class struggle in India. It is extremely important and urgent to forge broad unity and defeat fascist RSS/BJP. It would be a sheer illusion to build an egalitarian, peaceful and prosperous India without defeating Hindutva fascists. The political and ideological silence is no longer a choice for us. History tells us as witness that defeat of Hindutva fascism is certain and inevitable. Therefore, the only choice is to fight and defeat Hindutva fascists and their ideological narratives in India.

MANIFESTOS FOR MASS MOVEMENTS FOR THE FUTURE AND SURVIVAL OF INDIA

Mass movements are not always oppositional movements. The mass movements can be offensive, defensive and alternative at the same time. It offers progressive alternatives to face and recover from various crises. Mass movements establish lasting solidarities between different social, religious, cultural, economic, political and professional groups. It helps to overcome the old barriers and established fault lines of regressive societies. Mass movements shape our present and fortify our progressive future. India desperately needs a mass movement today to save itself from the ruining path paved by the predatory, neoliberal and capitalist Hindutva forces. These forces are the products of upper caste and class alliance represented by the RSS and BJP. It truly serves their purpose of empowering higher caste and class people in India under the veil of fake nationalism of the RSS and BJP. These forces further aggravate the structural malaises in Indian society. Therefore, Indians are in a critical movement in the history, and need to decide on various critical questions that is affecting the future of national life, peace, prosperity, unity, integrity and progress of India.

The people's manifesto for India's future depends on secular, liberal and democratic mass movements based on following five concrete ideological pillars of policy proposals.

Rebuilding Society

Indian society is destroyed by centuries long *apartheid practices* based on *Hindu caste order* which was institutionalised by the British colonialism and strengthened by the Hindutva politics. The caste discrimination denies the constitutional *citizenship rights* and works as an impediment in the growth of egalitarian society in India. The anti-Muslim politics of Hindutva forces led by BJP and RSS has destroyed the existing *social solidarity* between Hindus and Muslims by promoting the politics of hate and Islamophobia. The lynching and genocide of Muslims in India led to an environment of fear, which created the trust deficit in Indian democracy. The innocent Indian Muslims are made to feel as foreigners in their own land. The regional discrimination of North-East Indians, Kashmiris, tribals, Dalits, women and rural poor is a threat to national unity and integrity. Therefore, the pan-Indian mass movements for alternatives need to understand, acknowledge, apologise and rebuild the trust based on equal citizenship rights as enshrined in the Indian Constitution. The alternative manifestos for mass movements need to incorporate ideals of anti-caste movements and ensure to end Islamophobia and defeat all forms of social discrimination. It should vigorously oppose all attempts to solve the economic crisis by discrimination and scapegoating on caste, religion, gender, sexuality, regional and racial grounds. Social solidarity and peaceful coexistence can only rebuild the society and economy in India.

Rebuilding Economy

The centralisation project within Indian Constitution helps in the growth of capitalist economy in India. The financial decentralisation and autonomy of the states are important to revive cooperative federalism in India which can promote cooperative economy. The centralised economic planning for development and economic growth based on the ideals of neoliberal capitalism further marginalised the lower caste, tribals, farmers, rural and urban poor. The national parties like the Indian National Congress and BJP followed this ruinous path. There is absolutely no difference between BJP and Congress when it comes to economic policies. But when it comes to valiant defence of corporate capitalism, BJP stands out in open. The economic policies pursued by the BJP government led by Narendra Modi marginalise the masses. It ruined all regulatory mechanisms to support the capitalist classes. It provides tax breaks and stimulus packages to the rich and destroys livelihoods and employment opportunities for many. The economic austerity is not an economic policy, but a political choice followed by the BJP government to empower the capitalist elites in the country. The falling wages, growing unemployment, plummeting health, rising food insecurities and diminishing welfare state are the net results of economic policies pursued by the Modi-led BJP government in India.

The visions and missions of the mass movements in India need to develop broad united national campaign against liberalisation, privatisation and globalisation of Indian economy to stop the rampant exploitation of national resources and working classes. The non-sectarian social-solidarity-based economic policies and taxation for the welfare of one and all should be the foundation of all public polices for development in India. They will help to rebuild public services like health, education, public transportation and communication infrastructure in India. The sustainable economic growth depends on progressive nationalisation of economy, state control and intervention in market operations to maintain the quality and price of essential services. It is important to extend all supports by the state and governments to the farmers to increase agricultural production. The public ownership of all-natural resources can help to mobilise internal resources for industrialisation, economic growth and development in India. *Agriculture and industry* are two sectors that can generate mass employment and provide livelihoods to the masses in India.

Ensure Affirmative Actions to Reinstate the Legitimacy of Indian Constitution

The ideals of equality, liberty and justice are three non-negotiable pillars of Indian Constitution with liberal, secular and democratic ethos. But the legitimacy of Indian Constitution is under question due to the compromised actions of the constitutional institutions under the BJP government led by Modi and guided by the RSS. The failure of the state and government has created a constitutional void in India where hopelessness and injustice rules over the poor, Muslims, lower caste and farmers. So, it is important to reinsure citizenship based on individual liberty and equality before law as a non-negotiable right irrespective of caste, creed, religion, gender, sexuality and region. The centuries long caste oppression and gender inequalities, decades long marginalisation of Muslims, tribals, Dalits and women demands affirmative actions to ensure equality in letter and spirit of the Indian Constitution. The mass movements need to ensure the principles of affirmative actions for all marginalised communities in order to develop a truly pan-Indian alternative that focuses on people.

Rebuild the Environment

There is growing natural disasters in India due to over-exploitation of nature that pollutes the environment in large scale. The rural communities, urban and rural poor, farmers and forest dwellers are the worst victims of natural disasters due to *global warming and environmental destructions*. These communities need to participate in developing policies in environmental protection and become the shareholders of *sustainable developments*. The economic and social sustainability depends on environmental sustainability. So, the mass movements need to focus on environment by promoting *green politics and green economy* where citizens are both shareholders and policymakers.

Rebuild Peaceful Neighbourhood

Land and territories exist for people. The boundaries and demarcations are designed by people based on their own convenience. There is no point of going for war to protect it. Deaths and destitutions defeat the purpose of individuals, states and societies. The non-allied nature of Indian foreign policy was destroyed by the BJP-led Narendra Modi government. It ruined India's external image and relationship with neighbouring countries. The manifestos for the mass movements need to engage with cooperative foreign policy based on ideals of *peace, development and non-militarisation.* The peaceful neighbourhood can rebuild international trade and greater market integration based on each other's social and economic needs.

It is also important to *forge broad unity* among all liberal, secular, progressive and democratic people, and peaceful struggles, campaigns and movements in India. It is important to facilitate broad alliances and joint actions in different local and regional struggles without top-down approach. These broad proposals focusing on *people and environment* can take India in a democratic path of peace, progress and prosperity.

Chapter 5

Culture, Crime and Capitalism

In the world of ideology-free zone of politics, the question 'of morality and immorality in popular and mainstream political traditions' is becoming irrelevant. The incompetent governments, helpless states, visionless leadership, directionless politics, weak judiciaries and compliant media organisations are the net output of amoral and illiberal politics. The moral critique of political system does not yield any electoral dividends for radical politics within democratic system. Irrespective of ideological formations, the political system is designed in such a way that exploits people and stands with the capitalists and upholds the interests of the propertied class through corrupt means. It looks as if there is a clear bifurcation between politics and morality in praxis. The moralistic cults based on hard work, honesty, sobriety, sexual propriety, thrift, nonviolence, truth and other Gandhian, Ambedkarite, Marxist, Mandelian and Martin Luther King's shared and collective values in politics are becoming obsolete and considered to be liabilities in politics.

The deepening of moral crisis in politics is an extension of utilitarian values incorporated in the society during early industrial revolution and patronised during managerialist-led market revolution during twentieth and twenty-first centuries. The moral dumbfounding cultural effect in politics is further accelerated by the growth of fictitious online social, economic and cultural life in the age of information technology. It ensures mass melancholy of the obsolete and immoral self-serving politics of brutal capitalism, which hides behind democracy and individual freedom. It does not guide people and society towards peace, progress and prosperity due to its immoral political landscape. The immoral politics is based on illiberal ideas and practice, which divides the society and people on moral questions. In 2012, psychologist Jonathan Haidt has published his book *The Righteous Mind: Why Good People Are Divided by Religion and Politics*. He has outlined moral foundations of politics based on ideals of care, fairness loyalty, authority, sanctity and liberty. According to Jonathan Haidt, these moral qualities are intuitive and integral to human beings. But in reality, there are collective material foundations, which help to develop these moral qualities in human beings. These qualities are products of everyday experiences of working classes in their workplace and their interactions with fellow workers that ensure these moral qualities in working population.

What are the political alternatives before the working-class masses? How to ensure morality in politics? The answers to these questions are complex but not difficult to answer.

It is time to bring back mass politics rooted in class, dedicated to class and led by working classes. The concept of class politics is no longer confined within organised industrial zones. The trade unions used to organise these workers in their workplaces. The trade unions and working-class people have played a major role in wage bargain movements in the workplace to anti-colonial and anti-capitalist struggles. The working classes have played a major role in democratisation of society and in enlarging individual liberty and citizenship rights. The working-class morality in politics has shaped morality both in radical and mainstream politics. The work and the workplaces used to be the source of working-class consciousness, which shaped political movements, ideologies and leadership based on working-class morality.

In the age of information-technology-driven economic system, there is disintegration of work and workplace. The working-class people and their workplaces are scattered all over the places from the bedrooms of garment workers to the bathrooms of information technology workers. The work has entered into every step of worker's life and individualised work and working culture. The workers as citizens are alienated both from their workplace and fellow workers, which helped to develop depoliticised consciousness and growth of anti-politics machine. The capitalism and its political systems treat individuals as orderly objects and not as citizens and human beings with rights and liberties. Such an economic, social, political and cultural transformation in work and workplace led to the growth of professionalisation of technocratic politics shaped by the ruling and non-ruling classes to uphold their own interests. It promotes culture and politics of competitive immorality based on selfish-self-interests. The authoritarian megalomaniacs are controlling the state and government in defence of their capitalist masters.

Moreover, the separation of market from producers and consumers has helped for the growth of market-led democracy, which diminished citizenship rights and trying to convert citizens into self-interested and self-satisfying customers only. The customer-driven politics based on self-interests has dismantled the collective foundation of politics, state and governments.

Citizens are disinterested clients of a democratic state and government, where the capitalist classes rule and promote immoral politics. The moral crisis in politics is framed as crisis of state, government, secularism, multiculturalism, socialism and democracy. Such analysis hides the failures and vulnerabilities of capitalism and its immoral political projects. It promotes capitalism as only alternative and there is no other alternative to authoritarian capitalist doctrine. The moral crisis in politics has huge detrimental impacts on working-class needs and desires. The moral crisis in capitalist politics is an opportunity for working classes to revitalise their political project by mobilising different sections of working classes both in their organised and unorganised forms. The collective political movements of working classes based on working-class morality can revive the revolutionary politics to save democracy and individual freedom.

The universal nature of working-class experiences produces shared universal political morality and promotes politics of solidarity, cooperation and fraternity. The working-class internationalism can defeat the immoral politics of neo-imperial wars and neocolonial economic system to establish world peace based on shared prosperity. The revival of working-class politics and working-class morality can defeat the immoral alliance of reactionary religious forces, conservative and right-wing politics and illiberal market economy. The emphasis on working-class morality needs to evolve with secular and scientific ethos while directing addressing everyday life issues of people, animals and environment. The working-class morality can inspire people to organise themselves as a collective struggle for political, social, cultural and economic transformation in the society. The politics based on working-class morality can only achieve the politics of transformation based on egalitarian and secular values.

ADIVASIS, ANTHROPOLOGY AND ITS SWADDLING

The executive committee of the International Union of Anthropological and Ethnological Sciences (IUAES) has decided to withdraw its collaboration with the KISS University to organise the World Anthropology Congress *2023* in its campus. The decision of the executive committee is a product of 'mounting national and international pressure' from academic, activists and civil society networks. Who are these academics, intellectuals and activists? What are their caste, class location and professional base? They seem to be both subjective and objective outsiders to the predicaments of indigenous and working people. The decision to drop KISS University for hosting *World Anthropology Congress 2023* may appear to international audiences as the right ethical stance. However, a closer understanding of the local context reveals that it is not only short-sighted but also incisively reactionary. The justifications behind such a decision look inadequate and lack progressive vision. The decision is a disservice to the progressive character of Anthropology as a discipline and emancipatory knowledge traditions within it. The decision denies accessibilities to knowledge, infrastructure and available opportunities to learn to indigenous people, the very same people it claims to serve. This decision gives more space to Hindutva right-wing forces to Hinduise indigenous communities without any restrictions.

The World Anthropology Congress 2023 in the KISS University would have been a great opportunity for the 30,000 indigenous students and their teachers to learn the limits of factory schools, dangers of privatisation and Hinduisation from the critical researchers and anthropologists across the globe. It would have been a great opportunity to expose the economic logic of Hinduisation as a cultural and political project of the Hindutva fascists and their crony capitalists during the conference. It was an opportunity lost for both the participating anthropologists and for the students and staff members of the KISS, Utkal, Sambalpur and other universities in Odisha. *The Indian Anthropological Association* has lost an opportunity for progressive intervention within the limited available opportunities in India today.

There is no doubt that most of the private universities, residential schools and colleges are functioning like corporate businesses. These institutions treat their living and non-living infrastructures like profitable and portable car parks. The curriculums are designed to serve the market forces undermining the intellectual integrities, secular and scientific knowledge traditions and sanctity of the educational institutions. The privatisation is a bane for working classes, in general, and indigenous and rural poor, in particular. Factory schools are the products of marketisation of education. The privatisation and marketisation of education are not sustainable as it destroys every foundation of education, training and knowledge. The Indian private educational institutions are bastions of Brahmanical-Hindu-hierarchical-social order based on caste, class, gender, urban and rural marginalisation. The marginalisation of poor is written within the rotten structures of private educational institutions. Both private and public educational institutions in India are facing four threats: fear of authoritarian government, funding crunch, Hinduisation and loss of academic independence under Modi-led BJP/RSS government in New Delhi.

The conditions of schools, colleges and universities are very poor in Odisha. The lack of academic infrastructure is visible from the collapsing boundary walls to dust-filled bookshelves in the libraries. The hostels, classrooms, conference halls, laboratories to lavatories mark the failures of state and governments in funding quality education. The situation is more deplorable in the tribal areas of Odisha. There is no educational institution in Odisha with world-class facilities and funds to organise and manage large international conferences like the World Anthropology Congress 2023. The neoliberal economic and educational policies destroyed public education and paved the path for the growth of privatisation of education in India. The KISS University is not an isolated example. It is the product of the system but within all valid criticisms and limitations, KISS University provides free accommodation, food, dress and every other education facility for indigenous students from class-1 to postgraduation degree. The KISS University has produced and facilitated some amazing sport stars and Olympiads among indigenous students. What would be the future of these students without the KISS University?

With all its limitations and valid criticisms, the KISS and KIIT Universities have academic infrastructure to organise and accommodate international conferences like World Anthropology Congress 2023. It is naïve to oppose it in the name of a critical stance against factory schools, corporate funding and Hinduisation. Every state- and government-funded schools in Odisha celebrate Hindu religious festivals. Even the state- and government-funded schools in tribal areas of Odisha celebrate different Hindu religious festivals. There is a serious distinction between celebration of Hindu religious festivals in the schools and Hinduisation of indigenous communities. The first one is a slow poison of Hindu socialisation and the second one is cultural and economic genocide of indigenous communities by the RSS and BJP, which helps the mining corporations to exploit natural resources in the tribal areas of Odisha. There is still little progressive space within the KISS University, the progressive anthropologists and their organisations must engage with it to expand emancipatory ideals. The search for puritanism is a dangerous game in emancipatory politics, which helps right wing, reactionary religious and market forces.

Neo-traditionalist anthropological museums and neoliberal Hindutva laboratories are unnecessary evils. These forces cannot protect indigenous culture and their economic future. The indigenous communities can only sustain their culture, social and cultural identities better by accessing all modern health and educational facilities provided by the state and government. The indigenous communities can write their own political and economic narratives by getting exposed to the power structure that exploits them in their everyday life. They do not need guidance from the salary-seeking social servants from the republic of *People Like Us (PLU)*. Scientific and secular education is crucial for resistance to neoliberal Hindutva and all its infrastructures. The liberals, progressives and secular activists and intellectuals must use every little opportunity to expand emancipatory ideals for marginalised communities in particular and people in general. If the progressives do not engage with little liberal spaces, it will be captured by the religious reactionaries like Hindutva forces.

Anthropologists (the objective and subjective outsiders) have made enormous stride to recover their discipline from the lineages of its colonial past and neotraditional present for a progressive future. Anthropology has played a major role in shoddy shaping of knowledge in binary terms. In this frame, European knowledge entails philosophy and science whereas knowledge from outside Europe is branded as ethnography. The colonial legacies of such dubious distinction continue to percolate to local level and destroy pluriversal foundations of indigenous knowledge in different parts of the world. The anthropological knowledge has helped to conceptualise and categorise people as 'native', 'foreigner', 'original inhabitants' and 'immigrants'. Such categorisations are not only socially sterile but also intellectually bankrupt. It gives breathing space to the right-wing politics to thrive.

Anthropology as a discipline continues to evolve and separate itself from such ruling-class seraglios to enhance emancipatory power of people and their knowledge traditions. It is only possible via progressive engagements and not by disengagement with existing environment. Freedom of indigenous people and sustainable future depends on progressive engagement with all available spaces. It is within this context, the executive committee of the *International Union of Anthropological and Ethnological Sciences (IUAES) and Indian Anthropological Association* must rethink on their decision. Let Anthropology grow beyond its narrow silo to reclaim its radical promises for people, let anthropologists guide us in a progressive and emancipatory path free from reactionary forces in society, culture, religion, politics and economy. There is no ideal option here. Be with the liberal devil to defeat the neoliberal Hindutva fascists.

FACTORY SCHOOLS FROM INDUSTRIAL REVOLUTION TO MODERN UNIVERSITIES

How did factory schools develop? Why did factory school develop? What does factory schools do? What is the relevance of factory schools today? The answers to these questions come from the history of factory schools, which reveals its immense impact not only on our educational system but also on our society, culture, economy, politics and individual lives. The historical perspectives are important to understand the predicaments of the factory school model of educational systems today.

The factory schools were established by the Christian missionaries in early seventeenth-century America. The spread of Christianity by 'converting people' and 'controlling their natural resources' were twin objectives of these missionary-run factory schools. In the early days of industrial revolution in eighteenth and nineteenth centuries, the factory owners have established factory schools to develop skilled and productive workers for expanding their industrial outputs and profits. The sense of charity and Christian religious values has also influenced the factory owners to provide basic education and minimal leisure time for token welfare of factory workers. For example, Hannah Greg (née Lightbody) was the wife of Samuel Greg who established a factory school within the campus of the Quarry Bank Cotton Mill. The mill was established in 1784 on the outskirts of Manchester in a village called Styal, in the banks of the Bolin in Cheshire, England. It continues to run till today. The mill is not only the living witness to industrial revolution in England but also preserved the horrors of working conditions and miserable lives of workers and the history of the factory school. Hannah Greg's life was shaped by Presbyterian and Unitarian Christian theology, which inspired her to establish the school and look after the worker's children and a large number of pauper and orphaned children, who were working in the Quarry Bank Mill for 18 hours per day. It helped the mill to develop their own skilled workforce and increased their productivity. The Greg's family was also involved in slave trade and pretended to care for workers in their factory by establishing school for the workers and their children. It was a public relations exercise to control workers.

Robert Owen, the father of utopian socialism and pioneer of cooperative movement, has also established factory school near the New Lanark mill and experimented his socialist ideas on educational and social reforms. He established the Institute for the Formation of Character at New Lanark in 1818, which provided free education from infancy to adulthood. The institute has helped to increase the quality and standard of goods produced in his factory. Based on his experiments, he argued for radical factory reforms for worker's welfare. His ideals have not only transformed industrial revolution and politics in Europe during nineteenth century but also continue to have huge significance in contemporary world.

The factory schools have played significant role in increasing productive power of labour and shaping industrial revolution and politics in Europe. The factory owners were the biggest supporters of the *Elementary Education Act of 1870*, which has expanded the factory schools with the universalisation of education in England. The essence of factory schools was to produce benevolent, docile, productive and skilled labour force as per the requirements of the industrial capitalism. The European colonialism has used the experience, spirit and essence of factory school models of education in different colonies in Asia, Africa, Americas and Oceania in the pursuit of interests of the colonial capitalism. The European companies have sponsored Christian missionaries to help in the expansion of colonialism with the help of setting up religious schools and health centres. The educational curriculum in colonial and Christian missionary schools was designed to uphold European power, dominance and work ethics of Christianity. The model and location of factory schools were moved from industrial centres to non-industrial rural areas, other religious missionaries have also followed the path to shape the social and moral values of the people concomitant with the requirements of the religious denominations, societies, states and governments.

The state-led 'factory school' was originated in the early nineteenth-century Prussia, where educational curriculum, methods of teaching and learning were standardised and regimented as per the requirements of the state and governments. The idea of education was impersonal to promote professionalism and efficiency. The individual interests, needs, desires and creativities were domesticated and conditioned as per the requirements of the ruling and non-ruling classes. In this way, the formal and modern educational system has emerged from factory schools, which continue to serve the elites and capitalist classes in different forms for the last two centuries. The Prussian factory school model and the spirit of its educational system survived from class education to mass education in the Lancaster system, Madras system, Glasweegian and Mannian systems to Bologna processes, which promised to bring coherence to higher education systems in Europe. Alvin Toffler in his book *Future Shock* (1970) has condemned such educational practices, where mass education works like a complaint ingenious machine that teaches collective discipline, crushes creativity and socialises students with repetitive labour and hierarchy.

The RSS-led Vidya Bharati Akhil Bharatiya Shiksha Sansthan runs one of the largest private educational networks of more than 25,000 *Saraswati Shishu Mandir* schools with over 45 million students in India. It works like Christian missionary schools based on factory models. It is funded directly by corporations and indirectly by the governments in India. The Hindutva mythology and reactionary ideology of the RSS determines the curriculum of these schools. In the name of Indianisation of education, it promotes debauched Hindutva politics and bigoted cultural outlook devoid of secular and scientific ethos. The ideals and values of factory school model of education define the educational system promoted by the RSS. It does not empower people. It domesticates people for its political project that is concomitant with the interests of the Indian and global capitalist classes.

The unfettered growth of capitalist globalisation and liberalisation of economy led to withdrawal of welfare state and rise of privatisation of education in twenty-first century. Many corporations are opening their own educational and research institutions to pursue both business and create workforce for their industries. The privatisation and corporatisation of education transformed public education into a business, where educational curriculums were shaped by the market forces as per their requirements. The syllabus of banking, finance and insurance education and training is shaped by banking and insurance industries. The Computer Science education is shaped by the requirements of the Silicon Valley. The Medical Science and Chemistry curriculum are determined by the requirements of the pharmaceutical corporations. The way Christian missionaries were funded by the colonial corporations, in the same way, NGOs and charities today are funded by the corporations under their corporate social responsibility funds to shape education by establishing schools and research institutes as per their requirements. Most of the British universities are registered as charities and receiving huge research funds to expand corporate interests and public opinions in support of ruling and non-ruling establishments. There were always aberrations which question the power and stand with people within and beyond the frameworks of modern factory schools.

The factory school model of education has transformed and atomised educational system based on the priorities of capitalism. The marketisation and corporatisation of education has transformed students as cash cows, teachers as shopkeepers and educational institutions as shop floors. Such an educational system is neither representing the life experiences of people nor their everyday requirements. It produces skilled professionals, who work like orderly objects with disciplined hands and closed lips. The social, economic, cultural and educational alienation is the net outcome of such an educational system practised worldwide.

The educational system is designed in such a way that the students from the rich families and urban areas are getting unfettered access to education and educational infrastructure, whereas the students from disadvantaged backgrounds in terms of class, caste, tribe, gender, race, region, religion, poor and rural areas suffer greatly. Such a system produces professional meritocratic society based on inequality. Therefore, affirmative actions are not enough, it needs a complete overhauling of this skewed educational system run by the ruling and non-ruling-class establishments. The availability and accessibility to education is becoming an impossible mission for the poor in the age of privatisation. It is a structural indictment of class-divided society and bourgeois state within capitalism.

The democratisation of education and curriculum based on needs of people, communities and society and the accessibility, affordability and availability of scientific and secular education is central to egalitarian social and economic transformation. Education is not only a social desire but an organic need of common people based on their natural and inalienable human rights. The radical, revolutionary, progressive and democratic forces must use every available opportunity to claim the right to free and scientific education. The radical and revolutionary upsurge was an inadvertent outcome of factory schools, which helped social transformations all over the world. The radical movements and revolutionary political parties have used education as a tool of revolutionary transformation of society. It is time to shape and decolonise educational institutions and curriculum from Eurocentric worldview, reactionary religious and market forces enforced by factory schools in different forms.

As the onslaught of reactionary religious and market forces grow on education, it is important to use every available opportunity to promote liberal, secular, scientific, rational, democratic and radical agenda of education based on people's needs and desires. Yes, it is time to break away from the factory school model of educational system for the sake of education, people and society. Engagement and progressive interventions are twin keys for student- and teacher-led educational systems based on local, regional, national and international requirements of people, animals and environment.

ZOOMING THE DEATH OF TEACHERS AND TEACHING AS A PROFESSION

In search of profit, the growth of managerialism and marketisation of education crippled the abilities of teachers and destroyed institutions of learning all over the world. The managerialist revolution in education is designed to transform education as a commodity for sale by privatisation. The processes of commodification and privatisation of education is central to the principles of market in education for profit. Educational institutions are becoming certificate-selling supermarkets, which treat students as cash cows and teachers as salesperson. The introduction of league tables and rankings based on metric-driven 'evaluation of teaching, learning, student satisfaction, and research impact' promotes the culture of Taylorism to implement values of efficiency, productivity and output, which destroys the critical and creative space within teaching and learning. Management-led teaching and learning gives a false sense of democratic space with the idea of peer review culture, where control is exercised in such a way that it looks as if it is a means of professional growth and development for one's own good. It degrades the moral foundations of teaching and learning as a profession for public good.

Educational environment is further destroyed by managerial culture of command, communication and control system in which teaching is managed by people who never taught in their life and research is managed by people without any form of exposure to research. Such a system creates an incompetent, unethical, unprofessional managerial class in education sector that eats away the soul of education. These incompetent tickbox managers are given power to mismanage the place by which they can create their own workload by organising constant useless meetings. These managerial classes pretend with confidence as if they know the issues of teaching and research. These manager's Shakespearean acting skills in the meetings can seriously put professional actors in doubt. The rhetoric, diction and language of the managers sound as if they care of students and staffs. In reality, they only care about their salary-seeking positions and promotions. They run public-funded educational institutions like their own family firms.

The growth of managerial parasites in education destroys the collective culture of knowledge, where teaching is a learning process and learning is a process to produce knowledge and skills. Teachers and students learn from each other without thinking about essentialist and functional approach of the managers, their workload model for staffs and contact hours for students. Such a profound negative transition in education sector is not only a challenge for students and staffs but also a threat to education itself. It has enormous negative impacts on women, working classes, LGBTQ and ethnic minorities. It is becoming an alienating experience for students and staffs working within marketized education sector.

The pestilence of coronavirus spread gives breathing space to managers by shifting the focus from the perils of managerialism and failures of marketisation of education to question of sustainability of market-led educational institutions. Instead of addressing the long-standing issues within education sector, the managerial elites find instant solution by offering massive online courses. It changes the very foundation of teaching and learning in a classroom environment. Online classes in the Zoom, Microsoft Team, BlueBotton and other web conferencing applications can never replace classroom teaching. It only further accelerates existing problems of education sector.

The classroom challenges shape teachers and teaching as a profession. The distinctive pleasure of teaching in a classroom comes from the students who shape the art of teaching. It takes a long time to internalise teaching skills and develop as a teacher in the laboratory of classrooms. Every class adds new experiences both for the students and the teachers. The online platforms can never recreate the teaching and learning environment that a classroom offers. The interactive and participatory pedagogy of teaching and learning dies its natural death in online platforms where teachers look at students as dots in computer screen. The classroom offers limitless possibilities to engage with students, their excitements and their boredoms. So, online teaching and learning is not only short-sighted but also reductionist that destroys the organic space between a teacher and the students. In this way, COVID-19 pandemic has triggered a severe crisis within the traditional pedagogy of teaching and learning.

Teachers and students are not zombies. The zooming online is a medium of interaction and not a teaching and learning method. Any attempt to replace classrooms with online platforms destroys the very idea of teaching and learning. Technology and virtual leaning environments enhance the abilities of a teacher and a student. It cannot replace a teacher. The etiquettes of classroom teaching instil qualities like determination, focus, peer interactions, intercultural communication skills, debating abilities, public speaking and engagement skills via eye gaze. These are invaluable skills for the students and teachers. These set of important skills are more valuable in life than curriculum-driven skills and certificates. The managerial class is drunk with the bad cocktail of ignorance and arrogance so much that they failed to understand the importance of these skills.

The managerial stubbornness of market logic in education and its failures are under the carpet of the pestilence-infused crisis management. It is disempowering for students, teachers and few academic leaders. On the one hand, this crisis is an opportunity for managerial class to hide their failures. On the other hand, the COVID-19 pandemic is also exposing the limits of marketisation of education. It is revealing the thoughtless and distorted managerial response to crisis. It is an opportunity for students and teachers to refuse the culture of business as usual in post-pandemic education sector. It is not the individualised, selfish and brutish managerialism but the struggle for alternatives that come from collective experiences and understandings. The survival of teachers and teaching as a profession depends on how we steer the struggle for alternatives within and outside the education sector. It can offer a better tomorrow for critical and creative space for teaching and learning in a post-pandemic world if we fight against the twin evils of managerialism and marketisation of education. It is important to remember that education is not merely essential for employment but a tool of emancipation.

RIGHT-WING POLITICAL AND RELIGIOUS FORCES AND MASS MORALITY

The reactionary upheavals are taking place in different parts of the world with diminishing democratic culture in twenty-first century. The conservative alterations are pushing humanity into the darkness of dictatorship in the so-called glory of god, gold and national greatness. The god is represented by religious right-wing forces to capture gold or resources for the capitalist forces and national greatness is represented by cultural and religious reactionaries. There is a strong synergy between these forces to consolidate unchallenged capitalist system. The religious groups are represented by right-wing forces in politics. These reactionary forces demand that people need to follow certain cultural, social, provincial and religious norms. They try to impose food codes, dress codes and marriage codes on the masses. From food habits to sexual preferences, the conservative forces try to impose the idea of national, linguistic, regional, cultural and religious chauvinism.

Why do these forces demand such uniform moral values in the twenty-first-century world? The answer to this question is central to understand the inherent race, gender, caste, class and capitalist character of religious forces. The so-called exclusionary nationalist and religious propaganda is a veil that hides the fascist and capitalist character of these conservative forces.

The centralisation of economic and political power and the construction of cultural and religious norms are significant tools of social regulation of life and domestication of labour power. The idea of democracy, empowerment and diversity threatens capitalism and its market forces. It also threatens the religious, reactionary and fascist forces. The centralisation of politics and uniformity of cultural norms help both political and economic elites in the world. The religious philosophy provides ideological foundation for such an alliance between right-wing religious forces and capitalism, where the workers and the masses can imbibe ascetic attitude to the labour and its outcomes. The mass morality derived from the ideals of religious philosophy disciplines both individual labour and the labour of the masses as well. It domesticates the workers in such a way that workers feel as if there is nothing external to their work. Their work only decides their fate and future. But in reality, it is the capitalist class and religious ruling class that suppress the desires and aspirations and exploit their labour power for the production of capitalist profit. The neoliberal economic policies are celebrated by capitalist classes and their market forces. Capitalism produces profits for the few and miseries for the masses. Religious forces help in the processes of naturalisation and normalisation of miseries by outsourcing it to fate written by god in religion. The right-wing and religious forces provide strong irrational platform of mass morality for the success of capitalism as a social, economic and cultural system.

The deepening of capitalism ensures expansion and universalisation of religious mass morality to accommodate and solve its contradictory characters. Capitalism maximises religious morality with the help of reactionary religious forces in politics and society. It is easier for capitalism to manage capital and labour conflicts if more people surrender themselves and their labour to the unquestionable religious and moral justifications. The ascetic attitude of the masses is an unavoidable essential for the survival of capitalism. It supplements existing right-wing institutional arrangements of capitalism from the state, political parties and government to judiciary and religion. Religion infused with mass morality provides stability to the fragility of capitalism and helps to cover up its inherent internal contradictions. Mass morality also forces people to work obediently, which help capitalism to grow by rationalising exploitation of labour. The taming of labour power is central to the growth of capitalism. It uses science and technology for its growth but forms unholy alliances with reactionary religious and right-wing forces to control the masses with irrational morality in the name of god, religion, culture and nationalism.

The construction of mass morality removes all social and religious barriers to exploitative and violent capitalist accumulation processes. The mass morality is embedded within a broader framework of capitalism, which provides religious justifications to naturalise inequalities. There is nothing moral about capitalist system that promotes exploitation of human beings and degradation of environment. Capitalism is not only amoral but also promotes competitive culture of consumerism that destroys all existing moralities and goodness of human beings essential for future survival. The consumerism promotes monetised, individualist, selfish culture, which destroys idea of love, peace, commitment of human being for fellow human beings and nature. In this way, the construction of mass morality within capitalism serves its own purpose at the cost of the quality of human lives, society and nature.

Religion is not a precondition to morality. The moral inclinations are products of human experience with life and livelihoods. Morality exists independent of religious indoctrination. Moral concerns are human concerns. There is no morality without human concerns. The religious and right-wing forces use this innate relationship between human beings and morality to expand the regimes of mass morality with the help of organised religion. The organised religions institutionalise morality within social, economic, political and cultural context. It domesticates the masses for the ruling and non-ruling capitalist classes. These forces blame atheists, rationalists and secular forces for the decline of morality. In this way, religion-led mass morality works as a safety valve for the immoral capitalist system.

As the religious and right-wing forces accelerate their regimes of mass morality, the human predicaments continue to growth. The hunger, homelessness, hateful climate and all other forms of inequalities continue to grow. The emerging right-wing and religious forces strengthen the capitalist exploitative system. There is sprawling silence in the gloomy political, economic and cultural sky, which attempts to devour everything, that is progressive, liberal and democratic. The people who fight for the rights, liberty, equality and justice are imprisoned and silenced by the ruling classes. But the silence and silencing are prelude to all revolutionary upsurges in history. The flames of silence do not die with fascist uproars. It waits to gather momentum of the radical storm to burn down fantasies of fascism and all its reactionary brethren in politics, economy, society and culture. It is the revolutionaries who write the history of the masses and drive society into the territory of prosperity and peace for all.

INDIAN CONTRIBUTIONS TO BRITISH MUSIC

In the dark times,
Will there also be singing? Yes, there will also be singing.
About the dark times.

Bertolt Brecht

These historic lines are prophetically relevant today as we witness the forward march of right-wing and reactionary forces in India and in the UK. These forces are destroying the multicultural mosaic of our society and all other progressive achievements of the century. As the British Home Secretary Priti Patel is advocating for a new reactionary, and anti-working-class immigration bill, it becomes imperative to reinstate some of the historical debates to bring back some sense and sensibilities to political debates in Britain. And, it is also important for the Indians to realise that Hindutva forces were the colonial collaborators. The Hindutva politics led by Modi is destroying the working-class internationalism established within mystic, multicultural and musical traditions in India. The BJP hides all its failures by false propaganda in India and the Conservative Party hides all its failures and inefficiencies by patronising racist and anti-immigrant sentiments.

The British colonialism has not only siphoned out $45 trillion from the undivided India but also continue to benefit from the contemporary India. Indian diaspora and Indian companies contribute nearly £87 billion pounds to the British economy in 2020. Politically speaking, the anti-colonial struggles for independent India have made enormous contributions for the deepening of democracy and in the making of welfare state in the UK. The boiled British food tastes better with Indian spices. Indian contribution to British economy, politics, society and culture in past and present is well-established. From the Crown Jewel, chicken tikka masala to musical chutney, the undivided India's contributions to British economy, culture and society continue to be significant. The people from the Indian sub-continent have contributed immensely to British music culture. It needs to be documented and popularised at a time when British masses are misled by conservative politics of narrow nationalism.

The working-class ideals are becoming anathema in British politics. The corporate media demonises class politics and undermines working-class contributions to culture and music. There is continuous attack on working-class culture and heritage. So it is essential to define class both in economic and cultural terms while articulating the class foundation of British music and Indian working-class contributions to its growth and development. The idea of pure British music was a myth. It was primarily romantic and opposed to mechanistic lifestyle promoted by the industrial economy. It was represented in Matthew Arnold's *Sweetness and Light*. The British folk songs and music halls were the products of working-class cultural lives before the *Rock and Roll* music, which took over the industrial and post-industrial Britain. It led to the growth of mass culture, Americanisation, and commercialisation of music with the help of the BBC radio. The *Rock and Roll* also created a sense of music community, progressive subcultures and countercultures among youth in Britain. Lonnie Donegan's magical guitar and banjo in the *Chris Barber Jazz Band* led to the growth of the *Skiffle craze*, which introduced African and American music culture in Britain. The *Elvis, Bing Crosby and Beatles* have transformed the music and entertainment industry in Britain. David Simonelli's book brings back the focus on the working-class foundation of British music. It provides wonderful narratives on the *Working Class Heroes: Rock Music and British Society in the 1960s and 1970s*.

The Beatles were influenced by Indian music and exponent of Indian sitar. George Harrison has added sitar to John Lennon's *Norwegian Wood* (1965) for the first time. He later used North Indian *ragas, sitar and tabla* in songs like *Love You To* and *Within You Without You*. Jess Beck has simulated Indian sitar to give a psychedelic feeling to songs like *Heart Full of Soul* (1965) and *Shapes of Things* (1966). Brian Jones has borrowed the droning effects in the songs like *Paint It Black* (1966), *See My Friends* (1965) and *Fancy* (1966) from Indian *sitar*. The *Kinks*, the *Rolling Stones* and other music bands were not only influenced by Indian folk and classical music but also used it creatively to add exotic romantic feelings to their songs. John Lennon's stunning song *Tomorrow Never Knows* reflects Indian religious philosophy as outlined in the *Bhagavad Gita* (*songs of god*). The legacies continued in Robin Williamson's romantic hippie masterpiece like *The 5000 Spirits or the Layers of the Onion* (1967) and *The Hangman's Beautiful Daughter* (1968) which were also influenced by Indian and African musical traditions. His albums like *In Search of the Lost Chord* (1968), *Om* and *On the Threshold of Dream* (1969) absorbed the mystic religious culture and its philosophy in India. Jonathan Bellman's chapter on 'Indian Resonances in the British Invasion, 1965-1968' documents Indian influence on British music in his edited volume *The Exotic in Western Music*.

During this period, Freddie Mercury destroyed the cultural boundaries. He was central in the establishment of the famous British rock band called the *Queen*. The band's most popular song *Bohemian Rhapsody* is considered as one of the greatest rock songs of all time. Channi Singh's *Alaap* (1977), Sheila Chandra's *Ever So Lonely* (1982), Joi Bangla's *Desert Storm* (1991), Apache Indian's *Boom Shack-A-Lak* (1993) and Cornershop (1997)'s rendition of Asha Bhosle in *Brimful of Asha* and *The Fat Boy* are some of the classics of English music influenced by Indian musical traditions. The *drum, tabla* and *bass beats* in Talvin Singh's *OK* (1999) and Nitin Sawhney's

Beyond Skin by *Outcaste Record* (1999) are fine examples of musical journeying of two music traditions together. The Panjabi MC's *Mundian to Bach
Ke* (2002), MIA's *Arular* (2005), Jay Sean's *Dawn* (2009), Naughty Boy's *La
La La* (2013) and Zayn Malik's *Pillowtalk* (2016) are some of the pioneering
contributions to British music. Thankfully BBC acknowledges the creative
journeying of the Asian sound from *Alaap* to *Zayn* and their contribution
in shaping the British music. All these musicians and brands paved the way
for cultural integration in Britain by breaking social and cultural stereotypes
and prejudices. Their contribution in the making of modern Britain cannot
be measured in economic terms. The contemporary Indian musicians from
Hindi, Punjabi, Tamil and Bengali music industries continue to collaborate
with the British music industry and produced some of the most memorable
tunes and songs.

However, the history of undivided India's impacts on British music goes
beyond nineteenth and twenty-first centuries. Sir William Jones's essay *On
the Musical Modes of the Hindoos* has documented the impact of Indian
music on British musical traditions during eighteenth century. *The Study of
Primitive Music* by Charles S. Myers has identified the unique influence of
South Indian music on British music during early nineteenth century. A.H.
Fox Strangways was a leading member of the Folk Song Society, which was
founded by Cecil Sharp. His book *The Music of Hindostan* argued that Indian
music deserves more analytical attention from the mainstream English music.
Thirty Songs from the Punjab and Kashmir by Alice Coomaraswamy and
Ananda Coomaraswamy archived the apprenticeship between English musicians under the guidance of Indian music teachers like Abdul Rahim. The
Hindu and Sikh *Kirtans* (shared musical recitations), the songs of the Bhakti
(devotion) movements, *Tawaifs* (courtesan) and *Ustads* (Muslim masters) in
undivided North India had also significant impact on British music culture.
Ernest Clements's book (1913) attempts to reconcile the different musical
traditions in India and England. In this way, the Islamic and Hindu mysticism,
liturgies and Vedic hymns influenced Gustav Holst, Ralph Vaughan Williams
and Cecil Sharp, who were three leading figures of folklore movement in
British music.

Music originates in one place especially by people of working-class
background with different social, cultural and religious orientations but it
transcends the boundaries of nation states. Therefore, it is limiting to analyse
music by taking geographical location as a referent point. The English and
Indian aristocrats like the British Home Secretary Priti Patel undermine the
working-class contributions to different fields of everyday life including to the
field of music. Like chicken tikka masala, musical chutney in British music
is a product of its interactions with African, Asian, American and Caribbean
music traditions. Free movement of people helps in forging musical and

social bonds but the Conservative Party's immigration policies in the UK and Modi's reactionary politics in India attempt to destroy all achievements over the years. Transcendental working class and their internationalism is the only alternative for a sustainable future for India and Britain today, if these two countries bother to learn from their own folklore of mystic musical traditions.

CELEBRITY CULTURE, PROPAGANDA AND CAPITALISM

The triumph of capitalist chimeras based on false propaganda and its criminal follies at the millennium raises several questions on the rise of celebrity culture of fame and fortune. The celebrity cultures use popular culture and establish its grip over public imagination on different issues in the society, politics, economy, culture and religion. The celebrity culture shapes people's ideas, interests, everyday needs and desires by the means of mass adulation, identification and emulation of well-known faces: the celebrities. These three qualities are central to the idea of propaganda in which celebrities and celebrity cultures play vital roles. Edward Bernays (the nephew of Sigmund Freud) has written a book called *Propaganda (1928)*, which laid the foundation of twenty-first-century advertisement and marketing industries. The celebrity cultures serve the purposes of the ruling and non-ruling elites. Both American politicians and corporations used the ideals of propaganda for their ascendancy in the form of public relations exercise with the help of celebrities. The politicians use propaganda to win elections and corporations use it for profit maximisation.

The mysterious abilities of the invisible weapon called propaganda have played a major role in shaping public desires and opinions, which derives its historical and philosophical lineages from European colonialism. *Colonialism as a civilising mission* and *Sun never sets in British empire* are some of the classic examples of false propaganda in the making of colonial and imperialist Europe. The Nazis and fascists were adherent admirers of propaganda as a weapon to manipulate and control the masses. The organised manipulation of mind is the core of celebrity culture, which diverts people's attention from everyday hardships and other ugly realities of life. These genealogies continue to inspire the twenty-first-century capitalist propaganda led by celebrities across the globe.

The American corporations like the American Tobacco Company, Procter & Gamble, General Electric and many other media outlets have used propaganda as a tool with the help of celebrities to expand their businesses. The American Tobacco Company has used the ideals of Edward Bernays to overcome cultural barrier to smoking by combining smoking with female empowerment, freedom and personal choice. The female celebrities led by Bertha Hunt have flaunted their 'smoking touches of freedom' in the form of a protest by smoking during 1929 Easter Parade. *The New York Times* captioned it as *Group of Girls Puff at Cigarettes as a Gesture of 'Freedom'*. This so-called emancipatory logic has led to huge growth of female smokers and smokers among college- and university-going students. The tobacco market and its profit increased significantly. The Procter & Gamble has used Edward Bernays to organise soap yacht race in the Central Park and National Soap Sculpture Competition to expand its shop business as cleaning up act. Similarly, the Beech-Nut Packing Company's unhealthy food was branded as 'Hearty Breakfast' in the name of freedom of choice within the culture of consumption. The celebrities and celebrity cultures have played a major role in these master spin acts of corporate capitalism and transformation of American society.

The history of celebrity cultures from the Bronze age, silver screen to the age of social media keep redefining boundaries of popular culture, that is concomitant with the requirements of the ruling and non-ruling capitalist classes. The modern celebrity cultures are represented by performative language in which consumers adore the celebrities, fantasise their lifestyles and trust the products they advertise. There are few celebrities who lend their voice for peace and prosperity for all. There are very few celebrities in cinema and sports, who stand with the struggles of marginalised communities and fight against all forms of injustices and exploitations. However, celebrity culture is an integral part of capitalism, which glorifies individualism over collective values. The idea of utility, pleasure and satisfaction is central to the celebrity culture that is synchronous with commercial interests of corporates. The celebrities celebrate meritocracy, which is primarily the benefits of being within a network of power and wealth. There is nothing new in the bemoaning of celebrity culture. Thomas Busby questions celebrities as pretty women with nice dresses in his book *The Age of Genius* (1786). *It has highlighted the hollowness of celebrity culture, which continues to resonate with the exhibitionism of modern celebrity culture. In 2020, Busby would have written on celebrities as people with beauty without a brain and heart.*

There are two forms of celebritisation in history. From eighteenth to nineteenth century, celebrities were known for their sacrifices and contributions to society, science, literature, politics, history, economy and philosophy. The celebrities came from all walks of life and people continue to idealise and celebrate their lives till today. These celebrities have helped the processes of progressive social transformation with their ideas and actions. The twentieth- and twenty-first-century celebritisation is an art of constructing an individual as an object of desire for mass consumption with the help of propaganda. Such celebrity cultures are detrimental to celebrities themselves.

It commodifies the creativity of celebrities and their other abilities. From sports to cinema and in many other fields of life, celebrities are treated like commodities based on their popularity. Their popularity defines their value in the market. These celebrities are primarily from the world of cinema, TV entertainment industry and sports. There is no more glamour attached to the works and contributions of scientists, historians, philosophers and poets. The mass media and their propaganda play a major role in the making of these celebrities in terms of praise, validation and reproduction of consumable celebrity identity with social, cultural, political and economic currency. Their names are associated with brands and values. The commercialisation and commoditisation of celebrities betray their followers as everyone finds out quickly that the fair is not lovely for the skin. The hollowness of celebrity industry alienates celebrities from their own work and separates them from their fellow beings. The alienated celebrity culture forces celebrities to live a parasocial and lonely life. The glamour world of celebrity culture is alienating experience for all and results in mental illness and suicides. And alienation is an integral part of capitalism, which is suicidal.

The capitalist celebrity culture is an organised plunder of creativity in the name of hero or heroine worship. The available alternatives are in the processes of democratisation of fame and fortunes, celebration and socialisation of all kinds of creativities, moving away from marketisation and objectification of arts and artists and humanising celebrity status. Such transformations can ensure sustainable future for creative industries to survive all onslaughts of capitalism and its celebrity culture of consumerism. History is the witness to the greater glamour in the works of greater common good in the society than the narrow celebration of unabashed individualism. The aesthetic of fashionable 'self' only survives with others and not in isolation. The ordinariness of creativity does not domesticate but inspire the masses to celebrate and emulate creative culture. It is only possible if celebrities can write their own narratives and transform themselves from intimate strangers to socially concerned and politically committed citizens by ending their self-isolation and breaking their tinsel ghettoes. The power of creative performance survives in mass interactions and consumed in a patriarchal class, caste and racial hierarchy.

MR IRRFAN KHAN: THE ACTOR WHO EXPLAINED LIFE ON CINEMA SCREEN

As the sun sets in the gloomy sky, I sit down to write my scattered thoughts and shattered feelings after reading the death of one of my favourite actors in contemporary times. Mr Irrfan Khan's death justifies the poetic prediction of T. S. Eliot; April is truly the cruellest month in the memories and desires of life. It is death that eclipses all and outlines the limitations of human life. But human creativity outlives the body and shines in the history, in the making and unmaking of human stories, and their fate within everyday struggles of life which shines in cinema screens because of abilities of an actor. These abilities separate Irrfan from other fellow actors of Hindi cinema.

Acting as a profession is notorious for microscopic scrutiny and preoccupations. The success of a film depends on the synergy of many other people in a film set but the actors carry all the burdens of failure. It is a ruthless profession that takes toll on life of actors who take acting seriously as an art. Mr Irrfan Khan falls within such a tradition of cinema. His presence in a film set breeds confidence in all involved in the film making. His commitment is unparallelly distinctive in the film industry. All his films are testimony to his incredible abilities of an actor.

Mr Irrfan Khan has achieved pinnacles of success in the world of cinema within and outside India. The tinsel club of Hindi cinema in Mumbai is known for its nepotistic approach, where family lineages take primacy over acting talents. Mr Irrfan Khan was among the few actors who managed to demolish the entrenched glass ceilings with sheer qualities of acting. He did not stop there. He went on to create his own space in the fables of cinema in Hollywood. He is among few Indian actors with global reach. He left his incredible trademark in the world of cinema and theatre within fifty-three years of his life. Fifty-three is not the age to go but everything comes to an end in the Shakespearean play of life. But Irrfan Khan has left this world too soon.

Mr Irrfan Khan's death is an immense loss to the world of cinema. He is among the rare breed of Indian actors who can tell stories with movement of his eyes. His acting can tell stories in silence. In these stories, he will survive and continue to inspire both actors and film makers to move beyond commercial logic of cinema and entertainment. When commercial logic sets the stage of cinema, he pushed the boundaries and significance of cinematic art. From the beginning of his creative career, he has been telling a counter-narrative undermining commercial bid for storytelling and acting.

Unlike some others, Irrfan Khan achieved his wider recognition without revolting against mainstream commercial cinema. He used the platform to promote a new culture of cinema where cinema as an art and it did not die in search of commercial success. He did not follow the culture of acting determined by the mainstream market logic of cinema. His unflinching commitment to acting in cinema led to his commercial success. Awards and glories did not stop him in search of good cinema. His curiosity continued to grow with the growth of his popularity as an actor. His composed public appearances are glaring examples of his personality. He never projected himself bigger than the stories of his films. He did not promote himself larger than life like other actors of Bollywood. His humble behaviour reflects his attachment with his humble beginning. These qualities are rare among his contemporaries. In the death of Mr Irrfan Khan, the stake here is not who would uphold the legacies of his style of acting, sense and sensibilities but who would remain standing in the folklores of acting, cinema and memories of audience after the curtain falls in theatres of life. His name is the answer. His journey from Jaipur to Mumbai via Delhi ends in his death but legacies of his footprints in silver screen will continue to tell stories to entertain the masses.

As India and Indians in en masse mourn the death of one of their finest actors, the outpouring of sorrow and love for Mr Irrfan Khan restores my hopes on the idea of inclusive India on such an unusual day. In his death, people like me realise that it is not all lost to the politics of hate practised by the Hindutva fascists in India. It will be a befitting tribute to Irrfan Khan, if all people mourn the same way for common Muslims, Dalits and activists who were killed, butchered and lynched by the Hindutva vigilante groups. It would be truly amazing tribute if we mourn the same way during the deaths of women, migrant labourers, tribals, workers and farmers in India due to the policies of this government led by Narendra Modi.

Irrfan's family life reflects the beauties of liberal and secular India which is under threat. It would be a tribute to his life to uphold liberal and secular traditions of India as a republic. His death reminds us that it is a death that defines our lives. It is better to live life with a purpose and principles than travel in the glittering flow of power and money. Adieu Irrfan.

RISHI KAPOOR BEYOND SILVER SCREEN

There was no escape from acting as it was in his blood; he did not struggle for fame and fortune as it came with his family lineages, Rishi Kapoor wrote in his memoir. Acting was not a profession for him. His passion for life was embedded within acting. He was undoubtedly one of India's finest actors. He not only inherited the legacies of acting from his illustrious family but also represented progressive lineages of the Indian People's Theatre Association (IPTA). His unfiltered and fearless defence of India's liberal, secular, democratic and constitutional values separates him from other actors from the pretentiousness culture of Bollywood.

After Modi became the prime minister of India, many leading actors within Bollywood crowd either voice their sympathies with Hindutva politics or maintained cowardice silence, but Rishi Kapoor did not share this self-serving trend. He opposed the lynching of Muslims, journalists, rationalists and stood with secular forces in India. The terms like 'anti-nationals', 'traitors' and 'go to Pakistan' are used to describe anyone opposed to Modi government. These three phrases became the most favourite slogans of the Hindutva fanatics in defence of the Modi government. The emanating climate of hate and fear did not deter Rishi Kapoor to openly oppose the reactionary politics promoted by Modi government. He said openly that he is not a minion of BJP.

Rishi Kapoor did not calculate loss and profit while taking a firm position against Islamophobia and bigotry. He declared himself as a beef-eating religious Hindu and faced the wrath of cow vigilantes and other Hindutva fanatic groups. He opposed beef ban and argued audaciously that the culture of consumption should not be linked with religion and spiritualism. Religion is different from food habits of people. He was trolled for being pro-Muslim by the Hindutva zealots, but he stood to his ground. When Hindutva fundamentalists are tearing apart, he unapologetically stood firm in the defence of multicultural ethos of Indian society and its cosmopolitan outlook.

Rishi Kapoor was an unapologetic ambassador of peace between India and Pakistan. He loved Indians as much as he loved the people of Pakistan. His ancestral home is in Pakistan. So, his relationship with Pakistan runs far deeper than films. He requested the Government of Pakistan to convert his family home into a museum. He wanted to visit Pakistan eagerly but died with this unfulfilled dream. His commitment to peace processes between two countries defines him as a public figure in India. On 19 March 2020, he wrote in his twitter handle about his feelings for the people in Pakistan as coronavirus spreads all over the world. He wrote that 'people of Pakistan are also dear to us. Once we were one. We are concerned too. This is a global crisis. No ego matter this. We love you guys. Humanity zindabad'. The narrow silo of ruling-class narrative of nationalism was unattractive to him. He truly lived with Indian ideals of universal brotherhood and peace.

Self-criticisms are rare among leading actors in glittering self-confidence within the world of cinema. But Rishi Kapoor is unique. He did not spare himself. In the memoir, he candidly confessed about the mistakes in his life. He openly criticised himself in public. Indians are shocked and India is grieving as one of most important cultural icon is now gone. It is unconceivable loss to the world of Indian cinema. But a fine actor survives in the silver screens after his death. The memories of Rishi Kapoor as a person continue to inspire us as a progressive and liberal citizen. He was enchanted by life to entertain and bring smile to the masses and divert their attention from the ugly realities of their everyday life. India lost him when Indians need him the most. It is important to celebrate his poignant legacies beyond films.

CRIME, JUSTICE AND CAPITALISM

The right-wing henchmen and their liberal brethren provide moral justifications for extrajudicial deaths during colonial plunders and imperialist wars.
From Iraq wars to the killing of Osama Bin Laden and from honour killings
to domestic violence, police encounters and custodial deaths around the
world are part of the same genealogy that justifies violence on moral grounds.
Colonialism as civilising mission, imperialist wars for democracy and human
rights are products of unfounded moral discourses shaped by the ruling-class
propaganda. The moral arguments continue to provide justifications to institutionalise violence and patronise it in the name of nationalism, religion, community and caste honour. The masses fall into such false intellectual narrative
and celebrate such extrajudicial, structural and institutionalised violence as
justice. It has shaped the Orwellian proverbial expression: *Those who live by
the sword die by the sword. Those who do not die by the sword die of smelly
diseases.* Such a violent social formulation derives its cultural legitimacy
from Christian theology. The Gospel of Matthew echoes it by saying 'sword
shall perish with the sword'. The patronage of violence is an integral part of
most of the world religions. The idea of god and religions will perish without
cherishing the ideals of violence and fear in the name of justice. In this way,
normalisation and naturalisation of violence as justice derives its legitimacy
from religious and moral discourses, which is antithetical to ideals of justice.
    The moral foundation of extrajudicial killing as justice is not new to the
world. The modified version of the Hammurabian code and Anglo-Saxon culture of crime, evidence, punishment and justice continues to resonate in the
twenty-first-century judicial praxis. The origin and growth of crime and its
moral foundation is intrinsically linked with ascendancy of private property
from feudalism to finance capital. The economic construction of society and
transformation of individual as a mere producer and consumer in support of
capitalism both in its old and new forms led to the rise of crime. The culture
of consumerism has promoted a culture of competition, where realisation of
one's own self-interest is the supreme goal. The capitalist transformation of
need-based culture to a desire-based culture with the help of advertisement
industry, which has destroyed collective foundations of society. The ascendancy of capitalism has increased the wealth without diminishing miseries. It
has led to the concentration of wealth in the hands of few, and growth of huge
social and economic inequalities in the society.
    The rotten capitalist system continues to produce miseries for many and
prosperity for the few. Laws are made by the capitalist classes to protect
their own interests. The Corn Laws were made to uphold the interests of
landed aristocracies, mercantile classes and industrial bourgeoisie in early
nineteenth-century England. The legacies of such laws continue to exist today

in different parts of the world. The special economic zones, industrial zones, agricultural zones, export and import zones are classic examples of policies, working conditions and labour laws, which disempower the working-class masses and empowers capitalist classes. The strong-security state and conformist bourgeois judiciary is important to provide protection to the private properties of capitalist classes. The capitalist system not only produces crime, it also uses organised criminal gangs to promote its regimes of capitalist profit accumulation.

Historically, alienating capitalist system is an organic incubator for crime and criminals. There is nothing new in the criminogenic character of capitalism. The law is used and interpreted differently to different classes of people. As a result of which American prisons are overflowing with black, ethnic minority and working-class population whereas Indian prisons packed with lower caste, tribal and poor population. The criminals have their classes. The punishments and prison cells are different according to their class location of the criminals. If criminals are rich and powerful, the law takes a different course whereas law takes its own course with poor and vulnerable. The unequal availability and accessibility to police, law and judiciary did not help society to grow in an egalitarian way. The police, law firms, solicitors, judiciary and prisons did not deliver justice. These judicial institutions of law and order did not help to eradicate social and economic problems of our times. It has rather helped to consolidate the power of the capitalist elites while the masses continue to suffer in different forms of miseries.

The contemporary capitalism is organised around ideals of illiberal and undemocratic governance of the society in which citizens are free consumers and wage labours. The ideals of individual liberty, freedom and rights are cosmetic covers to criminogenic face of capitalism. The capitalist societies do not overcome the problem of crime, but it opens up in frontiers of crime every day in different stages of its development. The culture of crime and punishment is an integral part of the proportional retributive judicial system with bourgeois spirit in which 'popular/elite consciousness and an element of desire for revenge' plays a key role in shaping laws to regulate crime and criminals. The capitalist judicial system is based on the perceived notion of 'good' and 'bad'. Such a system disciplines the citizens and does not destroy the crime and criminals. It does not reform the criminals or did not provide the environment for the criminals to develop their abilities to reform themselves. It normalises and naturalises the culture of crime within retributive judicial system that complements capitalism. The moral foundations of retributive justice derive its legitimacy from major religions of the world. There is nothing modern about it. It is feudal, medieval and barbaric in letter and spirit. The social, economic, religious and cultural conditions that produce crime and promote criminals continue to thrive under capitalist patronage. Such a system moves the society into an unending darkness of injustice.

It is time to understand and unravel the innate goodness and human values in human beings, which are destroyed by capitalist cultures. Crimes and capitalisms are unnatural whereas love and peace is natural to all human beings in all societies. The cosmetic vicissitudes of capitalism and its actuarial justice cannot solve the problems of crime. The world needs new language of penology by addressing the alienating capitalist conditions that produces and patronises crime and criminals. The establishment of a crime-free society is possible and inevitable. It depends on our abilities to struggle for an egalitarian economy, democratic society and non-discriminatory governance based on progressive politics of peace and prosperity. Such decriminalised transformations depend on unwavering commitment of people's struggles to ideals of liberty, equality, fraternity and justice for all. These ideals are indivisible to establish a crime-free, punishment-free and prison-free society based on harmony and love for each other.

OLIGARCHIES OF MAINSTREAM MASS MEDIA IN SERVICE OF CAPITALISM

In early fifteenth-century Europe, news used to be political, economic, military and diplomatic messages of the ruling classes. There was no mass media. It was often the voices of the businessmen and ruling elites circulated within their own networks. The revolutionary upheavals and democratisation of society during nineteenth century led to the growth of mass media. People used mass media to fight against all forms of exploitation, injustices and inequalities. The mass media has also played momentous role during the struggle against feudalism, colonialism and apartheid. Mass media is vital in the growth of liberal, secular, democratic, progressive and scientific ideals in the society. Therefore, it is the historic responsibility of mass media to report on realities of everyday life and consider fact as sacred in professional journalism. Yellow journalism is no journalism. But idealism and principles are dead within mainstream capitalist media.

From the early twentieth century onwards, the mass media is not only manufacturing consent but also works as an agency of the ruling and non-ruling elites to hide alternatives from the masses. The old world of yellow journalism is transformed into news and opinions for sale in a post-truth world. It spreads fake news, misrepresents everyday realities, twists facts and shapes opinions like a marketing or advertisement industry. The mainstream media works as a propaganda machine for the people with money and power. The uncritical reporting and ruling-class biases are obsequious.

There is limited space for debates and disagreements in the media today. The editorial pages and opinion pieces are sponsored by the market forces that are concomitant with the requirements of neoliberal capitalism and its governance models. The essence of neoliberal capitalism and its affiliated media is to create domesticated and uncritical mass audience and destroy critical voices representing people. The idea is to create and mass-produce social, cultural and political values that accept the dominance of illegitimate authority and power. It is the market monopoly that controls the media today. The market monopolies are controlled by oligarchs of mass media. There are six companies – Comcast, Disney, Time Warner, Fox, CBS and Viacom – which control almost all 90 per cent media in the United States and other parts of the world.

The *National Amusements* is a multinational media conglomerate owned by Sumner Redstone and Shari Redstone. These two people control more than 170 networks, reaching out to more than 700 million people in more than 160 countries with the help of a company called the Viacom. It is one of the largest media conglomerates in the world. It controls print, electronics and internet media outlets. It also controls movies, video games, TV shows and many other creative industries like music. These companies shape public taste in culture, consumption and voting behaviour.

The *Walt Disney Company* is known as *Disney*, which controls hundreds of media and entertainment outlets. It is one of the leading multinational mass media and entertainment conglomerates which played a major role in shaping capitalism with American dreams. It helped to transform the need-based society into a desire-based society with the help of its advertisement and animation industry. It has promoted a culture of self-gratifying fantasies of individualism. It is also responsible for producing popular cultural narratives for the naturalisation and normalisation of American and global capitalism.

The Time Warner is known as the Warner Media LLC, which is another largest mass media and entertainment conglomerate. This conglomerate has used individual privacy data for its financial gain and played a major role in destroying net neutrality. The Comcast is another largest media and entertainment conglomerate, which played a major role in shaping American and world politics. It has huge budget for political lobbing, and it funds electoral campaigns in the name of universal political action. It traps consumers with its political projects and propaganda. This media corporation is opposed to universal media access. The News Corporation is owned by media mogul, Rupert Murdoch, who controls media and publication outlets in five continents. The News Corporation is known as the predatory capitalist media, which destroys media diversity and democracy. It upholds the power of the capitalist market. Similarly, the Sony Corporation is another leading multinational conglomerate which controls largest music, entertainment and video-game business. These media corporations uphold the voices of the capitalist class and supress the interests of the working-class masses.

The large media corporations are a threat to the democratic and liberal values of the societies across the globe. In pursuit for profit, the mainstream mass media has formed its alliances with reactionary religious, nationalist, undemocratic, illiberal and fascist forces across the globe. It negates every founding principle of mass media. These media corporations and their affiliates promote a culture of no alternative to capitalism in politics, economy, society and culture. These forces hide the economic, social and cultural realities of everyday lives within capitalism and promote capitalist myth. Facts are no longer the foundation of journalistic analysis. It is all about spreading falsehood of market forces by spreading consumer culture as only culture where individuals can realise their free choices. These media houses are responsible for transforming citizens as mere customers in a society driven by profit. In this way, mass media destroys the society based on solidarity, love, share and care by celebrating unabashed hedonistic individualism. Mass alienation is the net outcome of capitalism-led corporate mass media.

It is imperative for people to detox themselves from the propaganda machines of the governing elites and find their own alternatives. It is time to reclaim the founding principles of mass media by representing the predicaments of the masses. The masses can organise themselves to create cooperative media organisations to uphold their voices and represent their interests while promoting liberal, democratic, secular and scientific ethos in the society. This is only possible when people can control their own narratives by establishing people's media free from corporate cultures. *Vox Populi, Vox Dei* is the only alternative to defeat the toxic culture of capitalism and its mass media, which destroys lives, livelihoods of the masses. It serves power and tame voices of people. The powerful mass movement can crumble the palaces of media moguls and their oligarchic empire of propaganda and profit. The cooperative media owned by people is the only alternative to uphold *Vox Populi*.

IDEOLOGY BEHIND CHARACTER ASSASSINATION

What is character? Character indicates totality of feature of an individual's personality, courage, commitment and outlooks from righteousness to humility. The material or physical representations or moral frameworks are not character. Class, gender, race, sexual orientations, religious practice and moral values do not represent character. Character is a commitment to one's own self, to one's own family, friends, society, state and beyond. And character assassination is as old as human civilisation.

The character assassination manifests itself in different ways by spreading factually incorrect information, rumours, lies, misquoting, misrepresentation, silencing, acts of vandalism, name-calling, mental illness, creating false perceptions and sexual deviance. These are discussed in detail in Martijn Icks and Eric Shiraev's edited volume *Character Assassination throughout the Ages*. The criminal tribes, underdeveloped rural poor, dirty working classes, unhygienic lower castes, characterless women and brainless blacks are some of the examples of stereotype-based character assassination campaigns against different groups of populations in the world. The Nazi regime has flourished by discrediting Jewish population. The anti-terrorism campaign has shaped post-9/11 world by demonising Muslims. It is often used against women, working classes, minorities, and revolutionaries to tame their creativities and emancipatory potentials.

Why do people follow the strategy of character assassination? Is it for the sake of defeating or winning in an argument? What are the aims and objectives of character assassinations? Is it spontaneous or pre planned? Is it a mechanism of self-defence? Is it a product of anger, revenge, frustration and jealousy? Who fears character assassination and why? Who are the victims of character assassination? These are some of the questions central to understand the ideology behind character assassination. The time, place, people and their social, political, cultural and religious conditions shape the ideology of character assassination. From politics to personal lives, from villages to cities and from corporate world to literature, character assassination continues to be an intoxicating strategy adopted by both opponents and friends alike in different stages of life.

Character assassination as a form of smear campaign is an old and powerful strategy of social, political and cultural control of individuals and their freedom. Character assassination is a deliberate attempt to demoralises a person or a community by destroying their image with the help of spreading rumours, lies or facts to reduce their abilities to actively engage with themselves and with their fellow beings. It hurts the victims by diminishing their reputation and achievements in public eye, which disables the victims to achieve their goals successfully. In 1950, Jerome Davis published a book entitled *Character Assassination* which outlines 'fear, ignorance, envy, suspicion, malice, jealousy, frustration, greed, aggression, economic rivalry, emotional insecurity and an inferiority complex' as reasons behind character assassinations. Jerome Davis was a sociologist and a labour organiser. His book is an autobiographical reflection on self-defence against personal attacks.

There are different types of character assassinations, but the objectives are very similar. The idea is to discredit the abilities, integrity, charisma, intellect and power of an individual, a group or an institution. It often leads to deaths and destitutions. Character assassination is a dangerous strategy of demonisation, which silences people and their voice of reason. Therefore, it is important to understand it and fight back to ensure truth to prevail. Silence is not an option in the age of post-truth world dominated by the mass production of fake news. The reactionary ruling classes run character assassination campaign against the alternative forces to control and monopolise state power and control the society without facing any radical challenges of transformation.

The fascist forces indulge in character assassination of the past leaders to legitimise their politics of otherness and hegemonise their power over public. Harriet Flower has coined a concept called 'memory sanctions' in her book *The Art of Forgetting: Disgrace and Oblivion in Roman Political Culture*. The idea of 'memory sanctions' is 'deliberately designed strategies that aim to change the picture of the past, whether through erasure or redefinition, or by means of both'. The forward march of neoliberal authoritarianism led by the right-wing forces use this strategy by rewriting history and abusing progressive past and defame radical leaders to establish their reactionary rule. The collective memory is a threat to neoliberal authoritarianism. Therefore, the world is witnessing erasure of history, humanities and social sciences, weakening of scientific research, and onslaught on reason as non-merit goods. Character assassination of people and their past is the best way to domesticate them as per the needs and desires of the powerful. Character assassination as a tool, it has served the ruling and non-ruling elites and powerful for centuries to limit alternatives to flourish.

In the age of digital platforms, social media enables speed assassination of character without any time lapses. It is dangerous for peace and prosperity. Truth is the greatest causality of character assassination. It is a big business today. The public relations agencies, advertisement industries, mass media and other propaganda machines are net beneficiaries and enablers of character assassination to generate revenue. Therefore, it is apt to call character assassination as a self-help product and tool of patriarchal capitalism to control, domesticate and emasculate individual freedom and creativity. It tames the voice of science and reason within the cacophony of mass media: the voice of ruling and non-ruling classes.

Therefore, the radical politics and progressive ideology need to conceptualise 'character' as commitment for fellow human beings, nature and animals. Such a conceptualisation and its praxis can fight and defeat the character assassination as a reactionary and ruling-class strategy to uphold individual dignity and collective spirit of human essence.

INTELLECTUALS AS LUMPEN HERDS
IN THE UNIVERSITIES

Once upon a time, universities were the places where intellectuals, teachers and students as a community of learners used to reflect on everyday realities, learn the skills to use it in their professional life, discover the knowledge to understand them and dissect the complexities of society. They also used to practise their utopian dreams in pursuit of knowledge for the greater common good. However, universities are no longer bastions of academic freedom to produce knowledge to understand the past, analyse the present and face the challenges of the future. The universities are behaving like a commodity market today. Universities are becoming degree-selling supermarkets, where teachers and students are cash cows for the university managers. The neoliberal authoritarian governments consider higher education expenditure as a burden on the state. But at the same time, the governments are treating higher education as a profit-making corporate sector. Such contradictions are integral to capitalism as a system. The funding cuts due to austerity measures are forcing university managers to follow their political masters or the agenda of the funding bodies. The idea of independent research, teaching and learning activities are becoming anathema. The teaching, non-teaching staff members and students in the universities are treated as numbers in the Excel sheets of managers. These managers are alien to the idea of research and teaching. Their managerial bluffs continue to be the rulebooks of the university management. It is like quack's medicine. It does not heal but aggravates the crisis.

Moreover, these managers try to manage staffs and students exactly the way they manage university buildings, computers, chairs, tables and other non-living assets. All are resources to be used for accumulation of profit in their eyes. These managerial classes in alliance with ruling and non-ruling classes have destroyed the idea of universities as centres of knowledge production and dissemination for the progressive future and egalitarian growth of the society. The managerial classes have transformed university intellectuals into lumpen herds. The culture of intellectual compliance has cultivated both fear and faith in management. The managerial pressure to pursue uniformity and conformity in the name of process-driven quality assurance has ruined the diversities of knowledge production within the universities. The idea of debates, discourses and the democratic culture of disagreements are destroyed within the process-driven matrix of research rankings, teaching frameworks and learning objectives. The slogans of 'employability', 'business and industry partnerships' and 'knowledge transfer skills' are new marketing tools of managerial gimmicks to attract students to the universities, where knowledge production is secondary to essentialist set of skills for jobs. Such managerial strategies have transformed universities and other centres of higher learning into vocational training centres. The teaching and non-teaching staff members are new slaves within universities.

Such transformations did not happen overnight. It does not reflect the success of managers, managerialism and marketisation of universities. It shows the utter failures of intellectuals both as individuals and as a group. The puerile careerism and individualism among intellectuals have allowed managers to divide and supress intellectuals and destroyed the collective foundations of knowledge production and dissemination within and outside universities. As a result of which universities are no longer a community of learners but a place of transaction between the sellers (teachers) and buyers (students). The interactive culture is replaced by exchange relationships driven by market forces within university campuses. The fancy glass door buildings, smart classrooms, hi-tech libraries and airport-like coffee shops are looking good but make tired students and staffs feel like solitary car parks. The reasons are obvious that the transactional relationships are essentialist and exchange relationships are functional with limited expiry date. It does not help to form a critical mass or a meaningful bond among community of learners.

How did intellectuals land themselves in such a situation within the universities? What is the future of universities? What is the future of university students and staff members? The answers to these questions need deeper self-reflections by the university intellectuals both as individuals and as a group. The meaningful transformation of universities in a progressive path depends on honest and critical self-reflection. It is urgent and inevitable. There are two significant issues that need closer look by the university intellectuals for a meaningful self-reflection and critique. The first issue is around the works of intellectuals and their relationship with production within larger economy. The second issue involves the relationship between intellectuals, their role and location within class-divided society.

The deepening of capitalism during nineteenth, twentieth and twenty-first centuries led to the growth of a professional intellectual class (tutors, lecturers, readers, professors, fellows, researchers and their hierarchical reincarnations) within universities. This professional class is not homogeneous group but the intellectuals within it behaved like herds as if they are different from the working-class masses. The intellectuals have started normalising such a superficial notion by theorising that university intellectuals do not produce anything with immediate use and exchange value. Therefore, university intellectuals are different from the working classes and their class interests are different from each other. Such a myopic understanding was further propagated by the bourgeois media to weaken the working-class struggles for emancipation.

In reality, Computer Science curriculums in the universities are shaped as per the requirements of the Silicon Valley. The Wall Street and insurance companies decide the nature of Banking, Finance and Business Management Studies curriculum in the business schools. The International Relations, Politics and Security Studies are shaped by the NATO and other security formations of the state and non-state security agencies. The pharmaceutical corporations decide the nature of Chemistry and Medical Science curriculums. The dominant nationalists, religious and reactionary forces are trying to control and rewrite the curriculums of Languages, History, Philosophy, Archaeology and Anthropology to suit their goals. There are always exceptional universities and alternative programmes of studies, and few university intellectuals try to promote critical Social Sciences, Humanities and Natural Sciences. But these alternative and critical attempts are branded as non-merit and nonprofitable good for market-driven university programmes. It is clear that university intellectuals do not have control over their programmes. The university intellectuals do not have control over their own labour because once they produce a programme, teaching material or publish a research paper, it belongs to the university. Such trend reflects medieval feudalism within modern universities. The university intellectuals are micro and macro managed by the capitalist forces to achieve their larger economic goals. But still, the university intellectuals behave like lumpen herds and betray their own class; that is, working class both in terms of its foundation and location.

Marx and Engels in *The German Ideology* have argued that 'the class which has the means of material production at its disposal, has control at the same time over the means of mental production at its disposal' (1989: 64). The material production of goods and services for use and exchange value cannot be separated from mental production of ideas. There is commonality of class interests and class relations between the manual and mental workers as they produce value together, and capitalism misappropriates it and weakens the working class by dividing it. Universities merely reflect the capitalist social order and economic processes in the larger context. The university managers behave like lumpen proletariats and the university intellectuals behave like lumpen herds betraying their own class interests. The marketisation of universities led to the growth of industrialised minds, industrialised degrees and programmes in the service of dominant capitalist forces. The work creates consciousness if workers get time to reflect. The process-driven university teaching and research assignments give very little time to the university workers to reflect and resonate their consciousness with working-class consciousness. The university intellectual snobbery would end with working-class consciousness. But university intellectuals are attached to dominant capitalist classes partly due to marketisation of universities and partly due to the lack of class consciousness. The assimilation of university intellectuals within capitalist system is detrimental to interests of the intellectuals themselves. It reproduces exploitative capitalist-class relations.

It is within this context the university intellectuals must reclaim their role in the society, question the power that controls their labour and find their class foundation and class location within working-class politics of radical transformation of capitalist society. The future of universities, students and staff members in particular and society in general depends on the way intellectuals fight to disentangle themselves from the marketisation of universities. The independent universities and independence of intellectuals depend on emancipation of working-class masses from capitalist plunder. As long as the university intellectuals believe in their false notion that they are not part of the working class, their intellectual freedom will be an illusion within capitalism. Therefore, it is in the interests of the intellectuals to form unity with their working-class brethren and fight capitalism. It is the unadulterated responsibility of university intellectuals to think beyond themselves and their interests within and outside the university campuses. It is time to reconnect with the revolutionary legacies of working-class intellectuals. The collective and progressive struggles always offer alternatives and ensure emancipation of the masses.

REGIMES WITHOUT REASON AND CONSCIENCE

The world is silently witnessing the erosion of democratic, progressive, secular and liberal cultures of governance. The contemporary governments are becoming more authoritarian and threaten the multicultural mosaic of societies around the world. The governing and non-governing elites falsely argue that democracy breeds inefficiency and creates functional barrier to the animal spirit of profit-making and entrepreneurial activities. The majority of people are conspicuously silent. The pandemic has taken away the limited space for resistance to the on-going authoritarian ordeals. From Washington and Westminster to Beijing, Brussels and New Delhi, the authoritarian cultures define the operational character of the governments. These Machiavellian authoritarian regimes are not only against freedom and democracy but also spread bigotry. The silent coup of reactionary forces is accelerated by rewriting of history, imposition of neoliberal economic policies, removal of all institutional and legal barriers to the lynch mob of market forces. The governments are not bystanders but active facilitators of authoritarian regimes as a dominant reality in society, politics and economy.

There is a commonality of authoritarian regimes across the globe. These regimes follow a common conservative cult called 'nation first'. This 'nation first' reactionary political and economic dogma derives its philosophical lineages from social and religious conservative thoughts, that in essence argues to protect, promote and glorify moral traditions of the past. The conservatives and authoritarian ideologues argue that the values of the past can provide solutions to the present predicaments of the society. The knowledge of the past is more valuable for the present. The past glories and successes are the life and blood of contemporary authoritarian states and governments. The conservative ideals are opposed to change and prefer to maintain status quo. Edmund Burke as a philosopher is the patron saint of conservative philosophy for last three centuries. His philosophy continues to provide political justification to authoritarian and conservative regimes of today. Burke was opposed to the idea of any form of revolutionary change in the society as it destroys the traditional fabrics of good society. Such an ideological framework is a deliberate strategy to avoid accountability and supress citizenship rights and liberties. There is a relentless attack on the democratic and multicultural ethos in politics, often led by governments with conformist outlooks devoid of conscience and compassion.

The contemporary conservative politics is a reaction against the aggrandisement of neoliberal capitalism, which consolidated wealth in the hands of few and marginalised the masses. The capitalist classes have formed an alliance with the conservative forces to further consolidate their power and wealth. The government formed out of such an alliance does not represent the interests of the marginalised masses. As a result, the world is confronting miseries amid plenty. The forward march of reactionary and authoritarian governments across the globe is based on the politics of maintaining social, cultural and religious order of the past in the name of national, ethnic and religious glory based on conquest and dominance of minorities and working-class population. Such irrational, illogical and authoritarian outlooks define conservative philosophical praxis.

The conservative governments use the state power to implement their authoritarian agenda of governance devoid of conscience and compassion. These forces are not only hostile to critical public opinion but also supress any form of dissent within a democratic culture. Democracy dies its natural death without the voices of dissent and debates. The idea of mass obedience to authority is central to authoritarian governance model practised by conservative governments across the world. The authoritarian regimes and their ideology of mass obedience kill the innate conscience and compassion within human beings. The idea of dominance, hierarchy and subjugation becomes the organising principles of authoritarian states and governments under which majority of the people suffer. As a result, the banality of authoritarian evil becomes normal and natural in the society, which produces totalitarian leaders without conscience and compassion. Such leaders use every opportunity to lead and dominate the masses by using state power. The governments become hostage to such leaders and their ideological cult. The compassion and conscience tend to restrict individuals in the misuse of power, but the authoritarian cult leaders do not have any such restrictions in the use and abuse of power. The authoritarian leaders are revengeful, manipulative, unsympathetic and untrustworthy. These social and psychological characters are products of conservative and capitalist societies. From Americas, Africas to Europe and Asia, the world is witnessing such characteristics in leaders ruling these continents.

The pandemic fuelled economic crisis is ravaging the world, but the governments are mute spectators in the United States, United Kingdom, India, Brazil, Iran, Mexico and many other countries. The leaders and the governments in these countries show little compassion and conscience in discharging their democratic responsibilities for their citizens. The global health crisis has revealed that these authoritarian regimes promote the propaganda of 'nation first' but in reality, these leaders betray the very people who elect them to power. These governments and leadership stand with the capitalist class to further consolidate their wealth even during the global health and economic crises. The political and economic profiles of authoritarian governments show that these right-wing regimes are really without any form of human or animal conscience. The right-wing regimes and their leaders are motivated by fear and use it to rule the massed by spreading prejudice. The aggressiveness in authoritarian leaders is a product of fear; the source of the desire to dominate with the medieval mindset. These leaders use fake news and misleading information to manipulate and control the masses.

Why do people vote leaders and regimes without any reason and conscience? Why do people support dictatorships? Why do people support their own subjugation? The Stockholm syndrome, political ignorance, illiteracy, poverty, love for strong leaders and so on are some of the silly reasons based on superficial analysis. The alternative to such a right-wing, reactionary and authoritarian shift in society, politics and economy needs dispassionate analysis on the causes of such a transformation. It is impossible to fight authoritarian regimes without understanding the foundations of their support and reasons behind the causes of its growth. The capitalist delusions and growth of anti-politics culture of entitlement led to the rise of authoritarian regimes with the help of reactionary religious and market forces. In spite of flagrant erosion of democratic space and deepening of crises, the popularity of authoritarian regimes and their leaders did not decline. It is a serious cause of concern while reimagining alternatives. Foxy electoral strategies are not enough for radical social and political transformations to defeat authoritarian psychopaths. The survival of democratic, liberal, progressive and multicultural values depends on radical alternatives produced in impending people's struggles. People's struggles are incubators of ideas and inventories of alternatives. There is no other sustainable alternative to struggles based on compassion and conscience.

FREEDOM IN THE AGE OF NEOLIBERALISM
AND RIGHT-WING POLITICS

The world is facing its deepest crisis after the world wars. The legitimacy of Westphalian international systems and their postwar reincarnations are falling apart. The political parties are losing the public trust and people question their legitimacy. The states and governments are becoming hostages and facilitators of neoliberal capitalism, where people live in an environment of non-freedom and market oligarchs enjoy absolute freedom. The states and governments are exhibiting authoritarian and fascist tendencies. There is a huge rise of right-wing forces in society and politics. The neoliberal capitalist order is further aggravating the economic crisis. The masses are in the midst of a distinct period of crisis in contemporary world, where masses suffer in miseries and few people live in island of prosperity. It has exposed capitalist utopia. The decades of wage stagnation and declining privatisation of public resources, liberalisation of protective rules and regulations led to the concentration of political and economic powers in the hands of few. The world is witnessing the highest form of material inequalities in history. Economic marginalisation, social alienation and political despondency are three defining products of neoliberalism, which provides life and blood to the right-wing forces.

The growth of right-wing politics is playing the fundamental role in reproducing and naturalising growing economic, social and political inequalities in the world. It did not happen overnight. It is neither an accident nor a natural phenomenon. The large-scale acceleration of inequalities and marginalisation is a product of neoliberalism: a project of capitalism. It has transformed the society by dismantling its collective foundations. The unadulterated celebration of individualism led to the rise of a society where individual actions are shaped by the ideals of utility, pleasure and satisfaction. These three features have become the foundation for the celebration of idealised individual achievements. The adoration of 'successful self-made men and women' has become gold standard for social, economic, cultural and political acceptance in the society. Selfishness has become a virtue. The elites and their advocates have deployed such a neoliberal narrative to destroy the collective consciousness of people by which they exercise their illegitimate authority. The pestilence of loneliness and depression are the net output of neoliberalism.

Moreover, neoliberalism shaped popular consciousness that is separate from their material and social realities. It detached people from their own past and present to sustain and pursue the idea of 'there is no alternative' to neoliberalism. The neoliberal patronage led to the rise of religious and cultural right-wing forces in politics. These forces gave new meanings to individual life by promoting the idea of subjugation, supremacy, deaths and destitutions in the name of national interest. It has become a strategy of governance and control mechanism. Such a strategy led to the rise of supercilious freedom on the one hand and diminishing individual liberty on the other hand. The right-wing and reactionary forces assault the very idea of freedom that neoliberalism claims to promote. Such repulsive rise of contradictions is an integral part of neoliberalism as a project of capitalism.

Friedrich Hayek in his book *Road to Serfdom* (1944) argued that the government planning is destroying individual freedom. Hayekians have taken the argument further by arguing that state and society act as obstacles of individual freedom. The *Mont Pelerin Society* was supported by million-aires and founded by Hayek to promote neoliberalism as a doctrine. The Hayekian legacies continue to reflect in the mission, vision and functions of the *Cato Institute, American Enterprise Institute* and *Heritage Foundation* in Washington D.C., the *Institute of Economic Affairs, Centre for Policy Studies* and the *Adam Smith Institute* in London and many other neoliberal think tanks around the world. These organisations and networks are funded by bankers, industrialists and billionaires to promote neoliberalism in the name of individual freedom and democracy. These think tanks promote the idea that free market and its culture of consumerism facilitates individual freedom. In his book *Capitalism and Freedom* (1962) Milton Friedman has argued in defence of economic freedom in a liberal society under competitive capitalism. His philosophy laid the foundation for market democracy which is opposed to very idea of democracy itself. Such an elusive idea of freedom for the sake of market became the foundation for the growth of capitalism since last two centuries. It is time to bust the myth.

Neoliberalism as a project conceals the limits of market and capitalism more and ensures curbing of individual freedom both as a consumer and as a citizen. Freedom is not atomised individualism as promoted by neoliberalism. Our freedoms are interrelated and depend on each other. It is a process of collective realisation or collective surrender. So, it is important to decouple, rescue and articulate the idea of freedom and its collective spirit from the neoliberal and right-wing forces. Such a process depends on our collective desire to learn from the everyday realities of people and their interconnected experiences under different ruling regimes of capitalism. The concerns of people, their collective consciousness and way of finding alternatives for determining themselves as 'being' and 'becoming' need to be articulated without institutional and structural barriers. The realisation of 'self-determination' both in its individual and collective form is the foundation of freedom and democracy that neoliberal capitalism and right-wing forces destroy. The pluralist traditions of freedom and democracy are posing existential threats to capitalism and right-wing forces. Because both these forces depend on mass-produced essentialist and functionalist claims, which domesticates freedom and democracy as per their myopic and illiberal world view.

Moreover, neoliberalism in history shows its affinity with dictators and authoritarian governments. The neoliberal economists from the Chicago School provided all their skills to Chilean dictator Augusto Pinochet in revamping Chilean economy that ruined the lives of the masses. The American political theorist Wendy Brown in her book *In the Ruins of Neoliberalism* (2019) argued that neoliberalism laid the foundation for anti-democratic politics in the Western world by dismantling the political and social basis of individual life. Melinda Cooper in her book *Family Values: Between Neoliberalism and the New Social Conservatism* (2017) has explored the unholy alliance between neoliberalism and conservative politics. Such an alliance promotes reactionary family values and moralities, which curtails individual freedom and dignity to promote market forces. The iron lady of neoliberalism in Britain Margaret Thatcher once remarked that 'economics is the method: the object is to change the heart and soul' that is concomitant with the unchallenged interests of the market forces. Such an ideological narrative breaks down society as a mere collection of self-interested individuals. It destroys democratic solidarity and social order in pursuit of freedom for the market.

In this way, neoliberalism and non-freedom are intertwined and integral to each other. The democracies are disciplining the citizens to pursue the interests of the capital. The welfare state is being transformed into security states to protect the interests of the capitalist classes. The operant commitments of the governments are to shift power from labour to capital. Such an unfair process is taking place globally by normalising neoliberal onslaught on both individual and collective spirit of freedom. The objective is to continue the dominance of capitalism as an unchallenged global system. The propaganda machines of the capitalist classes are on overdrive to transform individuals into consumers and transform need-based society into desire-based society. Such transformations are important for the survival of capitalism. It solves internal contradictions of capitalism due to overproduction. It liberates capitalism from crisis and imprisons labour within precarity of a desire-based society in search of illusive freedom. The realisation of individual freedom and dignity depends on individuals' abilities to disentangle themselves from the economic clutches of neoliberal capitalism and political clutches of right-wing politics. There is no other way to achieve individual freedom that gives meaning to life both in its singular and collective visions.

Conclusion

Musings of the Lockdown Alternatives

The pandemic-driven lockdowns have triggered worldwide growth of unemployment, hunger, homelessness and poverty. The speed of economic descent in world economy is extraordinary. The world is sleepwalking into greater economic depression of the century and its impacts will reverberate for decades. The COVID-19-pandemic-led economic crisis has been used by ruling and non-ruling classes to reconfigure the world economy to consolidate their wealth and punish the masses by spreading economic risks, insecurities and crises. The credit and consumerism-led economic booms are no longer relevant strategies even for the short-term economic recovery due to inherent decline of trust of the masses on the existing economic and political institutions within capitalist system. The economic and political institutions within capitalism have lost their legitimacy in public eyes during this pandemic. The foundation of production, distribution, exchange and consumption are four pillars of any economic system irrespective of their ideological orientations. These four economic pillars survive on the foundation of trust. All economic activities run on the basis of trust. The level of trustworthiness determines economic revival and sustainability in all economic systems.

The deepening of capitalism and its deceptive culture of propaganda for last three centuries has eroded trust in the society, politics and economy. Trust in society is a product of interdependence whereas trust in an economic system is a production of free and open interaction between consumers and producers. The growth of capitalism led to the separation of producers from consumers, which led to the declining of the culture of trust in economy. The fourth industrial revolution led by digital capitalism has further eroded trust in economy by structurally delinking producers from the consumers. The consumerism as a project of capitalism has completely transformed economic trust into brand trust. The trust in system is transformed into trust in commodities (brands) based on its advertisement, brand value, peer acceptance and social visibility and respect. The culture of consumerism and advertisement has personalised trust. But leverage of trust in businesses and economic systems has declined over time due to the fact that trust is mutual and collective. It cannot be personalised. The corporatisation, individualisation and personalisation of trust lead to diminished trust.

The culture of forgery is rampant with the growth of digital business, which further accelerated the decline of trust even on the bands (personalised trust based on class). The banks used to be the only economic institution within capitalist economic system, which was trusted by public. But the scandals of the Wall Streets and continuous failure to protect the consumer interests in different economic crises led to fall of trust on banking systems within capitalism. The devaluation and demise of trust led to the declining of abilities of various public and private institutions dealing with economic crises. The consumers and producers feel vulnerable due to lack of trustworthiness and transparency with the growth of digital revolution in economy. So, the short- and long-term economic recovery depends on revival of trust in economic and political institutions. It demands total systemic change and disengagement with capitalism as a system and its distrustful culture of plunder in which every producer and consumer experienced deception.

Is there any way to revive public trust in economic and political institutions? Can trust be rejuvenated and re-established? Is trust building possible in the post-pandemic world? The answer to these questions is emphatically positive. There is no other answer. Trust each other to survive in peace and prosperity or perish together with the culture of distrust spread by capitalism.

The digitalisation of world economy for last three decades has entered into every aspect of economic systems. The reversal or dismantling of digital economy is neither possible nor a progressive alternative. It is important to democratise and develop cooperative models of digital economy, where the producers and consumers can participate with egalitarian openness. The direct interaction between producers and consumers can create a socially embedded market and economic system based on trust, which can ensure a sharing and caring economy free from institutional exploitation. The experience of the Mondragon Corporation as an alliance of worker cooperatives based in the Basque region of Spain offers an alternative. The core of the Mondragon success story is based on trust; the trust between producers and consumers. The sustainable trust within the Mondragon Corporation is established by its workers, who are the shareholders. The corporation is owned by the workers and managed by the workers. Therefore, trust was an organic development based on direct interaction of workers both as producers and consumers.

Such alternative experiments are completely ignored and concealed by the mainstream media, the voice of capitalism. The data-driven digital economy within contemporary capitalism promotes devaluation of trust by controlling individual data on every aspects of individual lives. There is no dignity and privacy when individual data is controlled by corporations without any form of inhibition. The capitalist systems have also formed alliance with reactionary religious and politically authoritarian forces to further control individual freedom. It intends to use reactionary aspects of religions, cultures, nationalisms and communities to enforce trust in economic and political system. Such attempts create superficial and short-term trust. It is the material conditions of people that determine the level of trust in long term. The development and enforcement of trust cannot be outsourced to reactionary religious and political forces. Trust grows organically, it cannot be reproduced by propaganda and enforced for a long time by these forces. The growth of fake news and false propaganda about products in the market and policies of the government has further eroded the culture of trust in economy and politics.

The centralisation of data-driven and data-dependent digital capitalism is accelerating treacherous world economy free from trust. The loss of citizen's trust on state and governments, loss of consumer's trust on products and loss of producer's trust on markets create a state of anarchy, which helps for the growth and consolidation of security state and authoritarian governments concomitant with the requirements of the capitalism. Such an economic and political project has failed in history. Its failure is immanent, but its social and humanitarian cost is incalculable. Therefore, it is imperative for all thinking beings to work collaboratively towards trustworthy social and economic transformations based on mutual and collective trust. It is collective trust that helps in the mobility of both labour and capital without creating barrier for each other. It is a mutual trust which can aid the economy to revive its global momentum without capitalism. Trust is the non-transactional new currency with both use and exchange value. The revival of trust in economy and politics is the answer to the multiple forms of capitalism crises. Trust is important for long-term peace and prosperity.

IN DEFENCE OF UTOPIAS

The coronavirus pandemic has forced the world into an uncharted territory, where businesses suffer with unpredictability, and people look at the future with hopeless abyss. The fragile global, national and local systems are becoming more fragile, in which risks and crisis causing esoteric turmoil in human lives. The crisis is proliferating in every step of human lives, institutions and networks. The politics has lost its direction to serve people. The power structure does not show any sign to reform itself. It is a prelude to turbulent future. It is making every effort to subvert democratic rights and freedom of people. The reactionary and right wingers are competing to overtake each other in promoting the politics of bigotry. There is growing sense of alienation among people. It is chaos and crisis that define everyday lives in the world today.

Every crisis breeds hopelessness and utopian visions both in its progressive and regressive forms. Every ideology carries certain element of utopia. The regressive utopias are based on constructed propaganda to achieve certain goals of ruling regimes and capitalist classes. The regressive forms of utopias lack imaginations. The *American Dream, Sun never sets in British empire* and *Fair and Lovely* are classic examples of unscrupulous and regressive utopias that promote capitalism, colonialism, sexism and racism. The regressive utopias obscure social, economic and political realities. It demolishes individual needs, dreams, desires and priorities. It promotes capitalism within economic systems and totalitarianism and colonialism in politics. The global capitalist utopian vision has promised prosperity for last five centuries but failed to eradicate poverty and inequalities. It accelerated the processes of marginalisation and deprivation in a world scale. There is massive growth of wealth and miseries at the same time. It indicates that capitalism is based on false propaganda. There is no vision for the people within its utopian outlook. A trail of destruction defines capitalism and all its establishments.

The establishment always frames alternative social transformations as dangerous. In the annals of history, every time the masses have challenged the power structures; they were branded as radicals and criminals. The ruling and non-ruling elites have always considered socialism, communism, democracy or any progressive ideals as dangerous utopia. History reveals that the progressive utopian ideals help human beings to recover from the crisis. So, the human search for progressive utopias and turning them into reality takes societies forward. All social, political, cultural, religious and economic transformations have followed their path in search of utopias. The emancipatory ideals drive progressive utopian visions. Hence, the regressive and conservative forces are always opposed to utopian ideals because it destabilises their worldviews based on power and privileges. Utopias can breakdown the unitary worldview of capitalism and all its affiliated philosophies.

The Austrian-born British philosopher Karl Popper who considered himself as a critical rationalist but in reality, he was a conservative-liberal philosopher. His opposition and unstructured critique of utopianism in his books *The Open Society and Its Enemies* (1945), *The Poverty of Historicism* (1957) and *Utopia and Violence* (1963) helped the growth of reductionist technocratic politics. His so-called ideas of scientific rationalism provided philosophical foundation to the neoliberal social democracy and rational choice in economics. The spirit of reason, reform, criticisms and other ideals of open society die its natural death in a capitalist system, where utopias are considered as unproductive debauchery and destructive. This is the way capitalism socialises masses and organises itself as the only viable system that destroys the very arguments of Karl Popper for open society. It is utopia that promotes open society and democratic culture. The idea of human progress owes its origin within utopia. In defence of utopia, Thomas More has written a book called *Utopia*, where he argued that 'the only authentic image of the future is, in the end, the failure of the present'. His prophetic words established utopian traditions and continue to resonate with our times even 505 years after the publication of the book.

In reality, the capitalist utopias were hidden behind limitless rules and regulations within the darkness of bureaucracy because capitalism failed to deal with everyday challenges it produces. David Graeber in his book *The Utopia of Rules* argued about the capitalist establishment's 'refusal to deal with people as they actually are'. Therefore, it tends to promote consumer culture to convert people into customers, transforms social relationship into market-led exchange relationships and individual needs into desires. These changes are the foundations of fake *American dreams* of prosperity, which demands individuals to surrender themselves within their unbound desires. The unbound desires create conditions for unfree labour, which is the core of capitalism and its illicit economy.

In the face of unfettered capitalism in alliance with right-wing and reactionary politics, and climate change across the globe, it is difficult to imagine alternative utopias to end market domination over human lives. The plight, precarity and crisis due to the outbreak of coronavirus offer fertile grounds for radical transformation of the world organised around capitalism. It depends on the quality of our utopia and commitment to transform it into reality. The struggles for democracy, universal adult suffrage, citizenship rights, women's right and right to life, liberty and equality were utopias at one point of time. The struggle of human beings transformed these utopias into realities. The utopias are not just about idealisms for the future to deal with different crisis. It is also thinking about the present issues based on past experiences. Utopias are unseen platforms of mind, where people imagine a better world than the present one. The rejection of utopias limits human imagination for better. It pushes masses into a corridor, where they lost the ability to imagine the meaning of their existence based on their own experiences. Such a process helps in naturalising and normalising 'there is no alternatives' to exploitative and unsustainable capitalist system. Utopias are not manifestos for change, but it creates open space to imagine alternatives that facilitates change in the society. In the history of ideas, utopianism played a significant role in shaping our everyday lives. It is impossible to live with the challenges of the present and imagine the future without the utopias.

The coronavirus pandemic has revealed the capitalist delusions. It pushed human lives into disposable body bags. It is proved that deaths and destitutions are integral to capitalism. Therefore, the mosaic of progressive utopias needs to seek social, political, economic and ecological transformations to face the challenges of today and outline a sustainable future based on peace and prosperity.

IN DEFENCE OF LOVE JIHAD

'Love jihad' is an abhorrent, insidious, reactionary, patriarchal, misogynist and anti-Muslim political project of Hindutva forces to undermine liberal, secular and constitutional democratic society in India. The freedom to love and marry in India is a part of the right to life and liberty guaranteed by the Indian Constitution. It is further fortified by the Special Marriage Act (1954), which upholds the secular character of individual right to love and marry outside one's own religion and caste. The secular, democratic and constitutional rights are antithetical to religious lunatics. It is a threat to their well-established hierarchical authority over people. It is opposed to their unnatural and unscientific approach to life, love, marriage and society. So, the perverted Hindutva forces and their right-wing religious brethren among Muslims, Christians, Sikhs and casteist moral police find themselves in same boat opposing youthful spirit of Indians to love and marry outside their medieval social, religious and cultural order. These reactionary forces are the soul of honour killings. India's latest National Crime Records Bureau (NCRB) report has revealed that honour killings are growing rapidly due to these religious and caste lunatics.

The state and governments are supposed to be secular and protect the constitutional rights of Indian citizens. But in reality, the Hindutva-led governments are pandering to the beastly instincts of these right-wing religious, cultural, social and political groups. The BJP-ruled states are planning to bring legislation to make 'love jihad' illegal. The BJP and its debauched Hindutva family considers 'love jihad' as a trap of Muslim men to marry Hindu women and convert them into Islam, which will change Indian demography. Such Hindutva bogey of Islamophobic propaganda is not only statistically false but also dangerous for civil liberties of all Indians irrespective of their religious and caste backgrounds. The objective of such ideological propaganda is to malign Muslim communities and ensure caste-based hierarchal and hegemonic Hindu social, political and religious order, which is concomitant with other religious right-wing forces. The law against 'love jihad' is primarily against freedom of youth. It is fundamentally against progressive social and political transformation towards an egalitarian society in India.

'Love jihad' derives its ideological inspiration from the bigoted writings of M.S. Golwalkar and his ideas outlined in his book *We, or Our Nationhood Redefined*. Golwalkar has argued for purity of Hindu race. The Hindutva forces like Rashtriya Swayamsevak Sangh (RSS), Bajrang Dal, the Vishwa Hindu Parishad (VHP), Akhil Bharati Vidyarthi Parishad (ABVP) and BJP are following the footprints of Golwalkar and his reactionary ideals. The Brahmanical Hindu purity project of Hindutva derives its intellectual strength from the fraudulent works of U. N. Mukherji and particularly his book *Hindus: A Dying Race* was an inspiration for the Hindu Maha Sabha. The campaign against 'love jihad' by the Hindutva fascists today resembles the assertive mass mobilisation of Hindus by the Arya Samaj and other reactionary Hindu revivalist organisations during 1920s. The purification movement led by several Hindu organisations during that period echoes today. Love jihad is an extension of purity of Hindu race based on Brahmanical and patriarchal caste order, where women and men are subservient to its social, cultural, religious and political hegemony.

The perverted Hindutva forces watch porn in state assemblies, rape women, maim and lynch fellow Muslim citizens in the name of cultural and religious nationalism but preach about protecting women from 'love jihad'. There is a striking similarity between Muslim and Hindu fundamentalists when it comes to the idea of love and marriage. Their method of command and control of individual freedom follows similar ideological pattern. The goal of these religious groups is to oppose equality and liberty of individuals in the matters of their everyday lives. The spectre of love hunts the religious and right-wing groups because love is a great equaliser in the society.

The narrow silo of religion and capitalism destroys all material and spiritual foundations of love and life. Both capitalism and feudal religious forces institutionalise love for reproduction. In capitalism, love depends on caste, class and racial compatibilities to preserve their inheritance with the help of marriage for reproduction, accumulation, dominance and preservation. The religious forces promote love as an idea of purity and honour confined within women in particular and men in general. These forces tend to locate purity and honour in food habits, dress, body and sexuality. The domestication of love and its institutionalisation is central to both capitalism and feudal religious forces. It destroys human beings' organic love and relationship with fellow human beings, nature and animals.

Love jihad need to be a social, cultural, religious and political project of all progressive, liberal and democratic forces in the society. Interfaith, interreligious, inter-racial, inter-caste and community marriages are central to defeat the reactionary religious order, which reinforces and sustains all forms of inequalities. Therefore, struggle for equality is a struggle to defend the idea of 'love jihad'. Love is the only way to overcome different caste, class and gender barriers. Love can only create shared space of peace and collective security. Love can only defeat the capitalist project of commodification of human lives and liberties. Love can only defeat capitalist pandemic of loneliness and help human beings to overcome alienation in a capitalist society.

The collective struggle in defence of 'love jihad' is important to reject Hindutva-led Islamophobia and ensure Indian youth's constitutional right to love and marry whomever they like and divorce whenever they want. Love and relationships are not supposed to be a non-living entity or unchangeable commodity in the name of stability, family and society. 'Love jihad' is a potential weapon against all forms of bigotry. Love can be used as a tool of all emancipatory struggles. Love, live and laugh to launch a continuous and united struggle against all religious and reactionary forces for the sake of peace and survival of human lives. In every pages of history, love always wins and the power of kings and their empires always failed in survival test of time. Love survives within all odds of time.

LIMITS OF PURITANISM

The principles and ideological commitments in politics, culture, religion and social practices breed culture of puritanism both in its progressive and regressive forms. The transformation of society to lead an exemplary life is the core in the politics of puritanism as a movement of divinity. Both right-wing reactionaries and left-wing radicals use puritanism-like applied theology to the concerns of their followers. The confident control of individual conscience and sanctification in the name of purity is central to this gradual and subtle process of puritan socialisation. Such puritan praxis shapes individual rights, liberties, duties and obligations for the society, state, community and family in different stages of history. The puritan provocations change with the change of time, place and public opinion but certain unchanging core doctrinal elements of puritanism continue to exist in spite of growth of science and technology. In the idea of purity of race, religion, gender, sexuality, caste, language, region and nationalism, the puritans use core doctrinal elements to appeal to public for its legitimacy. The purity and coherence between thoughts and actions are central to the core of puritanism, which individuals and communities tend to practise as daily discipline in matters of all forms of relationships and interactions. Puritanism as an ideological force has influenced religious, cultural, political, secular, liberal, conservative and radical trends in the society.

The religious, right-wing and reactionary puritans have relied heavily on the idea of god and nationalism in their effort to exercise political authority, influence government policies and control the state by forming informal and voluntary associations with missionary spirit. It is the idea of god and religion that works as the core and heart of puritanism. Religions provide ideological foundation to puritanism as an ideology of conformism, which emphasised on 'work is god and god is truth' for salvation. Such a narrow puritan essence has helped to hinder working-class abilities to embrace emancipatory ideals of their own consciousness from their own work and workplace. Further, the religious puritanism has destroyed the organic relationship between the 'work' and 'worker' by converting it into a contractual language of 'Covenant of Works' and the 'Covenant of Grace' in Christianity. The spiritual relationship between the 'work' and the 'worker' was further destroyed by asking for desire-free work (Niskama Karma) in Hindu religion as outlined in the Bhagavad Gita. All major world religions follow this pattern of theological arguments, which are adopted by puritanism and its advocates. Any deviation is regarded as sin; a path towards hell and blind following is sacred; a path towards heaven. In this process, the glorification of god, complete surrender to work, unquestionable truth and morality has become the core of right-wing puritanism that helps to domesticate individual freedom, individual labour and community space in the service of power – rulers, industrialists and capitalists.

Similarly, the radical sectarians and democratic dissenters have also reconfigured puritanism as a revolutionary ideology of counterculture led by marginalised communities to transform existing social, political and economic order. The mechanical understanding of historical transformations and conceptualisation of revolutionary processes follow certain outdated and unchanging narratives like puritans. Class struggle as a revolutionary project needs to get away from the orientation of puritanism. Class struggle often demands political and ideological manoeuvres within different contexts. It is an adultery of ideas, people and strategies to uphold working-class values and interests. The revolutionary organisational structure, its mechanisms and style of functioning need to get away from everything that disciplines individuals and their creativity abilities. The idea of disciplining is the core of puritanism that drags revolutionary processes into the reactionary puritan path. The individuals find themselves in an environment of disorientation; be it in religious congregations or in revolutionary political projects. Puritanism provides simple and readymade answers to higher questions guided by puritan morality. In this way, puritanism and its frameworks create a theological understanding of human life and natural world. Puritanism discourages individuals for scientific scrutiny and inquiry into existing knowledge and its advancement.

The re-emergence of religious puritanism and its right-wing avatars are product of this larger philosophical terrain, which is concomitant with capitalism and its hegemonic control over individuals and communities. The domesticated labour is a central requirement for the growth of capitalism. The religious puritanism can only create conformist and subservient individuals. Therefore, capitalism promotes authoritarian and religious right-wing force in politics and society to nourish conformist and domesticated individuals, who live with limited resources with unlimited manufactured desires. The gap between reality and desire is so vast that individuals fall in line to fulfil the gaps in their life. Puritanism itself is a desire that exploits such a situation of unnecessary emptiness created by the capitalist system to control individuals and communities.

Puritanism fortifies the spirit of capitalism and ensures the survival of unequal economic relationships based on social and religious morality. The religious foundations of puritanism shape everyday lives by controlling our choices and freedoms in the name of morality devoid of any substance and materiality. Puritanism as a movement, it has sanctified the ruling class's virtues as natural social and political order. The ideas of subordination, hierarchy, exploitations and inequalities are normalised within puritan frameworks of divine order. In this way, puritanism is a detrimental ideology, which is against progressive social and political transformations. It is within this context, it is important to reject all forms of puritan ideals to pave a clear path for scientific inquiry for the advancement of knowledge for social and political change.

IN SEARCH OF 'UNITY, SOLIDARITY AND PEACE' IN A FRAGILE WORLD

The horrors of deaths, destitutions and common vulnerabilities due to the pestilence of COVID-19 have brought back the ideals of universal unity, peace and solidarity into the centre stage of a fragile world. These ideals are historically proved shelter during every crisis created by colonial, imperialist and reactionary nationalist adventures during nineteenth century, and productivist plunders of capitalism during twentieth and twenty-first centuries. The coronavirus pandemic has intensified the planetary dimensions of capitalist crisis that never experienced before in the world history. The crisis that the world is facing today is not a product of COVID-19, but it has only helped to deepen the existing structural crisis within capitalist system, which engineered to benefit the few at the cost of humanity. It is not an unavoidable destiny designed by the god. It is designed by few people and their concerted effort to control the productive and creative power of labour and natural resources across the world. There is massive growth of military infrastructure to pursue the objective of controlling human being by brute force.

The Bastille fortress prison was reduced to rubbles in Paris during the forward march of French Revolution with the ideals of equality and liberty that established unity among people. The solidarity of European workers with the people fighting against European colonialism had led to the deepening of democracy, freedom and equality. It has also confirmed that the ideals of transnational unity based on international solidarity are possible among the majority of people. The ruthless dictators, fascists and authoritarian leaders did not find a safe place to survive. The radical democratic movements have ended the enormous power of the kings and queens. All empires from Ottomans, Romans to British Empire collapsed in history and all dictators were defeated by people in search of peace.

The twenty-first-century world is experiencing new wave of authoritarian regimes seeking to enforce their reactionary visions on society, diminishing individual liberty and fraternity. It also promotes narrow religious, political and cultural cults that dismantle unity among people. The threat to humanity and universal peace continues to grow as the authoritarian regimes increase their military expenditure and reduced expenditure on health, education and other human welfare programmes. According to a report published by The Stockholm International Peace Research Institute (SIPRI), the total global military expenditure was $1917 billion in 2019. It shows 3.6 per cent rise of military expenditure from 2018 which was largest growth in a decade. The report published on 27 April 2020 revealed further that the total global military spending constitutes of 2.2 per cent of Global Gross Domestic Product (GGDP) in 2019. It is approximately $249 (Rs. 18,590.84) per person. The countries like the United States, China, India, Russia and Saudi Arabia are five largest spenders and account for 62 per cent of global expenditure. The China and India are among top three military spenders in the middle of the COVID-19 crisis.

The international disarmament treaties are falling apart. The international mechanisms to control arms trade is collapsing. The states and governments are increasing their defence budget. The world is facing global arms race in the middle of a disastrous pandemic. The growing military expenditure is an instrument of authoritarian regimes to impose order to be in power. But bombs and bullets did not help the society to progress. It is peace that established societies, states, families and individual lives. It is within this context, the struggle for peace is a weapon to end wars and military expenditures by which the states and societies can invest in the dignity of lives and prosperity of human health and education.

The world is confronting many annihilating challenges accelerated by the COVID-19 crisis. It is clear that the business-as-usual approach within existing political, economic and social structures cannot face the challenges. The states and governments irrespective of their political ideology work under a capitalist framework, that uses authoritarian strategies of terror, fear and repression directed towards the working-class population in different parts of the world. The national and global institutional architectures have failed to provide any form of alternatives to capitalism, which reproduces inequalities and exploits both labour and nature. The pandemic-led lockdown revealed the dialectical relationship between capitalism, patriarchy, reactionary religious fundamentalist forces and market domination on society. It is an alliance that plunders the world and puts humanity in danger. The regional, local and national march towards emancipation from such a regime is impossible. Therefore, it is time to think again in universal terms for all the people irrespective of their race, sexuality, gender, class, caste, religious and regional differences. In order to overcome the challenges of differences, it is important to build unity between different sections of society based on common experiences, vulnerabilities and dreams. The potential for unity among masses depend on collective consciousness and commitment to stand in solidarity with marginalised population and their struggles around the world.

However, the world has experienced and recovered from ruinous fragilities in history due to human commitment to the values of unity, solidarity and peace. It is time to sketch out the plans to reinforce these ideals to fortify the future and survive the present. The universal reconstitution of society, economy and politics is unavoidable necessity to face the contemporary challenges beyond pandemic. It is important to understand and acknowledge unfairly structured social, political and economic systems that grossly distort the word in which majority of people suffer for the pleasure of few. There are different economic, political and economic hierarchies based on different layers of privileges. The people who are the beneficiaries of such a system of privileges perpetuate inequality, discrimination and exploitation. The untangling of entitlement culture based on gender, race, sexuality, caste and class is important. Because this uncanny culture of entitlement has the capacity to survive within all ideological formations of state and governance, it produces privileged homo economicus which serves to uphold the capitalist system that endangers equality and liberty. There will be no unity, solidarity and peace without equality and liberty.

The world is prosperous enough to end poverty, hunger and homelessness but wealth is concentrated in the hands of few. The democratisation and community management of resources is the first step towards a sustainable future. The ecological justice and egalitarian distribution of wealth with universal values can ensure the progress for all, and establish unity, solidarity and peace. There is no other way but to perish together if the fragilities of world continue to grow. The peaceful coexistence is the only alternative. Therefore, the future of world depends on struggle for peace based on unity and solidarity.

LIMITS OF INTERSECTIONALITY
AND GLOBAL SIGNIFICANCE OF
#BLACKLIVESMATTER MOVEMENTS

On 25 May 2020, Derek Chauvin, a white American police officer, killed George Floyd, a forty-six-year-old black man in Minneapolis, Minnesota. It was on a broad daylight, the police officer pressed his knee on Floyd's neck like a coward trophy hunter. There were eighteen complaints against Mr Chauvin, the killer police officer. He is the first white officer to be charged for the murder of a black civilian in Minnesota. Eric Garner was killed by another white police officer in New York on 17 July 2014. 'I Can't Breathe' were the last words of both George Floyd and Eric Garner before their death. These are among many institutional murders that sparked worldwide protects against racism. It revealed the inherent and institutional structures of racism in the United States. The last words of George and Eric 'I Can't Breathe' did not die with them. These words became anthems of anti-racism protests and social justice movements worldwide.

The #BlackLivesMatter movement which emerged during 2013 continues to campaign against racism within and outside the United States. The #BlackLivesMatter movement derives its inspiration from historic political struggles for equality, liberty and justice. It continues to represent the legacies of historic anti-colonial struggles, civil rights movement, other progressive and radical social and political movements. The protests across the United States, European and other cities across the world depict racial discrimination, frustration and despair of the people of colour in the face of pervasive racism in different parts of the world. The black, Asian and minority ethnic communities face different forms of institutionalised discrimination and structural violence in their everyday lives in different parts of the United States, Europe and Asia. The white supremacy as an ideal owes its origin within the historical events of transatlantic slavery and European colonialism that still informs and underpins racial and other forms of discrimination within and outside the Western world. Therefore, movements like #BlackLivesMatter carry global significance.

The #BlackLivesMatter movement also opens up wounds of all other forms of discrimination in different societies across the world. The discrimination against Muslims, Kashmiris, lower caste Dalits and tribals in India; non-Bengalis and religious minorities in Bangladesh, Ahmadis, Baluch; Hindus, Sikhs and Christians in Pakistan; Tamils in Sri Lanka; Rohingyas in Myanmar; Tibetans and Uighur Muslims in China; and other forms of discrimination based on gender, sexualities, dress and food habits are unadulterated realities of our unequal capitalist world. The forward march towards an egalitarian and non-discriminatory world depends on people's resolve to fight against all forms of discrimination based on prejudice.

There is global upsurge of right-wing politics and reactionary movements, which patronise the politics of hate and othering. It breeds discrimination, violence and inequalities in different parts of the world. The liberal and right-wing commentators offer Eurocentric Lockean social contract as an alternative to re-establish peace and social order based on ideals of hierarchy and domination. The progressive, democratic and emancipatory political forces and their movements are divided on different ideological sectarian lines. The social, cultural, religious, racial, gender and economic divisions in the society echo within the weak and divided emancipatory political struggles. Many radicals, socialists and progressive movements consider identity politics the cultural logic of failed capitalism. They argue that identity politics destroys the unity of the working classes and marginalised communities fight against capitalism system. In reality, these two ideological trends of progressive and radical movements need to understand that race, ethnicity, gender and class intersect with each other within a capitalist system. Intersectionality helps to understand the existence of multiple and overlapping forms of exploitation, violence and oppression. This realisation is important to develop clear emancipatory political strategies.

The intersectionality of race, gender, class, caste, sexuality and other marginalised communities are important indicators to understand different layers of exploitations and oppressions within the hierarchy of capitalist systems. The different forms of identities-based discrimination, oppression and exploitation exist not in separation but in unity with different structures and processes of capitalism. The politics of intersectionality ignores the role of pre-existing unequal social relations in shaping conditions of production and reproduction within capitalism. The failure of class politics and defeat of revolutionary movements during 1990s led to the rise of intersectionality as an approach to understand exploitation and discrimination based on personal characteristics of individuals, that is, race, gender, sexuality, caste, region, territoriality and ethnicity. The postmodern and post-structural theories provide the ideological foundation to intersectionality identity politics.

The idea of intersectionality attempts to find alternatives within existing capitalist system that reproduces the gender-, caste- and race-based inequalities and exploitations results in precarity and proletarianisation. The existing architype of intersectionality debates and discourses have failed to locate the fluidity of power relations and sites of struggles against identity-based violence, exploitations, dominance and discriminations within and outside the communities. The intersectionality approach to movement is ahistorical as it does not look at the inherent and historical roots of different forms of exploitation with capitalism. So, deradicalisation is an inadvertent outcome of intersectionality as a political approach to emancipatory struggles.

The critiques of intersectionality do not reject and disregard the realities of multiple forms of power structure that exploits, discriminates and kills on the basis of individual identities. The ideas of identities are not just about atomised, abstract and individual self-reflections. It also involves individual identity's organic relationship and interactions with environment and fellow beings. The individuals build relationships with others to fulfil one's own desires and needs that give meaning to their lives. This generates the foundation of collective identity based on voluntary but natural relationships. These relationships are territorialised and de-territorialised by multiple identities created and destroyed as per the requirements of the neoliberal capitalism under globalisation. For example, the identity issues of displaced person, refugees, internal and external migrants and so on are direct or indirect products of capitalism. So, there are material conditions that shape identity politics. The mindless criticisms of identity politics are also dangerous. It is important to separate two different ideological trends of identity politics.

The growth of European reactionary nationalist politics led by the *British Nationalist Party* and *English Defence League* in the UK, *UKIP* in England, the *National Front* in France, *New Dawn* in Greece and *Jobbik* in Hungary are classic examples of reactionary identity politics that promotes cultural logic of failed capitalism. The politics of higher caste Hindus led by the BJP in India and white supremacists in Europe and America are reactionary identity politics, which needs to be discarded. The *Scottish Nationalist Party (SNP)* follows both regressive and progressive aspects of identity politics which adds to the complexities of identity politics. The four centuries of globalisation led to the normalisation of precarity, and the emancipatory labour and trade union movements have become wage-bargaining movements promoting representative careerism in the name of affirmative actions. Such approach helps in hiding the institutional discriminatory practices of capitalist structures led by the patriarchy of white supremacists in Europe and Americas and Brahmanical Hindu caste order in Indian subcontinents.

The Dalit and tribal movements in India, LGBTQ movements, anti-racist movements, women's movements and indigenous communities' movements to save their land, livelihood and forests are emancipatory identity politics. Therefore, it is important to embrace progressive aspects of identity politics, develop intersectionality and transcend differences as a political strategy to strengthen emancipatory struggles for liberty, equality, justice and fraternity. The progressive ideological engagements with intersectionality politics can reduce the isolationist approach of identity politics. It is impossible to fight racial, gender and caste discrimination without fighting capitalism. The academic left and their privileged politics must get on with it without creating further mirage of theoretical complexities. The struggle against racism, patriarchy, caste, sexism and all other forms of discriminations and exploitations are struggles against capitalism. Let the everyday realities of people with their subjective and objective conditions guide an organised and united struggle for alternatives to all dehumanising structures of capitalism. Finally, as the significance of the #BlackLivesMatter movement goes global with its open and inclusive approach, it is important to call for a border-less revolutionary internationalism based on experiences of local sites of struggles against all forms of inequalities, injustices and exploitations. The local, national, regional and global alliance of revolutionary collectives can only help in democratising the world and ensure peace and prosperity for one and all.

SIGNIFICANCE OF PROTEST AGAINST POWER FOR HUMAN PROGRESS

As social, economic and political Darwinism dominates the intellectual debates and discourses to naturalise and normalise capitalist exploitation and inequalities, survival of the fittest is becoming the new normal. The best human qualities based on love, peace, sympathies, empathies and coexis-tence are becoming the signs of human weakness in the rat race success and survival. In this process, human beings are becoming mechanised where life has become a project to achieve. Human beings are becoming orderly objects shaped by the market forces of capitalism, where success means achievements. The reversal of such a system is possible and important for the survival of all. The present and future of humanity depends on our abilities to protect the achievements and protest the ruinous capitalist path. History is the witness to achievements of protests against power by common people.

The time has come again to celebrate the idea of protest and sketch its sig-nificance in the history of human progress. Protests are individual or group expression of dissent both in its violent and non-violent forms. It expresses itself in the form of writings, poems, singing, rallies, demonstrations, resis-tance movements and revolutionary struggles. The history of protest is as old as the history of human civilisation. It is the protests against social, economic, political, religious and cultural power structures that shaped the idea of free-dom and human progress towards twenty-first century. The ideas of human freedom from bondages of slavery, feudalism, colonialism and capitalism are products of protests. The ideals of democracy, liberty, equality and fraternity are the products of different struggles in history. From French Revolution, October Revolution, anti-colonial struggles to women's movement and envi-ronmental movements in Asia, Africa, Americas and Europe revealed that protest against power is human progress. The organised and unorganised protests put pressures and pursue human beings to accept, accommodate and advance change. In this sense, protest is a powerful tradition of change that shapes our present and assures better future.

All these ideals of human progress are at the crossroads today. The uncertainties of today and questions of better future confront everyone. The rise of authoritarian states and governments, right-wing politics, reactionary religious forces, conservative leaderships, environmental catastrophes and wars are integral to capitalism, which undermines human lives and progressive values. Capitalism as an economic, social, political and cultural system is based on deception. It is corrosive as well. Is there any alternative to this worldwide capitalist system? The liberal, conservative and capitalist intellectuals argue that 'there is no alternative' to capitalism. Such an argument derives its philosophical foundation from Darwinian philosophy. They argue that deception and survival of the fittest is not unique to capitalism. It is a part of the natural world and integral to human evolution. So, capitalism cannot be immune to deceptions, inequalities, exploitations, deaths and destitutions. Such normalisation of reactionary trends in economy and society are accelerated by religious and political forces to re-establish capitalist world order in a post-pandemic world.

There are three trends of protest movements today. The first trend of protests demands to restore the past and celebrate all reactionary orders in the society based on patriarchy, feudalism, racism, superstitions and hierarchy. These protest movements today hide behind nationalism to achieve their goals. They use ethnic, cultural and religious idioms to popularise their reactionary goals. Even the progressive forces fall into these narrow populist and bigoted nationalist strands of protest movements. The second trend is the liberal version of the protest movements that intends to reform, revise and restore the capitalist order with a human face or compassionate capitalism as they call it. The liberal version is a dichotomous myopia that helps in maintaining the hegemony of the old and powerful forces of capitalism. There is very little qualitative difference between the reactionary forces of the first trend and the liberal version of the second trend. The liberal outlook is irrelevant as capitalist system does not show any sign that the system can be reformed. The third trend of protest movements is universalist, progressive, democratic and egalitarian in its approach. It demands a complete radical change of society. The third tend of the protest movements have shaped historic transformations of society and continue to inspire human progress. But these movements are in the weakest ebb of their own history but strongest alternative available based on historical experiences. The human progress depends on reviving the revolutionary protest movements with universal appeal to save humanity from different disasters ingrained within capitalism. The prelude to the post-pandemic world shows very regressive trends of human history. It is time to unlock and revive the power of human potentials for revolutionary protest movements for a sustainable future.

The predatory nature of capitalism cannot be reformed and revised as liberals claim. The predatory capitalism reproduces itself in different forms that promote consumerism in one place and religious fundamentalism in another place. It forms alliances with democratic and dictatorial forces at the same time. It can take the shape of social democracy in Europe and neoliberal authoritarianism in Asia and Africa. It is not an article of faith but systematic treadmill of miseries of the masses within capitalism in different forms. This is the revealing feature of capitalism over last three centuries. The world is in a very critical moment in its history. The revolutionary reconstitution of our society is the only alternative. As Rosa Luxemburg warned, the choice is between socialism and barbarism. The history is the witness to human prosperity and progress due to the sustained power of protest movements for progressive change. It is time to reclaim the history of protest movements to revive its present and fortify our future. If the progressive, democratic, socialist and left forces fail to organise successful protest against capitalist order, the future of humanity would decent into the barbaric stage of capitalism. Peace, solidarity and unity are three weapons of revolutionary protest movements against capitalist order which destroys our planet and our future. The collective and democratic struggle against capitalism and all its power structures is our only chance to ensure peace and prosperity for all.

THE TWIN ESSENCE OF OUR TIMES

The pestilence of COVID-19 has not only revealed the failures of capitalism but also exuberated over all institutions of capitalism. The culture of crisis and conflicts are organic to capitalism. Capitalist systems are antithetical to the idea of peace, prosperity and stability. The coronavirus-infused lockdown is a time to reflect on emanating crisis and conflicts across the world. Some capitalist predicaments are temporary, but most of them are annihilating for people and the planet. The capitalist crisis is producing meaninglessness of life and alienating environment, which treats people and planet as orderly objects to consolidate and expand the empire of profit. The profit-driven economy produces compliance culture of politics that destroys the idea of democracy and individual freedom to uphold the interests of the market forces.

The assaults on democracy, secularism, multiculturalism, reason, science, peace and stability have become everyday affairs within capitalism. The clients of Davos priests and capitalist powers led by Brussels, Westminster and Washington are on overdrive to reverse the trend, but they have failed to provide basic health, education, employment and food as fundamental rights. The dignity of life and citizenship rights is in shatters under capitalism. Capitalism and all its institutions are trying to recover from the crisis by expanding its support for imperialist wars, neocolonial modes of resource exploitation, authoritarian politics and reactionary religious forces in the society. These capitalist methods of survival put people and planet in danger. It diverts progressive nature of class conflicts with reactionary nationalist and religious forces. It obscures the future of humanity.

The world is facing major humanitarian crises today due to wars, global warming, pandemic and loss of sources of livelihoods for the survival of the masses. These crises owe their origin within capitalism as a result of over-exploitation of nature and human beings. Scarcity, famine, natural disasters are natural outcomes of profit-fetishised capitalist system, which reproduces crises and accelerates hunger, homelessness, poverty, inequalities and exploitation in world scale. Capitalism survives by destroying the creative abilities of individuals and regenerative abilities of nature. Therefore, capitalism cannot offer any form of alternatives for sustainable future of humanity.

As advanced capitalist countries in Europe and America suffer under capitalism and the pandemic of coronavirus, the countries like China, Cuba and Vietnam show their commitments and abilities to contain COVID-19 and ensure public health, security and safety of human lives. Socialist experiments with all their limitations show that people's lives are more important than profit-driven economic system. Therefore, it is time to revive alternative politics by expanding working-class struggles by forming local, regional, national and international alliances with all democratic, liberal and progressive forces all over the world. The sustainability of working-class struggle within a progressive path depends on the quality and size of the revolutionary communist parties to guide them. History of working-class struggles reveals that only revolutionary communist parties can transform class consciousness into class organisations and class struggles.

The future of people and survival of the planet depends on our abilities to organise people and communities under the red flag to overthrow capitalism. Communism is the only alternative to celebrate democracy and individual freedom in real sense, whereas capitalism promotes fictitious freedom and market democracy. It is only communists who can overcome narrow silos and develop class unity of intersectionality to fight different layers of exploitation and inequalities based on gender, race, caste, religion and sexualities. The class unity and struggles acknowledge individual differences and uniqueness. It is only communists who fight for a nuclear-free world. Communists fight for a world free from war, exploitation and inequalities. There is no other party, group or ideology but communists who talk about humanism, peace, prosperity, people and planet without borders. The current crisis is an opportunity to campaign for a bigger communist party based on mass struggles to ensure an alternative to capitalism. Peace within a communist society or perish within capitalism are two available paths. The choice is clear before us. There is no future within capitalism.

The twentieth century experienced the sparks of alternatives to capitalism with the rise of anti-colonial, anti-capitalist, anti-fascists and anti-war working-class struggles for peace and democracy. Each of these struggles were organised and led by the working classes in Asia, Africa, Americas, Europe and Oceania. The twenty-first century is the time to demand and reclaim the ideological perspectives and historical legacies of working-class struggles often led by the socialists and communists all over the world. The forward march of equality, liberty, fraternity and justice depends on our abilities to organise ourselves and fight against all forms of reactionary ideas and institutions established by capitalist system.

From the rice fields of Asia and Africa to the supermarket shop floors of America and Europe, it is only the working classes work and endure all the pain within the bondages of capitalism. The working classes can also organise themselves for their own freedom from capitalism that exploits them. The working-class consciousness, courage, discipline, endurance, morality and understandings are exceptional qualities in human history. Therefore, it is only the working classes, who can establish a just world free from exploitation and inequalities. A consistent, continuous and strong working-class struggle and a bigger communist party are twin necessities of our time. There is no other way but to fight locally, provincially and nationally to reclaim lost working-class glories of internationalism based on peace, solidarity and prosperity.

Bibliography

Bartolf, Christian, and Dominique Miething. "Gustav Landauer and the revolutionary principle of non-violent non-cooperation." In *The German Revolution and Political Theory*, pp. 215–235. Palgrave Macmillan, Cham, 2019.

Basu, Anustup. *Hindutva as Political Monotheism*. Duke University Press, 2020.

Bellman, Jonathan. "Indian resonances in the British Invasion, 1965-1968." *Journal of Musicology* 15, no. 1 (1997): 116–136.

Bellman, Jonathan. *The exotic in Western Music*. UPNE, 1998.

Bennett, Stuart, David S. Moon, Nick Pearce, and Sophie Whiting. "Labouring under a delusion? Scotland's national questions and the crisis of the Scottish Labour Party." *Territory, Politics, Governance* (2020): 1–19.

Bernays, E. *Propaganda*. Horace Liveright, New York, 1928.

Bohrer, Ashley. "Intersectionality and Marxism: A critical historiography." *Historical Materialism* 26, no. 2 (2018): 46–74.

Brown, Wendy. *In the ruins of neoliberalism: the rise of antidemocratic politics in the West*. Columbia University Press, 2019.

Burke, Edmund. "*A Vindication of Natural Society*. 1756." Glasgow: Fontana, 1975.

Burke, Edmund. *Philosophical Enquiry Into the Sublime and Beautiful: And Other Pre-Revolutionary Writings*. Penguin Books, 1999.

Busby, Thomas. "The Age of Genius." *A Satire on the Times* 8 (1786).

Call, Charles T. "The fallacy of the 'Failed State'." *Third World Quarterly* 29, no. 8 (2008): 1491–1507.

Christodoulaki, Ioanna. "The Rise of the Golden Dawn in Greece: Austerity and Its Impact on Democracy," edited by John Stone Rutledge Dennis Polly Rizova Xiaoshuo Hou In *The Wiley Blackwell Companion to Race, Ethnicity, and Nationalism*, pp. 227–243, 2020.

Clayton, Martin. "*Musical renaissance and Its Margins in England and India, 1874–1914*." Ashgate, 2007.

Cleland, Jamie. "Charismatic leadership in a far-right movement: an analysis of an English defence league message board following the resignation of Tommy Robinson." *Social Identities* 26, no. 1 (2020): 48–60.

Clements, Ernest. *Introduction to the study of Indian music.* London; New York: Longmans, Green, 1913.

Cooper, Melinda. *Family values: Between neoliberalism and the New Social Conservatism.* MIT Press, 2017.

Dave, Dhaval M., Andrew I. Friedson, Kyutaro Matsuzawa, Joseph J. Sabia, and Samuel Safford. *Black Lives Matter protests, social distancing, and COVID-19.* No. w27408. National Bureau of Economic Research, 2020.

Davis, Courtney, and John Abraham. *Unhealthy Pharmaceutical Regulation: Innovation, politics and Promissory Science.* Palgrave MacMillan, New York, 2013.

Desai, Radhika. "Marx's critical political economy, 'Marxist economics' and actually occurring revolutions against capitalism." *Third World Quarterly* (2020): 41: 1–18.

Eggemeier, Matthew T. *Against Empire: Ekklesial Resistance and the Politics of Radical Democracy*, Vol. 25. Wipf and Stock Publishers, 2020.

Fox-Strangways, Arthur Henry. *The music of Hindustan.* Mittal Publications, 1914.

Fromm, Erich. *Escape from freedom.* Macmillan, 1994.

Fukuyama, Francis. *The End of History and the Last Man.* Free Press, New York, 1992.

Fukuyama, Francis. *Trust: The Social Virtues and the Creation of Prosperity.* Free Press, 1995.

Fukuyama, Francis. *The Great Disruption: Human Nature and the Reconstitution of Social Order.* Free Press, New York, 1999.

Fukuyama, Francis. *The Origins of Political Order: From Prehuman Times to the French Revolution.* Farrar, Straus and Giroux, New York, 2011.

Fukuyama, Francis. *Political Order and Political Decay: From the Industrial Revolution to the Present Day.* Farrar, Straus and Giroux, New York, 2014.

Fukuyama, Francis. *Identity: The Demand for Dignity and the Politics of Resentment.* Farrar, Straus and Giroux, New York, 2018.

Golwalkar, M.S. "*Bunch of thoughts.*" Sahitya Sindu Prakashana, Bangalore, 2015.

Golwalkar, M.S. *Shri Guruji Samagra Darshan*, Vol. 4. Bharatiya Vichar Sadhana, 1974.

Golwalkar, M.S. *We or Our Nationhood Defined.* Bharat Publications, Nagpur, 1939.

Graeber, David. *Debt: The first 5000 years.* Penguin UK, 2012.

Graeber, David. *The utopia of rules: On technology, stupidity, and the Secret Joys of bureaucracy.* Melville House, 2015.

György, Károly. "Hungarian right-wing populism: nothing is what it seems." *International Union Rights* 27, no. 1–2 (2020): 12–13.

Haidt, Jonathan. *The Righteous Mind: Why Good People are divided by politics and religion.* Vintage, 2012.

Hancox, Dan. *The Village Against the world.* Verso Books, 2013.

Hayek, Friedrich August. *The road to serfdom: Text and documents: The Definitive Edition.* Routledge, 2014.

Hill, Jonathan. "Beyond the other? A postcolonial critique of the failed state thesis." *African identities* 3, no. 2 (2005): 139–154.

Hoffmann, Anna Lauren. "Where fairness fails: data, algorithms, and the limits of antidiscrimination discourse." *Information, Communication & Society* 22, no. 7 (2019): 900–915.

Huntington S.P. *The Clash of Civilizations and the Remaking of World Order*. Simon and Schuster, New York, 1996.

Huntington S.P. The clash of civilizations? In: Crothers L., Lockhart C. (eds), *Culture and Politics*. Palgrave Macmillan, New York, 2000.

Jahn, Egbert. "Is the policy of non-violence of Mohandas K. Gandhi a unique phenomenon, or is it of universal significance?." In *War and Compromise Between Nations and States*, pp. 97–115. Springer, Cham, 2020.

Kacki, Sacha. "Digging up the victims of the Black death" *Waiting for the End of the World? New Perspectives on Natural Disasters in Medieval Europe* (2020).

Kautsky, Karl. *Thomas More and His Utopia: With a Historical Introduction*. Lawrence and Wishart, 1979.

Kelly, Alfred H. "Darwinism and the working class in Wilhelmian Germany." In *Political Symbolism in Modern Europe*, pp. 146–167. Routledge, 2020.

Kissinger, Henry. "Henry Kissinger on the assembly of a New World Order." *Wall Street Journal*, 29 (2014).

Kissinger, Henry. *World order*. New York, Penguin Press. 2014.

Levi, Eugenio, Rama Dasi Mariani, and Fabrizio Patriarca. "Hate at first sight? Dynamic aspects of the electoral impact of migration: the case of Ukip." *Journal of Population Economics* 33, no. 1 (2020): 1–32.

Lummis, Douglas C. *Radical democracy*. Cornell University Press, 1996.

Mark, Karl, and Engels, Friedrich. *The Communist Manifesto*. Progress Publishers, Moscow, 1977.

Mark, Karl, and Engels, Friedrich. *The German Ideology*. Progress Publishers, Moscow, 1976.

Milton, Friedman. *"Capitalism and freedom." University of Chicago*, 1962.

Mohnhaupt, j. *Animals in National Socialism*. Wisconsin University Press, 2020.

More, Saint Thomas. *The Utopia of Sir Thomas More: In Latin from the Edition of March 1518, and in English from the 1st Ed. of Ralph Robynson's Translation in 1551*. Clarendon Press, 1895.

Morley, Christopher. "On laziness." 1920. *Quotidiana*. Ed. Patrick Madden. 18 Oct 2007. 20 Sep 2020. http://essays.quotidiana.org/morley/laziness/.

Myers, Charles S. "The study of primitive music." *The Musical Antiquary* 3 (1912): 121–141.

Nayak, Bhabani Shankar. "Colonial World of postcolonial historians: Reification, theoreticism, and the neoliberal reinvention of tribal identity in India." *Journal of Asian and African Studies* (2020): 0021909620930048.

Nayak, Bhabani Shankar. *Hindu Fundamentalism and the Spirit of Capitalism in India: Hinduisation of Tribals in Kalahandi During the New Economic Reforms*. Rowman & Littlefield, 2017.

Nayebi, Nima. "The geosynchronous orbit and the outer limits of Westphalian Sovereignty." *Hastings Science and Technology Law Journal* 3 (2011): 471.

Newsinger, John. *The Blood Never Dried: A People's History of the British Empire*. Bookmarks, 2013.

Okros, Alan. "Generational theory and Cohort analysis." In *Harnessing the Potential of Digital Post-Millennials in the Future Workplace*, pp. 33–51. Springer, Cham, 2020.

Orwell, George. *Down and Out in Paris and London*, San Diego. Harcourt Brace & Co., 1983.

Orwellian Proverbial Expression. *"Those who live by the sword die by the sword. Those who do not die by the sword die of smelly diseases"*.

Popper, Karl. "The poverty of historicism, II. A criticism of historicist methods." *Economica* 11, no. 43 (1944): 119–137.

Popper, Karl R. "Utopia and violence." *World affairs* 149, no. 1 (1986): 3–9.

Popper, Karl R. *The Open Society and Its Enemies*. Princeton University Press, 2020.

Popper, Karl R. *The poverty of historicism*. Psychology Press, 2002.

Putnam, Robert D. *Our kids: The American dream in crisis*. Simon and Schuster, 2016.

Raaflaub, Kurt A., Josiah Ober, and Robert Wallace. *Origins of democracy in ancient Greece*. University of California Press, 2008.

Rahim, Asma Ayesha, and Thomas V. Chacko. "Replicating the Kerala state's successful COVID-19 containment model: Insights on what worked." *Indian Journal of Community Medicine* 45, no. 3 (2020): 261.

Räthzel, Nora, Khayaat Fakier, and Diana Mulinari. *Marxist-feminist Theories and Struggles Today: Essential Writings on Intersectionality, Labour and Ecofeminism*. Zed Books, 2020.

Roy, Tathagata. *The Life & Times of Shyama Prasad Mookerjee*. Prabhat Prakashan, 2014.

Russell, Bertrand. *In praise of idleness, and Other Essays*. G. Allen & Unwin, London, 1958.

Sarkar, Sumit. *Beyond Nationalist Frames: postmodernism, Hindu fundamentalism, history*. Indiana University Press, 2002.

Shaffer, Ryan. "Foreign friends and British fascism: understanding the American friends of the British National Party." *Contemporary British History* 34, no. 1 (2020): 118–139.

Sharma, J. *Terrifying Vision: MS Golwalkar, the RSS, and India*. Penguin Books India, 2007.

Shelley, Percy Bysshe, Leigh Hunt, and Thomas James Wise. *The masque of anarchy*. Publication for the Shelley Soc. by Reeves & Turner, 1892.

Shevde, Natasha. "All's fair in love and cream: A cultural case study of Fair & Lovely in India." *Advertising & Society Review* 9, no. 2 (2008).

Simonelli, David. *Working Class Heroes: Rock Music and British society in the 1960s and 1970s*. Lexington Books, 2012.

Singh, Jakeet. "Religious agency and the limits of intersectionality." *Hypatia* 30, no. 4 (2015): 657–674.

Sonnino, Piera. *This has happened: an Italian family in Auschwitz*. Macmillan, 2009.

Stevenson, R.L. *An Apology for Idlers*. Penguin, New York, 2009.

Stikkers, Kenneth W. "Institutionalizing the common good in economy: Lessons from the Mondragon cooperatives." *Humanistic Management Journal* 5, no. 1 (2020): 105–115.

Stoner, Alexander M. "Critical reflections on America's Green new deal: Capital, labor, and the dynamics of contemporary social change." *Capitalism Nature Socialism* (2020): 1–18.

Strauss, William, and Neil Howe. *The Fourth Turning: What the cycles of History Tell us about America's Next Rendezvous with destiny*. Three Rivers Press, 2009.

Subramanian, Arvind, and Josh Felman. *India's Great Slowdown: What Happened? What's the Way Out?*. Vol. 369. CID Faculty Working Paper, 2019.

Szetela, Adam. "Black lives matter at five: limits and possibilities." *Ethnic and Racial Studies* 43, no. 8 (2020): 1358–1383.

Taylor, Keeanga-Yamahtta. *From# BlackLivesMatter to Black Liberation*. Haymarket Books, 2016.

Teschke, Benno. *The myth of 1648: class, geopolitics, and the making of modern International Relations*. Verso, 2003.

Thompson, Peter. "Margaret Thatcher: a new illusion." *Perception* (1980).

Toffler, Alvin. *Future shock*. Bantam, 1970.

Tsiamis, Costas. *Plague in Byzantine Times: A Historical and Medical Study*. De Gruyter, 2020.

Upadhyaya, Deendayal. *Integral humanism*. Bharatiya Janta Party, 1965.

Upadhyaya, Deendayal. *The Two Plans: Promises, Performance, Prospects*. Rashtradharma Prakashan Limited, 1958.

Wilkinson, Richard, and Kate Pickett. *The Spirit Level: Why Greater Equality Makes Societies Stronger*. Bloomsbury Publishing USA, 2011.

Zon, B. M. "From very acute and plausible 'to' curiously misinterpreted': William Jones's' On the musical modes of the Hindoos' (1792) and its reception in later treatises on Indian music." Routledge, 2006.

Index

About the Author

Bhabani Shankar Nayak is a political economist and working as Reader in Business Management and Director of MBA, University for the Creative Arts, UK. He taught in different universities in Sussex, Glasgow, Salford, York and Coventry. He is the author of *Hindu Fundamentalism and the Spirit of Capitalism in India* (2017) and *Nationalising Crisis: The Political Economy of Public Policy in Contemporary India* (2006). He has published five anthologies: *Nomad and Road*, *Dreams of Distance*, *Forbidden River*, *Abandoned and Unclaimed* and *Deceptive Sand*.

Lightning Source UK Ltd.
Milton Keynes UK
UKHW012338110122
396986UK00001B/18